Æthelflæd

The Lady of the Mercians

Tim Clarkson

First published in Great Britain in 2018 by
John Donald, an imprint of Birlinn Ltd

West Newington House
10 Newington Road
Edinburgh
EH9 1QS

www.birlinn.co.uk

ISBN: 978 1 910900 16 1

British Library Cataloguing-in-Publication Data
A catalogue record for this book is available on request from the British Library

Typeset by 3btype.com
Printed and bound in Britain by T. J. International, Padstow, Cornwall

CONTENTS

LIST OF PLATES

LIST OF MAPS AND PLANS

The historic (pre-1974) counties of southern and midland England

GENEALOGICAL TABLE

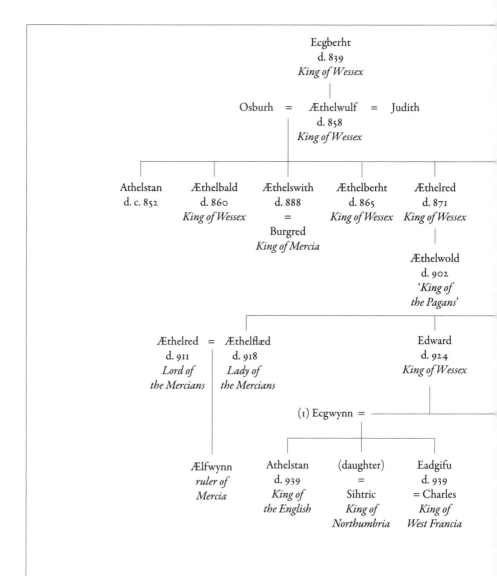

Ecgberht
d. 839
King of Wessex

Osburh = Æthelwulf = Judith
d. 858
King of Wessex

Athelstan	Æthelbald	Æthelswith	Æthelberht	Æthelred
d. c. 852	d. 860	d. 888	d. 865	d. 871
	King of Wessex	=	*King of Wessex*	*King of Wessex*
		Burgred		
		King of Mercia		

Æthelwold
d. 902
'*King of
the Pagans*'

Æthelred = Æthelflæd   Edward
d. 911   d. 918   d. 924
Lord of   Lady of   King of Wessex
the Mercians the Mercians*

(1) Ecgwynn =

Ælfwynn	Athelstan	(daughter)	Eadgifu
ruler of	d. 939	=	d. 939
Mercia	*King of*	Sihtric	= Charles
	the English	*King of*	*King of*
		Northumbria	*West Francia*

The royal dynasty of Wessex from the early ninth to the late tenth centuries

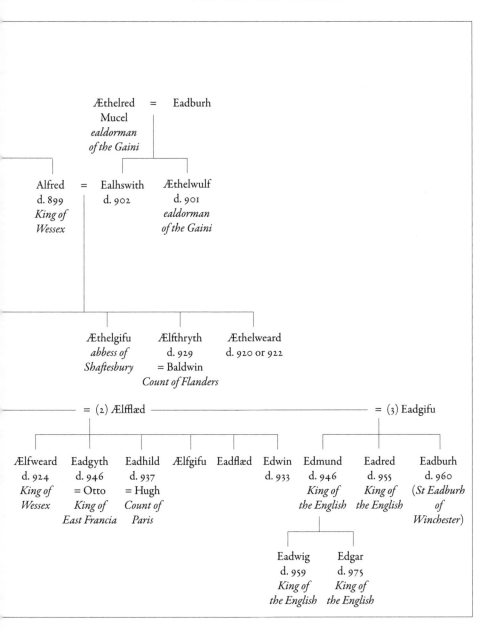

Æthelred Mucel *ealdorman of the Gaini* = Eadburh

Alfred d. 899 *King of Wessex* = Ealhswith d. 902

Æthelwulf d. 901 *ealdorman of the Gaini*

Æthelgifu *abbess of Shaftesbury*

Ælfthryth d. 929 = Baldwin *Count of Flanders*

Æthelweard d. 920 or 922

= (2) Ælfflæd

= (3) Eadgifu

Ælfweard d. 924 *King of Wessex*

Eadgyth d. 946 = Otto *King of East Francia*

Eadhild d. 937 = Hugh *Count of Paris*

Ælfgifu

Eadflæd

Edwin d. 933

Edmund d. 946 *King of the English*

Eadred d. 955 *King of the English*

Eadburh d. 960 (*St Eadburh of Winchester*)

Eadwig d. 959 *King of the English*

Edgar d. 975 *King of the English*

Early medieval Britain

1

INTRODUCTION

More than a thousand years ago, in the year 911, the Lord of the Mercians died. His name was Æthelred. He had ruled the western half of the Anglo-Saxon kingdom of Mercia, a kingdom whose monarchs had once dominated much of southern Britain. At the time of Lord Æthelred's death, those days of supremacy were long gone, for the eastern half of Mercia now lay in the hands of Viking warlords. So, too, did the neighbouring kingdoms of East Anglia and Northumbria. This had been the situation for more than thirty years, ever since the coming to Britain of a large Viking host known as the Great Heathen Army.

Neither the cause nor the place of Æthelred's death is known but his body was taken to the former Roman city of Gloucester, there to be entombed. His passing heralded one of the most remarkable moments in early English history, for his authority passed not to a man but to a woman. His widow, Æthelflæd, succeeded him as ruler of the Mercians. This was a highly unusual event in a period when kings and mighty lords were normally followed by male successors. Yet, despite her gender, Æthelflæd was no stranger to war and politics. Her late father was none other than Alfred the Great, the renowned king of Wessex who had spent much of his reign fighting Viking invaders. Æthelflæd had lived among warriors during her childhood and had known the hardships of life in military encampments. In adulthood, as the wife of the Lord of the Mercians, she had played an active role in government alongside her husband. After Æthelred's death, she stepped into his shoes as protector of his people, ruling them as he had done and leading Mercia's armies to war. It is in this military guise as a 'warrior queen' that she is now most recognisable to modern eyes. Sculptors and other artists often depict her holding a sword and wearing armour. Yet there is more to her story than tales of battles and alliances. She was a capable ruler at home: a founder of towns and cities and a patron of churches. Her legacy still survives in the western midlands of England, especially at places that benefited from her patronage. She is often commemorated there as 'Queen Ethelfleda', using a feminised form of her name that appeared in texts written long after her lifetime. Some of her contemporaries referred to her as a queen but others did not, and in the Old English language of her people she was usually known as *myrcna hlæfdige*, the Lady of the Mercians.

Chronological scope

This book is a biography of Æthelflæd and is mainly concerned with the events of her life. She was born towards the end of the 860s and lived for roughly fifty years before dying on 12 June 918. The main body of the book – comprising Chapters 3 to 7 – is devoted to the period when she was alive. It is preceded by the present chapter, which serves as an introduction, and by Chapter 2, in which the origins and early histories of Wessex and Mercia are outlined. Chapter 3 deals with Æthelflæd's childhood, taking the narrative as far as her wedding to Lord Æthelred in the mid-880s. The next three chapters cover the years they spent together, carrying the story through the final decade of the ninth century and on into the first decade of the tenth, up to the time of Æthelred's death in 911. In these chapters we see the close co-operation between Mercia and Wessex against the Viking armies who posed a common threat to both. Here we also see the final years of King Alfred's life and the first decade of the reign of his eldest son, a man known to history as Edward the Elder.[1] Chapters 7 and 8 look at the years of Æthelflæd's widowhood when, as the Lady of the Mercians, she won renown as an effective ruler and war-leader. The aftermath of her death in June 918 is examined in the ninth chapter, which looks at the relationship between her brother Edward and her daughter Ælfwynn who succeeded her as ruler of Mercia. The final chapter considers Æthelflæd's legacy by assessing her historical significance and by looking at how she is remembered today.

In a broader chronological context, Æthelflæd lived during the early medieval period, an era spanning roughly the fifth to eleventh centuries AD. In Britain, this is usually defined as starting with the collapse of Roman rule in the early 400s and ending with the Norman invasion of England in 1066. It represents more than half of the Middle Ages, the centuries of medieval European history between Classical antiquity and the modern era. In popular usage the early medieval period is sometimes described as the 'Dark Ages' because it witnessed the demise of Classical civilisation in the fifth century when groups of barbarians brought the downfall of the Western Roman Empire. Many historians now avoid the term 'Dark Ages', regarding it as misleading and overly negative. At worst, it conjures an inaccurate picture of post-Roman Europe as a primitive, brutal place devoid of the trappings of civilisation. Nevertheless, it is undoubtedly more familiar to the wider public than 'early medieval' and thus retains a certain usefulness. It continues to be used by historians and archaeologists in the titles of their publications and shows no sign of disappearing in the near future. A more specific term relating to Æthelflæd's era is 'Late Anglo-Saxon' (or 'Late Saxon'), encompassing approximately the mid-ninth to the late eleventh centuries. It is mainly employed here as a convenient label for archaeological evidence associated with the period.

Terminology

As far as we know, Æthelflæd spent her entire life in southern Britain, the part of the island below a line drawn between the great river-estuaries of Mersey and Humber. There is no evidence that she ever ventured further north, nor that she ever travelled overseas. Her everyday speech was Old English, the language of the Anglo-Saxons, the ancestral speech of the English language spoken today. In terms of cultural identity she was therefore an Englishwoman, albeit one living in a time when 'England' as a political entity had not yet come into being. She was born in a period when the Anglo-Saxons still lived in separate kingdoms rather than as a unified people under one monarch. Throughout this book, the term 'England' is used mainly in a geographical sense. As a political term it had little meaning in Æthelflæd's time and would be quite misleading if used in that way here. However, the adjective 'English' does not have the same ambiguity. 'English' and 'Anglo-Saxon' are essentially synonymous and both are used in this book. They describe the early medieval inhabitants of Wessex, Mercia, Northumbria, East Anglia and other places where the Old English language was a common tongue. Æthelflæd knew that she was a member of the population group described in contemporary Latin texts as *gens Anglorum* ('the English nation') and in her own language as *Angelcynn*.[2] Indeed, the concept of Englishness as a cultural label shared across political frontiers was already well-established before her birth. As an educated person she would have encountered it in the writings of the Venerable Bede, a Northumbrian monk of the early 700s who saw the English as a chosen people like the ancient Israelites. Traditions reported by Bede traced English origins back to the Angles, Saxons, Jutes and other North Germanic peoples who colonised parts of southern and eastern Britain in the fifth and sixth centuries. Most of the original colonists sprang from the Angles and Saxons so it was these two groups whose names were eventually brought together in the collective term 'Anglo-Saxon', itself apparently devised in the eighth century. Æthelflæd's father, Alfred the Great, nurtured a personal vision of English unity, aspiring to the grandiose title 'king of the Anglo-Saxons'. In practice, he exercised little real authority north of the River Thames. He was a scion of the royal dynasty of Wessex, the kingdom of the West Saxons. The heartlands of Wessex comprised the modern counties of Hampshire, Wiltshire, Somerset and Dorset but in Alfred's time the kingdom had expanded to include other territories along the southern coast. At the height of his reign in the 890s, Wessex encompassed the formerly independent kingdom of the South Saxons (whose name survives in abbreviated form as 'Sussex'), together with Surrey, Kent and parts of Essex (the land of the East Saxons). North of the Thames lay the territories originally settled not by Saxons but by Angles – Mercia, East Anglia and Northumbria – all of which were wholly or partly under Viking occupation during Alfred's reign.

The early Anglo-Saxon settlers who arrived from Germany in the fifth century supplanted an indigenous population of Britons, whose own power had steadily been pushed westward. The Britons spoke a Celtic language ancestral to modern Welsh. Many of them had long resisted the encroachment of the Anglo-Saxons, who referred to them as *wealas*, an Old English term from which our modern word 'Welsh' derives. In Æthelflæd's time, *wealas* could be applied to any group of native Britons, regardless of whether they came from Wales, Cornwall or the northern realm of Strathclyde. In this book, 'Welsh' is used exclusively to refer to the Britons of Wales. Their compatriots in other areas are referred to simply as Britons. The term 'British' is likewise applied to the Britons alone. It is not used here of the Anglo-Saxons, Scots or other inhabitants of the island of Britain. Æthelflæd herself would have understood this distinction very clearly, as would her contemporaries in any part of the island not under native British rule.

'Viking' is used in this book as an umbrella label for various groups of Scandinavians who raided and colonised parts of Britain in the Viking Age. This period is generally seen as running from the late eighth to the late eleventh centuries. We often picture the stereotypical Viking as a fierce warrior from Norway or Denmark, wielding an axe or sword and sailing the seas in search of plunder. Many of the Scandinavian raiders who harried the coasts of Britain and Ireland probably fitted this image, especially in the early 800s when the first wave of hit-and-run raids reached its height. By c.850, however, the raiding bands were coalescing to form larger armies whose leaders sought territory for conquest and settlement. Although the distinctions between Norwegian

('Norse') and Danish Vikings were not always clear-cut, contemporary writers believed that Ireland was colonised mainly by Norsemen and that the English lands were colonised mainly by Danes. Modern historians tend to follow this scenario and it is likewise adopted in this book.[3]

The woman whose story unfolds in the following chapters was born into a family whose everyday speech was Old English. Her name was formed in the same language, being a compound of *æthel* ('noble') and *flæd* ('beauty'). It is a fairly typical Anglo-Saxon female name incorporating two of the most common naming elements. In modern English it appears with the variant spellings Ethelfled, Ethelfleda and Æthelflæda, the latter two reflecting attempts to make the name sound more feminine. Ethelfleda is often encountered in Victorian and early twentieth century contexts, not only in printed publications but also in commemorative objects such as sculpture and signage. Until recently, it was probably the most recognisable form of the name in those parts of the English midlands where Æthelflæd ruled 1100 years ago. An imposing railway bridge at Runcorn in Cheshire, on what was once her north-west frontier, was named in commemoration of *Ethelfleda* in Victorian times. So, too, was a public garden created in the 1950s at Wednesbury on the outskirts of Birmingham. To a wider public Æthelflæd is now the more familiar spelling, largely because of its use in historical novels and, more recently, in a popular television series. Modern historians have been using this form of the name for many years and it is the one employed in the following chapters.

Familiar spellings of other personal names are similarly employed here, sometimes at the expense of consistency. An example is Alfred in preference to Old English *Ælfred*, where the former is so instantly recognisable that hardly anyone bothers to use the latter. The same logic applies to Edward being preferred over *Eadweard*, to Athelstan over *Æthelstan*, and also to certain modernised Viking names such as Guthrum. Some historians prefer to render Viking names as closely as possible to the original Scandinavian (Old Norse) forms, while others prefer Anglicised or Gaelicised variants. No particular convention is followed in this book, the sole justification for an inconsistent approach being that the author has used it before.[4] Thus, the Old Norse names *Rognvaldr* and *Sigtryggr* are here rendered Ragnall and Sihtric, these being Gaelicised spellings found in medieval Irish texts. Conversely, Old Norse *Ivarr* and *Ottar* are preferred over Gaelic *Imar* and *Ottir*. Guthrum, an Anglicised form of Old Norse *Guðþormr*, has already been mentioned. Another Anglicised spelling is Guthfrith for *Guðrøðr*, here used in preference over the Old Norse name and its Middle Irish form *Gofraid*.

The English chronicles

Our most important source of information on Æthelflæd is the *Anglo-Saxon Chronicle* (hereafter also *ASC*), a year-by-year record of events spanning the entire first millennium and extending into the twelfth century. It survives today in seven manuscripts. The original chronicle was begun in Wessex in the late ninth century, during the reign of Alfred the Great.[5] It differs from similar chronicles produced elsewhere in Western Europe by not using Latin for its annals or year-entries. Instead, its compilers wrote in their own vernacular tongue – Old English. They created not only a record of their own time but also of the remote past, drawing on older texts to present a history of the world from the dawn of the Christian era. Newer, contemporary entries were continually added, taking the story onward into the tenth century and beyond, right up to the Norman Conquest. Copies were made of the original chronicle from the outset, these being distributed to important monasteries in Wessex and elsewhere. The copies were kept current by successive generations of scribes, probably via official updates issued periodically from the West Saxon royal court.[6] Information sourced locally was also added, so that each copy began to reflect the geographical interests of the monastery in which it was held. In this way, several different versions of *ASC* came into being, each essentially a duplicate of the original but diverging in certain aspects. The original itself is lost so it is from the few surviving copies that we begin our reconstruction of Æthelflæd's story.

The oldest survivor is the so-called 'A' text, also known as the Winchester Chronicle. This was begun at the Old Minster in Winchester, the principal church of the West Saxon royal dynasty. Its first scribe made a full copy of the original chronicle up to the year-entry for 891. Other scribes then carried the sequence of entries on into the tenth century, often giving detailed information about kings and battles. Entries generally become less detailed for the eleventh century but by then the manuscript had been transferred to Canterbury, where it remained until the Reformation. At one time it was in the possession of Matthew Parker, archbishop of Canterbury from 1559 to 1575, and for this reason it is sometimes known as the Parker Chronicle. As the oldest surviving manuscript of *ASC* it is regarded as the standard version. Most modern editions and translations are based on it, with cross-referencing to other manuscripts where they give variant information.

The second oldest manuscript, known as the 'B' text, was written in the late tenth century. It appears to be a copy of the original chronicle up to 977, at which point its year-entries end. The location of the scribe is unknown but, by c.1050, the manuscript was at Abingdon Abbey in Oxfordshire. There it provided the basis for another copy known as 'C'. Sometime before 1100, the B manuscript was taken to Canterbury Cathedral where it was amended with additions and corrections, together with information of local Kentish interest. B and C are not identical, for C's scribes included data that is absent from B. More importantly for our present purpose, both manuscripts contain a sequence of year-entries relating specifically to Æthelflæd. These cover the period 902 to 924 and refer not only to Æthelflæd herself but also to her husband Lord Æthelred, her mother Ealhswith, her daughter Ælfwynn and her nephew Athelstan. The entire sequence is known as the 'Mercian Register', for it has a focus on Mercian rather than on West Saxon affairs. It is examined more closely under the next sub-heading.

Roughly contemporary with manuscript C is the so-called Worcester Chronicle or 'D' text, written during the middle decades of the eleventh century by scribes who had a particular interest in Northumbria.[7] Although they themselves seem to have been based at Worcester Cathedral, their immediate source appears to have been an older copy of *ASC* maintained in a Northumbrian church or monastery. This source had received the usual periodic updates from Wessex during the 900s but had also been supplemented with additional, northern material drawn from Bede's *Ecclesiastical History of the English People* (published in 731) and from a set of eighth-century Northumbrian annals. It also included an incomplete version of the Mercian Register with some entries omitted and others duplicated at different years. The arrival of the original Northumbrian manuscript in Worcester may have been due to a close relationship between the ecclesiastical dioceses of Worcester and York in the early eleventh century.

Manuscripts A to D are the ones most often referenced in this book. A is particularly useful in preserving the oldest known version of *ASC*, while B, C and D contain the Mercian Register with its special focus on Æthelflæd. The other manuscripts are less useful for our present purpose and can be described more briefly, beginning with the 'E' text. Sometimes known as the Laud Chronicle, this was written at the monastery of Peterborough in the early 1100s. It has some of the Northumbrian focus of D but does not contain the Mercian Register. Of all the surviving manuscripts it is the one with the latest year-entries, the final one being for 1154. Also from the early twelfth century comes the 'F' manuscript, a bilingual version of *ASC* in which each entry in Old English is followed by a Latin translation. It was produced at Canterbury in the period after the Norman Conquest when Old English had fallen out of favour as a language appropriate for official documents. In the new era of Norman rule the preferred medium of documentation was Latin, hence the use of both languages in F. With the manuscript known as 'G' we jump forward to the 1500s, when the dean of Lichfield Cathedral made a copy of *ASC* from a version written at Winchester five hundred years earlier. His Winchester source was itself a copy of the 'A' text with entries up to c.1012.[8] Finally, the manuscript designated 'H' is a one-page fragment from a lost twelfth-century copy of *ASC* that also probably originated at Winchester. It only has year-entries for 1113 and 1114 and thus lies outside the scope of this book.

The importance of *ASC* as a historical record has been recognised for more than a thousand years. Historians have mined its information from the time of its first appearance in the late ninth century. The first to do so, as far as we know, was the Welsh monk Asser, writer of a contemporary biography of King Alfred. Asser consulted a version of *ASC* that seems to have ended at the year 887.[9] He was well positioned to comment on the events of Alfred's reign, being himself a close companion of the king at the royal court of Wessex. About a hundred years later, a West Saxon nobleman called Æthelweard produced a chronicle of his own. Written in Latin, this was a translation of *ASC* supplemented with additions by Æthelweard himself. He was an ealdorman (literally 'elder man'), a high-ranking royal official, with close connections to the ruling dynasty. His work survives in a single manuscript that was badly damaged in a fire in 1731, leaving a sixteenth-century copy as the only complete version now available. Æthelweard's chronicle is a useful resource for the period covered in this book and is occasionally cited, even though it contains only a single mention of Æthelflæd.[10]

Moving forward to the twelfth century, we find *ASC*'s year-entries recycled in several English chronicles produced at this time. These were composed in Latin, by writers whose special interests coloured their works. One such chronicle, completed at Worcester Cathedral in the early 1140s, was compiled by several writers over a fifty-year period. Modern historians usually cite a monk called John as the main author, although some prefer an alternative attribution to Florentius ('Florence') who was probably involved at an earlier stage.[11] As Worcester lies in the western midlands, it is likely that Florence, John and their colleagues had access to one or more Mercian versions of *ASC* preserved in the cathedral library. Meanwhile, over in the eastern midlands, John's contemporary Henry of Huntingdon produced another chronicle. Henry probably used a version of *ASC* held at nearby Peterborough, for his year-entries show similarities with the above-mentioned Laud Chronicle.[12] Henry and the Worcester monks appear to have had access to other ancient sources that are now lost, hence their chronicles contain unique information not found in *ASC* or elsewhere. The same can be said of William of Malmesbury, another twelfth-century contemporary, who resided at Malmesbury Abbey in Wiltshire. William claimed to have consulted 'a certain ancient volume' which provided information unique to his writings. His most famous work is *Gesta Regum Anglorum* ('Deeds of the English Kings'), a history from c.450 to his own time. It contains stories about Æthelflæd and her family that are not found in other texts and so cannot be authenticated. Modern scholars are understandably wary of taking William's testimony at face value, especially as he does not explain what the 'ancient volume' actually was. However, as a native of the former kingdom of Wessex, living in a monastery associated with its kings, he may have had access to genuine traditions. This possibility makes his *Gesta Regum* a valuable source, albeit one that must be approached with care.[13]

The Annals of Æthelflæd

Manuscripts B, C and D of the *Anglo-Saxon Chronicle* contain the distinct sequence of year-entries known as the Mercian Register. The title was first coined at the end of the late nineteenth century by Charles Plummer in his magisterial edition of *ASC*. Plummer also described these entries as 'The Annals of Æthelflæd' because of their special focus on the Lady of the Mercians.[14] No other woman of the Anglo-Saxon period receives such sustained interest from a contemporary text. Indeed, only a small number of women appear in the entire corpus of chronicles from early medieval Britain and Ireland, with the majority receiving only a single mention. Æthelflæd is therefore a unique case. Her 'annals' begin in 902, the first being a notice of her mother's death. The next significant event is the repair of Chester's defences in 907, a project usually attributed to Æthelflæd despite her name not being mentioned. Her name is likewise absent from the entry for 909, which refers to the recovery of the bones of Saint Oswald from lands under Danish occupation. Again, the retrieval of these precious relics is thought to have been one of her ventures. She is first mentioned by name in an entry for 910 which reports that she ordered the construction of a burh – a fortress or fortified settlement – at a place called *Bremesbyrig*. The location is unknown but it probably lay in western Mercia, the territory ruled by Æthelflæd and her husband (and, after 911, by Æthelflæd alone). Subsequent entries describe her founding other burhs, many of them being identifiable today as places in the western midlands. Her military campaigns against Welsh and Scandinavian enemies are also mentioned, culminating in the capture of a major Danish stronghold at Derby in 917 and the surrender of another at Leicester in the following year. We are then informed of her death on 12 June 918. After her passing, we learn from her 'Annals' that her daughter, Ælfwynn, became the new ruler of Mercia. Within a few months, Ælfwynn was toppled from power during a forceful takeover by her uncle, King Edward of Wessex. A penultimate year-entry refers to Edward's construction of a burh at *Cledemutha* ('Clwyd-mouth') on Mercia's north-western frontier. The sequence finally ends in 924, the year of Edward's death, with the information that his son Athelstan was chosen by the Mercians as their king.

All these annals relate to Mercia. They begin with the death of Æthelflæd's mother, a Mercian princess. They end with the elevation of Æthelflæd's nephew to the Mercian kingship. In between, we are told of Æthelflæd herself, or rather of her military activities as fort-builder and war-leader. Since none of this information appears in the 'A' text of *ASC* it must have originated in Mercia, as an alternative narrative to the official version of events composed in Wessex. The entries up to and including 918 may have been written while Æthelflæd was still alive or in the immediate aftermath of her death. Whoever wrote them was keen to emphasise her lawful tenure of the authority she had inherited from her husband, pointing out that she ruled with divine approval.[15] We are informed that she governed the Mercians 'with rightful lordship', and that she founded burhs and defeated her enemies with God's blessing. This is in stark contrast to the parallel West Saxon narrative in *ASC* A, which highlights military co-operation between Wessex and Mercia without any mention of Æthelflæd. Her husband, Lord Æthelred, received slightly more attention from the West Saxon side but it looks as if she was deliberately ignored.

The Mercian Register's precise relationship with the official 'A-text' of *ASC* is hard to discern, for the relevant manuscripts (B, C and D) are later copies written long after Æthelflæd's time. One possibility is that a copy of the original ninth-century West Saxon chronicle, containing official updates as far as the year-entry for 914, was amended by a Mercian scribe. The latter would presumably have had access to a separate text which included information on Æthelflæd and her family, perhaps already set out in annal form. This material would then have been inserted into the chronicle copy, which went on to become the basis of the surviving B, C and D manuscripts. More, of course, could be said. More has indeed been said by specialist scholars who have examined the Mercian Register in detail. One striking suggestion is that the ultimate source of the 'Annals of Æthelflæd' was a Latin poem, essentially a history of her deeds composed in verse.[16] Meanwhile, in Wessex, the scribes attached to King Edward's court continued to update the official chronicle with reports of his achievements. They said little about Æthelflæd, either because her deeds would have drawn attention away from Edward's or because most of them took place in Mercia and had little impact on Wessex. Alternatively, Edward's scribes may have downplayed his sister's success because she had overseen Mercia's resurgence as an independent military power capable of pursuing its own destiny without West Saxon help.

Celtic sources

In Wales, Ireland and Scotland a long tradition of chronicle-writing in Latin reached back to the seventh century or earlier, when monasteries began to keep records of important events occurring in both the religious and secular worlds. The two main Irish collections are now the *Annals of Ulster* and the *Annals of Tigernach*, respectively preserved in manuscripts of the fourteenth and fifteenth centuries. Despite the late dates of their surviving versions, these two have been shown to be based on much older chronicles and are generally regarded as reliable. One of their common sources was a chronicle compiled on Iona, the tiny island off the western coast of Scotland where Saint Columba founded a monastery in the sixth century. Nevertheless, like all medieval texts they must be treated with caution. This means that we cannot simply accept their testimony at face value, especially if the information appears nowhere else.[17]

The year-entries in the Ulster and Tigernach chronicles are chiefly concerned with affairs in Ireland and northern Britain. They do, however, include occasional references to Mercia and Wessex. Æthelflæd's father, Alfred the Great, is not mentioned in either collection but she herself appears in an entry in the *Annals of Ulster*, where her death in 918 is noted. Such scant attention being paid by Irish annalists to the rulers of Anglo-Saxon territory is hardly surprising. All the more remarkable, then, that we find Æthelflæd as the central figure in several entries in another Irish chronicle known as the 'Three Fragments' or *Fragmentary Annals of Ireland* (hereafter *FAI*). This survives in a seventeenth-century copy of a lost fifteenth-century manuscript which in turn was based on an original compilation of the eleventh century.[18] Unlike the Ulster and Tigernach chronicles, *FAI*'s entries are in Irish rather than Latin. It also stands apart in its tendency to include detailed narratives rather than brief annals. What might be written in a line or two by the Ulster and Tigernach scribes is often turned into a picturesque story in *FAI*. Historians are rightly sceptical when they encounter this type of 'saga' material in a source that purports to be a factual chronicle. Some have gone so far as to disregard *FAI* as an unreliable witness, seeing its long narratives as little more than fictional stories. Others take a more optimistic view by allowing the possibility that the narratives might preserve kernels of authentic history, and this approach is adopted here. There is no doubt that *FAI* gives more information about Æthelflæd than any other source apart from the Mercian Register. Whatever we think of its reliability, its creators had a keen interest in the Lady of the Mercians and evidently admired her. Their primary focus, as we shall see in later chapters of this book, was on her dealings with Viking foes. To what extent their account reflects real history rather than imaginative storytelling is a question that must remain unanswered.

In Wales, the equivalent of the Irish annalistic collections is a Latin chronicle known as *Annales Cambriae*, the Welsh Annals. It survives in a number of copies, the oldest being a tenth-century compilation preserved in a manuscript of c.1100. The lost original seems to have been kept at the monastery of St David's where, from the late eighth century onwards, it was used as a contemporary record of events. Earlier material is thought to have been borrowed from chronicles compiled in Ireland and northern Britain to create a set of retrospective annals running from the mid-fifth to the late eighth centuries. The intention may have been to produce a chronicle not of the Welsh alone but of the Britons as a whole, hence the inclusion of year-entries relating to Strathclyde and to other places in what is now southern Scotland.[19] From the late 700s, the focus shifts more clearly to Wales. A few entries from this later period mention the English, and also the Vikings, usually in the context of hostilities with the Welsh. Æthelflæd gets a single mention in a brief notice of her death, as does her father Alfred the Great. Indeed, one characteristic of the Welsh Annals is their brevity. The entries tend to give far less information than those in the Anglo-Saxon and Irish chronicles. They nevertheless constitute a valuable source, sometimes providing unique information that adds to our understanding of an event recorded in other texts.[20]

A rather more controversial Welsh source is *The Historie of Cambria*, written in the sixteenth century by the Welsh cleric David Powel. It represents the finished version of a work originally begun by Humphrey Llwyd (1527–1568) as a compilation drawn from a number of older Welsh chronicles. The latter were believed to have been based on a lost original attributed to Caradoc of

Llancarfan, a twelfth-century monk best known for his *vitae* ('Lives') of ancient British saints. Powel augmented Llwyd's text with additions of his own, producing a narrative history of Wales from the seventh to the fourteenth centuries. There are several curious references to Æthelflæd which purport to shed light on her dealings with the Welsh. These are of interest because they include information found in no other source, but their uniqueness means that they cannot be authenticated.[21]

Anglo-Saxon charters

One way for an early medieval king to show his generosity was by making rich gifts to loyal henchmen or to favoured churches. Where the gift included a portion of land the boundaries and associated privileges were often set out in a formal document known as a charter. These documents preserve snapshots of specific moments in time and, whenever they survive, they become important sources of information for historians. From the Anglo-Saxon kingdoms approximately one thousand charters have survived, spanning a 400-year period from the late seventh century to the eleventh. They give fascinating insights into how land was divided and distributed. We often learn not only who bestowed the gift and who received it, but also who witnessed it and where it occurred. We see names of familiar places given in the forms used in Anglo-Saxon times, together with other names that defy identification on a modern map. The main issue facing anyone who wishes to use these documents is the question of authenticity, for only a handful of charters survive as originals. The rest are copies, some of which were written long after the Anglo-Saxon period. Moreover, not all the copies are accurate or genuine. Detailed analysis has shown that many contain errors and later alterations, while some are fakes masquerading as copies of genuine Anglo-Saxon texts. A fake charter might be drawn up in the fourteenth century, for example, to add fictional antiquity to a disputed claim of land-ownership. Those charters which are nevertheless deemed to be authentic – whether surviving as originals or copies, whether accurate or corrupt – obviously have a high value as sources of information.

About a third of the more-or-less authentic charters relate to Mercia, especially to lands associated with the bishops of Worcester.[22] Some refer to Æthelflæd as benefactor, beneficiary or witness. They tell us useful things about her status, her relationships with other members of the Mercian elite and her movements around her domains. Thus, in a charter drawn up in 901, we learn that she and her husband visited Shrewsbury on the River Severn where they bestowed land and a gold chalice on the nearby monastery of Much Wenlock.[23] Fourteen years later, according to a thirteenth-century copy of a charter, Æthelflæd was at the fortress of Weardbyrig to renew a land-grant for a Mercian nobleman. Although the venue itself cannot now be identified, the event can be dated with confidence to September 915. Here we see the widowed Æthelflæd as sole ruler of Mercia, accompanied by her daughter Ælfwynn who was then in her late twenties. The list of witnesses includes bishops, high-ranking noblemen and other senior figures. This kind of detailed information adds colour and depth to a story sketched only in outline by the chroniclers.

Archaeology and place-names

The modern landscape can tell us a great deal about the early medieval past, not least through physical artefacts and structures unearthed by archaeologists. Our knowledge of Æthelflæd has certainly been increased by this kind of tangible information. Evidence of activity in the late ninth and early tenth centuries has been found at a number of sites associated with her, chiefly from the burhs or fortified settlements that she and her husband ordered to be built. According to the Mercian Register, she and Lord Æthelred established burhs in various locations, often on exposed frontiers. In the present-day western midlands, physical evidence of these settlements has been found at several towns and cities, sometimes because of rather than in spite of modern urban development. Although such development often seems to obliterate traces of the distant past, its preliminary groundworks do enable archaeologists to see what lies beneath the present-day surface. Features dating from the Late Anglo-Saxon period can then be identified among layers of activity that in some cases reach back to Roman or pre-Roman times. Likewise, at some of the churches founded or endowed by Æthelflæd, archaeological evidence from her era has been discovered. In some cases a full-scale excavation is not always necessary, for the evidence may already be visible. We might encounter it as a finely sculptured monument carved by Mercian stonemasons or as tenth-century stonework preserved in a much later wall. From beyond Mercia we obtain other physical data that can be used to build up a broader context or to make useful comparisons. Archaeological information from the late ninth-century burhs of Wessex, built by Alfred the Great and used as templates by his daughter, is valuable in this way. Other comparisons can be made with settlements used by the Viking armies whom Æthelflæd and her husband confronted. Thus, in Danish-occupied eastern Mercia, the remains of houses and fortifications give useful insights into the economy and society of a mixed Anglo-Scandinavian population. We find ourselves peering behind the sparse record of the chronicles to see English and Danish people flourishing under the rule of Viking warlords and enjoying such benefits as new trading opportunities.[24]

Aside from archaeological data, we find the landscape yielding additional information via place-names ('toponyms'). The modern forms of many names can be traced back to earlier forms coined in languages such as Old English, Old Norse, Welsh and Gaelic. Analysis of toponyms and what they mean can tell us how land was used in early medieval times for different types of activity and by different groups of people. In the case of Old English names we learn which settlements grew up near a burh or fort (e.g. Burton) or around a river crossing (names with the suffix -ford) or beside a Roman road (names containing 'street', from Latin *strata*). Names ending in -ley like Hanley and Bewdley contain the Old English word *leah* ('clearing, glade') indicating a settlement associated with woodland. Other names commemorate an individual, perhaps the founder of the settlement, as in Birmingham ('village of Beorma's people') and Handsworth ('Hune's farmstead'). A number of toponyms recorded in Anglo-Saxon charters and chronicles are now deemed to be 'lost', meaning that we are unable to match them to places on a modern map. One such name has already been mentioned: the burh of Weardbyrig where Æthelflæd issued a charter in 915. Also unlocated are her burhs at Scergeat and Bremesbyrig. All three defy identification, despite many attempts to find them. A faint glimmer of hope begins to appear when we look closely at one of the names, for *scergeat* means something like 'boundary gap' in Old English. There could be several such gaps or passes around the boundaries of Æthelflæd's realm and, although we may never know which of them she chose for her burh, we might be able to narrow the search by examining their history and archaeology.

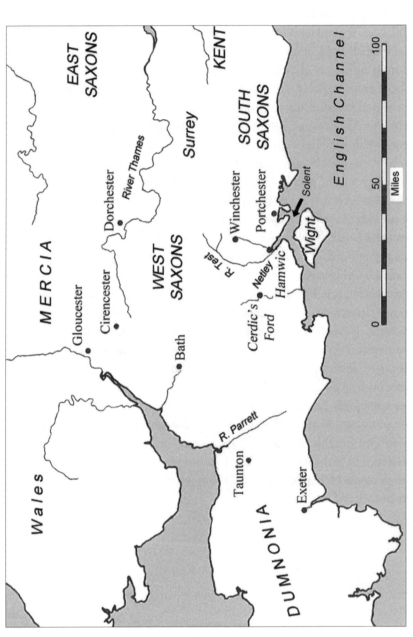

The origins of Wessex

2

KINGDOMS

West Saxon origins

Æthelflæd was born and raised in Wessex, the kingdom of the West Saxons. She was of West Saxon stock on her father's side, but her mother was a Mercian princess. West Saxons and Mercians alike regarded themselves as descendants of the original Anglo-Saxon settlers who had migrated to Britain in the fifth and sixth centuries AD. The migration was not so much a single event as a series of population movements spanning many decades. It saw groups of Germanic people leaving their homelands on the southern shores of the North Sea and heading for Britain. Their numbers are unknown but may have been quite significant, possibly in the tens of thousands. What social or economic circumstances drove them to leave their homes in southern Denmark and northern Germany is uncertain but many were perhaps lured to Britain by new opportunities arising after the end of Roman rule. According to later legends, some of the earliest settlers were invited by native Britons who hired them as mercenary troops. Others seem to have come as adventurers who seized British territory by force of arms. Although they had different origins as Angles, Saxons, Jutes or Frisians the settlers essentially spoke the same language and, as time went by, they began to regard themselves as one people.

The West Saxons adopted their name to distinguish themselves from other groups of similar origin like the South Saxons and East Saxons of present-day Sussex and Essex. Out of these early divisions the first Anglo-Saxon kingdoms arose, each an independent entity established in lands formerly under native British rule. Foundation-legends were devised to explain how each kingdom arose and to justify the status of a dominant royal dynasty. In Wessex, the legend begins with a man called Cerdic who supposedly arrived in Britain in the year 495. Landing on the south coast with his son Cynric and five shiploads of Saxons, Cerdic is said to have fought local Britons in what is now western Hampshire. These hostilities included a battle in which a British king called

Natanleod was slain. Afterwards, the Saxons seized a territory called *Natanleaga*, as far as 'Cerdic's Ford'. At some point, Cerdic's army was reinforced by the arrival of an additional group of Saxons led by his kinsmen Stuf and Wihtgar. To these newcomers he gave the Isle of Wight. Cerdic himself is said to have died in 534, bequeathing his kingship to Cynric. Meanwhile, according to another strand of the legend, a Saxon called Port landed in south-east Hampshire in 501. After slaying a high-ranking Briton, Port and his sons established a settlement of their own at *Portesmutha*. Nothing more is heard of them after that. Although shown as contemporaries of Cerdic they appear to belong to a separate legend.

The foundation-legend of Wessex is preserved as a series of entries in the *Anglo-Saxon Chronicle*. How much of it is real history rather than pseudo-history is a matter of debate. Some modern historians have questioned Cerdic's existence, seeing him as a fictional character invented by the creators of the legend. While such scepticism is understandable, Cerdic's central role might suggest that he was a historical figure. Unfortunately, we cannot say the same of the supporting cast, most of whom are extremely shadowy figures. Stuf and Wihtgar, depicted in the legend as Cerdic's kinsmen, fall into this category. Although they also appear in Asser's ninth-century biography of King Alfred, their historicity is very dubious. Asser describes them as the first English rulers of the Isle of Wight, identifying them as Jutes rather than Saxons. This is consistent with a tradition noted in the previous century by Bede who said that Wight was settled by Jutes who established their own kingdom there. Yet Bede makes no mention of Stuf and Wihtgar. The latter, in any case, looks suspiciously like a fictional eponym for Wight itself, which was known to the early English as Wiht. The island's name actually has an even older origin, deriving from Vectis, an ancient name used by the Romans (who pronounced the initial letter as W), and thus pre-dating the Saxon and Jutish migrations by several hundred years. Nevertheless, the eighth-century tradition that Wight's first English settlers were Jutes may have a historical basis. We know that the island was conquered by the West Saxons during a ruthless and bloody campaign in the late seventh century. Perhaps Stuf and Wihtgar and their alleged link with Cerdic of Wessex were invented at this time, to legitimise the West Saxon conquest?

Alongside Stuf and Wihtgar we should probably dismiss the British king Natanleod as another fictional figure. He was supposedly defeated and killed in 508, his death leading to Cerdic's takeover of an area called Natanleaga. The latter is almost certainly an early form of the Hampshire place-name Netley, the first element of which is thought to be the Old English word *næt* ('wet'). Such an adjective seems an apt description of the wetland known today as Netley Marsh. Rather than being an otherwise unrecorded Celtic personal name, Natanleod looks like a fictional eponym for the place-name Natanleaga. If there was a British king whom the Saxons defeated in the vicinity of Netley, his real name has evidently not survived.

Of all the spurious characters in the West Saxon foundation-legend the most obviously fictional is Port, supposedly the founder of Portesmutha (Portsmouth). The first element of the place-name has a rather more straightforward origin, being derived from Latin *portus*, 'a port'. On the edge of Portsmouth harbour stand the remains of Portchester Castle, a huge Roman fortress whose Latin name was Portus Adurni. Its massive walls – still standing to a height of six metres today – would have been an imposing sight to early Anglo-Saxon settlers, who learned its name from native Britons. The tale of a local Saxon leader called 'Port' must have arisen in folklore, eventually finding its way into the foundation-legend of Wessex. It is worth mentioning again that Bede regarded this part of southern Hampshire as having been settled by Jutes not Saxons. He noted that a memory of Jutish origins was still preserved in his own time, when the area had long been under West Saxon rule. As in the case of the Isle of Wight, we might be seeing here a formerly independent kingdom whose first rulers were of Jutish origin.[1] It is not beyond the bounds of possibility that the story of Port preserves a garbled but authentic folk-tradition of such a dynasty.

One curious observation about Cerdic is that his name appears to be of Celtic rather than of Germanic origin. It looks like a form of the native British name Ceretic (or Caradoc), borne by the famous King Caratacus who resisted Roman forces in Wales in the first century AD. In the early seventh century, a certain King Ceretic ruled a British realm in what is now West Yorkshire. This Ceretic's name was rendered as *Cerdic* by Bede, who wrote about him a hundred years later. We might wonder if Ceretic's namesake, the Cerdic who reputedly founded Wessex, was not so much a Saxon immigrant as an ambitious Briton. Perhaps he set himself up as an independent king, with Saxons among his entourage? Such a scenario is far from outlandish if we imagine local British families intermarrying with Saxon settlers to produce a hybrid 'Brito-Saxon' elite sharing political and economic interests. Unfortunately, the data is too limited to build up a coherent picture of Cerdic's true place in history. Moreover, it is possible that the geography of his career as presented in *ASC* is misplaced. It may be more accurate to envisage his original territory lying not in Hampshire but somewhere further east. Indeed, a case can be made for shifting the true origins of Wessex to the upper Thames valley, leaving Hampshire as a predominantly Jutish area which did not fall under West Saxon control until the late seventh century. In this alternative scenario, the upper reaches of the Thames are the real heartland of Cerdic and his immediate successors. Their initial expansion would then have been confined to this inland region, with their attention turning southward to Hampshire and the Isle of Wight only after the mid-600s. Such a picture fits well with archaeological evidence for early Saxon settlement around the upper Thames. It could also explain why the first West Saxon bishopric was founded at Dorchester-on-Thames in Oxfordshire rather than somewhere nearer the Hampshire coast.[2] Perhaps the story of Cerdic was relocated to Hampshire to promote a false belief that this was ancestral West Saxon territory, when its early colonists had actually been Jutes?

If Cerdic was a genuine historical character then the same might be said of his son Cynric. According to *ASC*, Cynric succeeded his father as king of Wessex and reigned for twenty-six years until 560. He in turn was succeeded by a son Ceawlin, to whom *ASC* assigns a reign of thirty-two years. A somewhat different chronology is given in the West Saxon Regnal Table, another text compiled in the late ninth century. This pushes the start of Cerdic's reign forward to c.530 and restricts Ceawlin's reign to no more than seventeen years. Whatever the true chronology, Ceawlin marks the point where legend begins to give way to real history. He is mentioned in Bede's *Ecclesiastical History* as a powerful over-king whose authority was recognised in other Anglo-Saxon kingdoms. From *ASC* we learn that he took a large amount of territory from the Britons, most notably by seizing the former Roman cities of Bath, Cirencester and Gloucester in 577. By the early seventh century, the West Saxon kingship was held by Cynegils, the first king of the 'House of Cerdic' to renounce paganism. He was baptised in 635 but his contemporaries in other kingdoms had already trodden the same path. In Kent, a royal family of Jutish descent had been Christian for a generation, having welcomed a papal mission as far back as 597. In the northern realm of Bernicia, ruled since the middle of the sixth century by Angles who had displaced a native British dynasty, Christianity was being vigorously promoted in the 630s by the pious King Oswald. It was Oswald himself who oversaw the baptism of Cynegils of Wessex, playing the role of godfather. Christianity was thereafter preached among the West Saxons, initially by Birinus who was appointed as their first bishop with his base at Dorchester-on-Thames. Although Cynegils and his people were somewhat late in abandoning paganism they were by no means the last of the early English to do so. Further east, their South Saxon neighbours were still worshipping

Germanic gods in the middle of the seventh century, as were the Jutes of Wight and Hampshire.

Gewisse

Three entries in the 'A' text of the *Anglo-Saxon Chronicle* include a royal genealogy showing Cerdic as the great-grandson of a man called Gewis.[3] The same genealogy appears at the beginning of Asser's Life of King Alfred but with Gewis shown there as Cerdic's grandfather. From *ASC* we learn nothing more about Gewis, but Asser adds that the Britons referred to the West Saxons as Gewisse because of him. This echoes an earlier statement by Bede who noted that 'in early days they were called the Gewisse'. At first glance, then, the terms 'West Saxon' and Gewisse appear to be synonymous, especially when eighth-century charters describe more than one king of Wessex as *rex Gewisorum*.[4] However, many historians now think that Gewisse originated as a name for early Anglo-Saxon settlers in the upper valley of the Thames, and that the leaders of this people subsequently took over Hampshire and other territories in the south-west. The same theory proposes that the term 'West Saxon' was coined in the late seventh century as a way of encompassing not only the Gewisse but also the Jutes and other groups whose lands they had recently annexed. It is certainly a plausible scenario and one that fits with the eventual disappearance of the name Gewisse. By the late 800s, it was apparently obsolete enough to be omitted from an Old English translation of Bede's *Ecclesiastical History*. As for Gewis himself, the most we can say is that he was probably a fictional figure, perhaps one invented to explain the name of the Gewisse in a foundation-tale that was later replaced by the Cerdic legend.[5]

After Cynegils, the next king of Wessex was his son Cenwalh, a pagan who soon converted to Christianity. Cenwalh founded a church at Winchester, the ancient Roman city that would eventually become the principal royal centre of the kingdom. In 658, Cenwalh won a victory over the Britons which extended the western boundary of his kingdom to the River Parret in present-day Somerset. Three years later, a battle against unidentified foes at a place called Posentesburh may have been an attempt to halt Mercian encroachment from the north unless it, too, was a conflict with the Britons. Interestingly, when Cenwalh died c.672 he was not succeeded by a male relative but by his widow Seaxburh. Cenwalh had previously been married to a sister of the powerful Mercian king Penda but had discarded her in favour of Seaxburh, provoking a Mercian assault on Wessex. According to *ASC*, Seaxburh eventually succeeded Cenwalh, although whether she held full authority is hard to say. Bede does not mention her period of rule, saying only that 'under-kings took over the government of the realm' after Cenwalh's death.[6] In this instance Bede may be wrong and the Wessex chroniclers may be right. If so, we are seeing the first instance of a woman holding sole authority in an Anglo-Saxon kingdom. This highly unusual scenario was to be repeated more than two hundred years later when Æthelflæd became sole ruler of Mercia. Of Seaxburh herself we learn almost nothing. Her origins are unknown but, whatever they were, it is possible that she was put forward by the Mercians – not by the West Saxons – as their preferred successor to Cenwalh. Mercia had already gained influence in lands adjacent to Wessex, notably among the Jutes of Hampshire and Wight and among the South Saxons further east. Installing a pro-Mercian queen on the West Saxon throne would have been a logical extension of this political strategy.[7] In the end, Seaxburh's rule was brief. She appears to have been deposed in 674, not by her husband's kin but by a different branch of the West Saxon royal house. A prince called Æscwine then took the throne. He fought the Mercians in the following year but otherwise had a short and uneventful reign that ended with his death in 676. The kingship then returned to the main branch of the House of Cerdic when Cenwalh's brother Centwine began to rule. He is credited with pushing the Britons back 'as far as the sea', a reference to successful military campaigns. However, his death c.685 led to another dynastic reshuffle which again saw power in the hands of a rival branch of the royal family. The new king was Cædwalla, an ambitious and energetic man who began his reign as a pagan until an intervention from the northern kingdom of Bernicia brought him into the Christian fold. The agent of his conversion was the pious Northumbrian bishop Wilfrid who persuaded him to rethink his religious preferences. Not only did Cædwalla heed this advice, he transformed himself into a zealous crusader against the remnants of Anglo-Saxon paganism. He brutally conquered the Jutes of Wight in 686, deposing and slaying their king and forcing the inhabitants to adopt Christianity.

Until he changed his religion, Cædwalla had been the last pagan ruler of Wessex. A place of importance nevertheless continued to be retained for Woden in the traditions of the royal house. This mighty Germanic god had long been revered by Anglo-Saxon kings as a forefather from whom all their dynasties were descended. In each kingdom a mythical bloodline was preserved as a royal genealogy running back through many generations to a period before the original migration to Britain. Even after they began to adopt Christianity, kings continued to trace their ancestry from Woden. This was no sentimental nod to the pagan past. It was deliberate propaganda, employing Woden's former status as a figure of supernatural authority to confer legitimacy upon those who claimed to be his descendants. A royal family that staked such a claim was making a strong statement about its own right to rule, even if its members were devoutly Christian.

Cædwalla's conquest of Wight brought the island permanently under West Saxon control. The same campaign is likely to have included the final acquisition of all of Hampshire. As we have seen, Bede implies that the population of these newly acquired provinces were Jutes. Other Jutish territory further west, in the New Forest and elsewhere, had evidently been annexed by Wessex some twenty years earlier. One important consequence of such gains was the opening up of new routes of access to maritime trade via the English Channel. Cædwalla's conquests east of the River Solent enabled the creation of a major port at the confluence of the Test and Itchen. This was Hamwic, also known as Hamtun, the forerunner of present-day Southampton. By the end of the seventh century it had developed into a flourishing commercial centre with international trading connections.

In 688, Cædwalla gave up his kingship to embark on a pilgrimage to Rome. He was baptised there by the pope but died one week later. His successor was Ine whose long reign lasted thirty-seven years and who is credited with drawing up the first West Saxon law-code. Ine's wife, Æthelburh, is likewise an interesting figure. According to an entry in *ASC*, she led a military campaign in 722 which resulted in the destruction of Taunton. This place had been built by her husband, who was still very much alive at the time. The context of her action may have been a revolt against his kingship by a rival claimant. *ASC*'s entry for 722 adds that a certain Ealdberht, known as 'the Exile', fled into Surrey and Sussex. Ine then fought against the South Saxons, slaying Ealdberht on their territory in 725. Perhaps Ealdberht was a West Saxon prince or nobleman who had mounted a challenge to Ine's authority? He may have seized Taunton as the base for an uprising until Ine's queen ejected him. We can infer that he was then given refuge by the South Saxons, who thereby incurred Ine's wrath. It is also worth observing that Æthelburh's assault on Taunton, the first recorded military venture by an Anglo-Saxon woman, foreshadowed the campaigns of Æthelflæd two hundred years later.

Like his predecessor, Ine went on a pilgrimage to Rome and died there. The reigns of the next five kings of Wessex coincided with a period of dominance by Mercia, the so-called 'Mercian Ascendancy'.[8] This is discussed in more detail below. In the meantime, we may note that the expansion of Wessex continued regardless, mainly through conflict with the Britons. Ine had defeated the British kingdom of Dumnonia (Devon and Cornwall) in 710, a victory that may have gained some territory, but twelve years later he had suffered a reversal at the hands of the same enemy.[9] Further West Saxon gains along the same frontier appear to have been made as the century wore on and, by 786, almost all of what is now south-west England lay under the rule of Cerdic's descendants. In that year, the kingship of Wessex passed to a man called Beorhtric. During his reign a new kind of foe made its first recorded appearance in West Saxon territory. The event was noted retrospectively in *ASC* under the year 789:

And in [Beorhtric's] days came for the first time three ships of Northmen from Horthaland; and then the reeve rode thither and tried to compel them to go to the royal manor, for he did not know what they were; and then they slew him. These were the first ships of the Danes to come to England.

The reeve's name is unknown but his rank shows that he was an important royal official. His violent death signalled that the Viking Age had come to Wessex.

Mercian origins

Æthelflæd's paternal ancestry was West Saxon: she was Alfred the Great's daughter and a princess of the House of Cerdic. On her mother's side she was of Mercian heritage. Asser tells us that her maternal grandfather was an ealdorman of the Gaini, an otherwise unrecorded people whose territory cannot now be located. They may have been an ancient Mercian group, with origins going back to the time of the earliest Anglo-Saxon settlements. It is possible that a memory of them still lingers in Lincolnshire, in the north-east of Mercia, where the town of Gainsborough has a name that might mean 'fort of the Gaini'. Just as the people of ninth-century Wessex identified as being of Saxon or Jutish stock, so the Gaini and other Mercian groups regarded themselves as Angles. Also of Anglian heritage were the eastern neighbours of the Mercians: the East Angles of present-day Norfolk and Suffolk. The Northumbrians, too, claimed Anglian ancestry. Their lands lay north of the Mersey and Humber estuaries, although the eastern part of this frontier was often disputed with the Mercians. The western part followed the course of the Mersey, a river whose name derives from Old English *mǣres ēa*, 'boundary river'. A related term is *Mierce*, 'Mercians', meaning literally 'march-dwellers, borderers'. From the late seventh century, *Mierce* was used as an umbrella term for the inhabitants of what are now the midland counties of England. The border from which their name arose is unknown but is less likely to have been the River Mersey than an early line of interface between Anglo-Saxon settlers and native Britons somewhere in the central midlands. The oldest Mercian heartland is thought to have lain in the valley of the River Trent and this is a plausible setting for the original 'march'.[10]

Unfortunately, the Mercians have bequeathed few records of their history. There is no detailed account of their origins, no foundation-legend comparable to the story of Cerdic in the *Anglo-Saxon Chronicle*. Instead, we must try to piece together various scraps of information, some of which appear in texts compiled no earlier than the twelfth century. Unsurprisingly, the result is an incomplete picture of Mercia's beginnings. A more-or-less authentic narrative commences with a king called Creoda whose reign appears to have spanned the years 585 to 588. Creoda was succeeded by his son Pybba, who was in turn followed by Cearl before the kingship passed to Pybba's son Penda in the early 600s. Both Cearl and Penda appear in Bede's *Ecclesiastical History* so their historical existence is not in doubt. Cearl's ancestry is unknown but Penda's is shown in a genealogy preserved in *ASC* and in other texts. Penda's line of descent is shown running back through five previous generations to a man called Icel who – if he is not simply a figure of legend – may have been active around the year 500. By the early eighth century, members of the Mercian royal dynasty were calling themselves Iclingas ('Icel's descendants'). If a Mercian foundation-legend had survived it may have identified Icel as the first member of the dynasty to arrive in Britain from the Anglian homelands across the North Sea.[11] Like the House of Cerdic in Wessex, the Iclingas traced their line back to the Germanic god Woden and continued to do so after they adopted Christianity.

Our knowledge of Mercian history before the seventh century is sparse. Although both Creoda and Pybba were probably real rather than fictional, little is known of them. Of Cearl, who seems to have emerged from a different family, we have only a brief glimpse in Bede's *Ecclesiastical History*. Bede states that Cearl gave his daughter in marriage to Edwin, a prince of the northern Anglian kingdom of Deira, who had been forced into exile by enemies from neighbouring Bernicia. Edwin eventually became king of both Deira and Bernicia in 617.

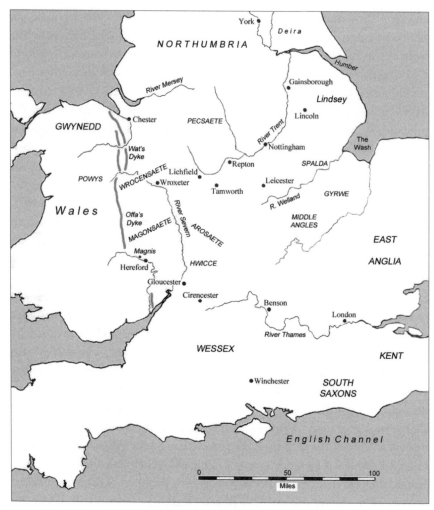

The origins of Mercia

He was a Christian, unlike most of his subjects who still worshipped the old Germanic gods. In 633 he was slain in battle against the Welsh warlord Cadwallon, king of Gwynedd, whose ally was none other than Penda of Mercia. Bede indicates that Penda had acceded to the Mercian kingship seven years earlier, in 626. To Bede he was an almost demonic figure, a heathen savage who contrasted sharply with pious Christian kings such as Edwin. Penda was a resolute pagan and remained so until his death. His long reign of some thirty years saw a major expansion of Mercian territory, driven by a string of military victories.[12] In 628, he fought the West Saxons at Cirencester, compelling them to seek an agreement with him. The resulting treaty seems to have transferred the territory of the Hwicce people of Worcestershire to Penda's overlordship.[13] On his northern frontier, Penda defeated and slew Oswald, the devoutly Christian king of Bernicia, and laid both Bernicia and Deira under tribute. A similarly bloody fate awaited the East Anglian king Anna, who fell in battle against Penda in 654.

By the middle of the seventh century, Penda was ruling a much larger Mercia than the one he had inherited from his forebears. An idea of its size can be gleaned from a document known as the Tribal Hidage, a list of territories in central England compiled at some point between the mid-seventh and the early ninth centuries.[14] The list assigns each territory a figure based on the number of hides, the hide being a measurement of land sufficient for sustaining one household. One territory, described as 'the first land of the Mercians', was assessed at the very high figure of 30,000 hides. It almost certainly corresponds to Staffordshire with parts of Warwickshire, Leicestershire, Nottinghamshire and Derbyshire.[15] Within this area lay the original domain of Penda's dynasty, including Tamworth – the main royal centre in his time – and Lichfield, where St Chad established a bishopric in 669.

Other territories annexed by Penda and his successors appear in the Tribal Hidage under the names of specific population groups. They include the Wrocensæte ('Wroxeter dwellers') of Shropshire, the Pecsæte in what is now the Peak District and the Arosæte who lived around the River Arrow in Worcestershire and Warwickshire. Many of these groups had been absorbed into the Mercian kingdom by c.700, either by military conquest or by the threat of it. One group seemingly absent from the list but certainly under Penda's control was the Magonsæte, a people of present-day Herefordshire who took their name from the Roman settlement of Magnis at Kenchester.[16] Penda assigned their lands to his son Merewalh, whom he installed there as sub-king. Over in the east, along the East Anglian border, the Tribal Hidage lists a scatter

of small groups whose lands were likewise brought into 'Greater Mercia'. They
included the Spalda, from whom the Lincolnshire town of Spalding is named,
and the Gyrwe who lived in the fenlands between Cambridgeshire and The Wash.
Most of these eastern groups seem to have been Middle Angles, a collection of
separate peoples who had never consolidated into a kingdom of their own.[17]
The various Middle Anglian groups were still living independently from one
another when Penda attached them permanently to Mercia. Only then did they
become answerable to a single authority, for Penda installed his son Peada as
their first king. It might not be too wide of the mark to envisage Peada's sub-
kingdom corresponding to the later ecclesiastical diocese of Leicester.

Mercia's expansion into the eastern midlands brought Penda into conflict
with the East Angles, whose lands he invaded. He slew their king and made his
successor a Mercian puppet. Penda was no doubt a man of fairly advanced years
when, in 655, he was destroyed by Oswald's brother Oswiu in the great battle of
Winwæd. His vast army, which included contingents from Wales and East
Anglia, was cut to pieces. His death led to a brief period of Mercian subjection
to Oswiu, who ruled Bernicia and Deira together as the unified kingdom of
Northumbria. Oswiu placed northern Mercia under his own direct rule, leaving
the southern part to Penda's son Peada. The latter had been sub-king of the
Middle Angles during his father's reign but was also Oswiu's son-in-law, having
married the Northumbrian king's daughter some years earlier. He had converted
to Christianity while Penda was still alive. After the Northumbrian victory at
Winwæd, large numbers of Peada's compatriots followed the same path, for
Oswiu sent Christian missionaries to preach among them. In 656, the first bishop
of the Mercians was appointed, with his see at Repton. The same year saw
Peada's murder by his Northumbrian wife. Why she killed him is unknown, but
the event no doubt disrupted her father's hold on Mercia. Anti-Northumbrian
sentiment eventually erupted in a revolt which saw the ejection of Oswiu's
henchmen and the installation of Peada's younger brother Wulfhere as king. For
a time, Wulfhere acknowledged Oswiu's superiority but, by c.665, he appears to
have shaken off the yoke.[18] Nevertheless, the success of Oswiu's missionaries in
bringing Mercia into the Christian fold meant that Northumbrian clerics were
always welcomed there. One of these was Chad, a Bernician monk who was
appointed as bishop of Mercia in 669. He moved the episcopal seat from Repton
to Lichfield, placing his church on the site of today's cathedral.

Wulfhere, like his father, became a powerful king whom other kings
recognised as an overlord. Unlike his father, he seems to have attained this
status partly by skilful diplomacy rather than by aggressive warfare alone.

Alliances, treaties and inter-dynastic marriages were his preferred tools. His own strategic union with a Kentish princess undoubtedly gained him an alliance with her family. That is not to say that he lacked an appetite for military campaigns: in 661, he raided southward as far as the English Channel and attacked the Isle of Wight. He then gave the island to the king of the South Saxons, whose conversion to Christianity he sponsored.[19] As noted above, the West Saxons were briefly ruled by a queen called Seaxburh in the early 670s. It is possible that she relied on Mercian support, which would have come from Wulfhere. Further west, Wulfhere obtained influence among the Hwicce, a people who had acknowledged his father Penda as overlord. They still had their own kings and provided a useful buffer on Wulfhere's south-west frontier, beyond which lay the Welsh and the West Saxons. The latter had good reason to feel nervous about Mercia's expansion, although their anxiety may have been relieved after Wulfhere launched an abortive attack on Northumbria in 674. His invasion ended in a defeat which forced him into a subordinate relationship with the Northumbrian king Ecgfrith, son of Oswiu. A dynastic marriage between Wulfhere's brother Æthelred and a Northumbrian princess was arranged at this time and was no doubt intended to seal the new political arrangement. Wulfhere's position was severely weakened and it is not known if he won or lost his final military campaign. This was fought in 675, against the West Saxons, but by the end of the year he was dead.

The kingship of Mercia then passed to Wulfhere's brother Æthelred who continued the family tradition of aggressive warfare. In 676, Mercian forces devastated Kent, a long-time ally of Northumbria. Three years later, on the banks of the River Trent, Æthelred scored an important victory over the Northumbrians, winning back territories lost by Wulfhere in 674. Among these was Lindsey, present-day northern Lincolnshire, a frontier region that had long been disputed between Mercia and Northumbria. Æthelred's reign lasted to the end of the seventh century and, unlike most kings of this period, he did not die in office but stepped aside to make way for a successor. His reason for giving up the throne is not recorded. It might have had something to do with the violent death of his Northumbrian wife in 697: she was murdered by Mercian nobles, perhaps an anti-Northumbrian faction who opposed her husband. Æthelred eventually withdrew from the turbulent world of high-level politics and may have became a monk. His successor Coenred did something similar, giving up the kingship and setting out on a pilgrimage to Rome.

Of the next king, Ceolred, little is reported. In 715, he fought a battle in Wiltshire against the West Saxon king Ine but neither the cause nor the result is known. He died in 716 and was succeeded by Æthelbald, a great-nephew of the mighty Penda. Æthelbald's reign appears to have been uneventful until 733, when he captured Somerton in Somerset from Wessex. By the end of the decade his attention had turned towards Northumbria, the bitter enemy of his seventh-century predecessors. Until then, no warfare between Mercian and Northumbrian kings had been recorded since 679, suggesting a period of peace in which old rivalries had cooled. The peace ended in 740 when Æthelbald launched a raid across his northern border. He is said to have been in alliance at that time with the Pictish king Onuist (Óengus) who was simultaneously at war with the Northumbrian king Eadberht.[20] The long-term outcome of these hostilities is unknown but, within ten years, Onuist and Eadberht had settled their differences to mount a combined assault on the Britons of the Clyde. In 741, Æthelbald turned back to the south, resuming his conflict with the West Saxons under their newly anointed king Cuthred. The end of this war may have seen Æthelbald reimposing his overlordship on Wessex, for he was able to call upon Cuthred for military assistance against the Welsh a couple of years later.

Hostilities between Æthelbald and Cuthred resumed in 752 when they fought a battle which Æthelbald won, his victory marking the start of the 'Mercian Ascendancy', a period in which the rulers of the midlands dominated their neighbours.[21] From the mid-eighth century to the early ninth, the southern English kingdoms of Kent, Sussex, East Anglia and the Hwicce were all subordinate to Mercia. We cannot be sure that Wessex should be added to this list, even though it appears to have been experiencing a period of dynastic uncertainty.[22] Æthelbald himself was murdered in 755 by unknown assailants. His successor Beornred was in turn toppled by Offa, a king whose reign of nearly forty years marked the high-point of Mercia's supremacy.

Offa's most famous achievement was his eponymous dyke, a massive linear earthwork marking the western boundary of his realm. Surviving sections still define the border between England and Wales, the best-preserved of these being testimony to the extent of Offa's power. Only a king who ruled with unchallenged authority could have commanded the human resources necessary for such a huge project. The earthwork's design shows that it was intended to face the Welsh, serving not only as a frontier but also as a demonstration of the manpower available to Mercia's greatest king. It is somewhat surprising, then, that the first reference to Offa's warfare comes late in his reign, in the year 776, with a retrospective entry in *ASC* noting a battle in Kent. This was almost certainly a Mercian defeat, although perhaps one not significant enough to uncouple the Kentish kingdom from Offa's overlordship. A more successful military campaign came three years later when he defeated the West Saxons to capture the settlement of *Bensingtun*, probably Benson in Oxfordshire.[23] This victory may have restored Offa's dominance over Wessex which had no doubt been jolted by his defeat in Kent. Alternatively, Wessex might not have been subordinate to Mercia at this time. Hence, although it is tempting to see the marriage of Offa's daughter Eadburh to the West Saxon king Beorhtric in 789 as a union foisted on Wessex by a dominant Mercia, this might not be the correct interpretation.[24] It was in this same year that the Vikings made their first documented appearance on English shores, killing one of Beorhtric's officials on the Dorset coast. There is no record of a similar incident on Mercian soil at such an early date. Indeed, the next report of a Viking warband on English territory described a raid by 'heathens' on the Northumbrian monastery of Lindisfarne in 793.[25] Offa died before the end of the century, apparently without encountering the new foes from Scandinavia. His successors, however, would not be able to avoid the coming storm.

Wessex, Mercia and the Vikings

The dark portents of 789 and 793 caused much anxiety to those directly affected but otherwise had little impact. Perhaps these early encounters with Vikings were regarded as isolated events rather than as the first signs of a looming catastrophe? Among the Anglo-Saxon kingdoms, the usual cycle of wars and dynastic strife went on as before. This had been the norm for three hundred years and showed no sign of abating as the ninth century dawned. In Mercia, Offa was succeeded by his son Ecgfrith who seems to have enjoyed amicable relations with his West Saxon brother-in-law Beorhtric. This friendliness continued after Ecgfrith's death and, in 799, his successor Cenwulf agreed a peace treaty with the West Saxons.[26] But Cenwulf was a man who nurtured predatory ambitions of his own. He had previously attacked Kent, his south-eastern neighbour, ritually mutilating its king in an act of extreme barbarity. In 802, he shattered the treaty with Wessex by sending a Mercian army over the border to attack Wiltshire, a raid which saw the invaders hurled back by local forces. Wessex at that time was ruled by Ecgberht, a king who seems to have had no further trouble from Cenwulf. His own ambitions surfaced in 825 when he ravaged the lands of the Cornish – the Britons of Cornwall. By then, Cornwall was the last surviving portion of the British kingdom of Dumnonia. The adjacent territory of Devon had already been conquered by Wessex and it was from there that Ecgberht's forces raided the Cornish.[27] In the same year,

Ecgberht turned his attention to the Mercians, whose long overlordship of the southern English was beginning to unravel. Ecgberht had a personal score to settle: in his youth he had been driven into exile by the mighty King Offa. So it was that in 825, at a place called *Ellandun* in Wiltshire, he won a decisive victory over the Mercian king Beornwulf.

The battle of Ellandun marked not only the end of the Mercian Ascendancy but also the birth of a much longer period of West Saxon dominance. Southern English territories that had previously acknowledged Mercian superiority now transferred their allegiance to the House of Cerdic. Ecgberht soon found himself recognised as overlord of Sussex, Surrey and Kent.[28] The rulers of these areas – essentially vassals who had previously answered to Mercian kings – were expelled and not replaced. The result was a greatly enlarged Wessex encompassing all lands south of the Thames, with Essex possibly a temporary inclusion north of the river. In East Anglia, a revolt against many decades of Mercian overlordship brought King Beornwulf to a battle in which he was slain by the East Angles. Much further north, the Northumbrian king Eanred is said to have submitted to Ecgberht in 829, in a ceremony at Dore on the Mercian-Northumbrian border. Whether this really was a submission or just an acknowledgement of Ecgberht's overlordship in the south is uncertain.[29] The West Saxon king was able to come so far north of his heartlands because he had defeated and deposed the new Mercian king Wiglaf some months earlier. In the end, Ecgberht's authority over Mercia turned out to be brief, for Wiglaf managed to regain power in the following year, perhaps after a revolt against West Saxon domination.[30] Ecgberht's position was weaker thereafter, but there would be no rebirth of Mercian superiority. Wessex retained control of all lands south of the Thames, including the formerly independent kingdoms of Sussex and Kent. Any lingering Mercian ambitions would, in any case, soon be crushed by Scandinavian warlords.

As we have already noted, the end of the eighth century and the beginning of the ninth brought the first Viking raids on the British Isles. Following the attack on Lindisfarne in 793, other exposed monasteries were similarly targeted. Iona, the pre-eminent religious house in northern Britain, was plundered in 795 and twice in the following decade. One of the small isles off the east coast of Ireland – either Rathlin or Lambay – was likewise raided in 795. It seems that the Irish and the peoples of northern Britain bore the brunt of Viking aggression at this time, with the documentary record implying that southern Britain was briefly left alone. The situation changed in 835 when a force of heathen warriors sailed into the Thames to attack the Isle of Sheppey off the north coast of Kent. The next year saw a large raid on the coast of Wessex by thirty-five shiploads of Danes.

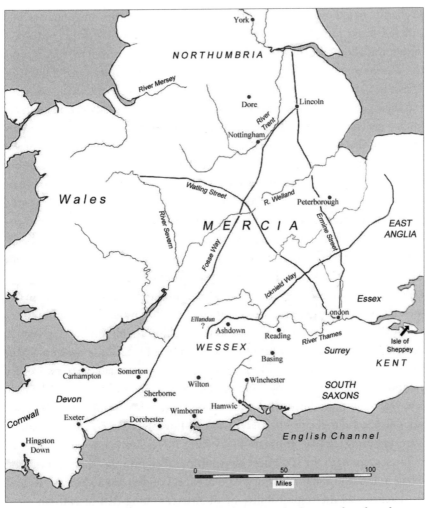

The early ninth century, showing the four great highways of medieval England (the Roman roads Watling Street, Ermine Street and Fosse Way, and the pre-Roman Icknield Way)

Ecgberht met these marauders in a battle at Carhampton in Somerset but suffered heavy losses, leaving the enemy in possession of the field.[31] In 838 a 'great pirate host' of Danes joined with the Britons of Cornwall to wage war on the West Saxons. In response, Ecgberht raised an army and marched to Hingston Down in Cornwall where he won a victory. He died in the following year and was succeeded by his son Æthelwulf, the father of Alfred the Great. In contemporary charters, Æthelwulf is described as king of the 'southern peoples', an indication that he had inherited his father's authority over all lands south of the Thames. One of his first actions was to divide his kingdom into two, assigning the eastern provinces – Kent, Surrey and Sussex – to his eldest son Athelstan while keeping the old West Saxon heartlands for himself. Relations with Mercia seem to have been fairly amicable during his reign, with hints of peaceful co-operation. A longstanding border dispute was settled in the 840s when lands around the upper Thames in what is now Berkshire were transferred from Mercian to West Saxon control, apparently without bloodshed. An exchange of expertise between Mercian and West Saxon mints implies a joint venture in the manufacture of coins and perhaps in other aspects of royal administration too.[32]

Æthelwulf soon had to face a new wave of Viking assaults on his kingdom. A raiding-fleet landed at the port of Hamwic but was beaten back by West Saxon forces under the command of an ealdorman. Less fortunate were two other ealdormen who were slain by raiders in Dorset and Kent respectively. The next few years saw more hostilities, with victory and defeat being tasted by both sides. Beyond Æthelwulf's borders his fellow-English in Mercia and East Anglia were enduring similar tribulations. Viking forces were now increasing in numerical strength. In 851, a fleet of 350 ships sailed into the Thames, bringing terror to London and Canterbury. At that time, London was a Mercian city and its defence was the responsibility of the Mercian king Beorhtwulf who had succeeded Wiglaf. Beorhtwulf was defeated by the Vikings, leaving the way open for them to pour southward into Surrey. It was left to Æthelwulf to halt their advance, which he duly did in the great battle of *Aclea* ('Oak Field'). At some point during this campaign his eldest son Athelstan, ruling as sub-king in Kent, seems to have died. Meanwhile, in Mercia, the kingship now passed to a man called Burgred. In 853, despite the Scandinavian menace, he sought and obtained Æthelwulf's help in subduing the Welsh. This new mood of friendship between two English kingdoms who had so often been bitter rivals was sealed when Æthelwulf's daughter Æthelswith became Burgred's wife.[33]

Also in 853, Æthelwulf sent his youngest son Alfred on a visit to Rome, accompanied by a large entourage. Alfred was then about four years old. He was introduced to Pope Leo IV who adorned him with the trappings of a Roman consul. This incident was later given 'spin' by Asser and the compilers of *ASC* who claimed that the pope had actually anointed Alfred as a future king of Wessex.[34] The young prince returned to Rome two years later, this time with his father. Before departing for this trip, Æthelwulf divided his kingdom between his two surviving elder sons, giving the eastern provinces to Æthelberht and the western heartlands to Æthelbald. This may have been intended as a temporary arrangement while he was away in Rome, for his visit to the holy city was a lengthy one. He spent a whole year there before returning home via the kingdom of the Franks, acquiring a new wife along the way. His bride was the Frankish princess Judith, daughter of King Charles the Bald and great-granddaughter of the renowned Charlemagne. However, when he came back to Wessex, he was dismayed to learn that his son Æthelbald was refusing to give up the western kingship. Seeking to avoid a civil war, Æthelwulf accepted the situation and set himself up in the eastern provinces, taking back the authority he had assigned to Æthelberht.[35]

Æthelwulf died in 858 and was entombed at Winchester in the royal family's principal church. In his will he cemented the partition of the kingdom between Æthelberht and Æthelbald, confirming these men in the eastern and western provinces respectively.[36] Æthelbald tried to strengthen his own position by marrying his widowed stepmother Judith but his untimely death in 860 saw the whole kingdom fall under Æthelberht's control. Æthelberht soon had to contend with a Viking assault on the Hampshire coast which brought marauders to the very gates of Winchester. Two of his trusted ealdormen drove the heathens back to their ships and calm was duly restored.

In 865, after a reign of only five years, Æthelberht died. His body was taken not to Winchester but to another royal church at Sherborne in Dorset, the seat of a West Saxon bishopric since 705. He was succeeded by Æthelred, the elder of his two surviving brothers, whose reign witnessed a significant change in the character of the Viking attacks. Where previously the raiders had used hit-and-run tactics, they now came intending to conquer and colonise. In 865, a huge force of Danes, known to modern historians as the Great Heathen Army, landed in East Anglia. It did not sail home to Scandinavia when its raiding was done but stayed over the winter. Its leaders forged an agreement with the East Angles, who even supplied the Danish warriors with horses for the new raiding season. After winter was ended, the Danes mounted their steeds and rode northward to seize York, the capital of the English kingdom of Northumbria. At that time, the allegiance of the Northumbrians was divided between two rival kings who were now obliged to put aside their quarrel. Combining their forces, they marched on York in March 867, seeking to expel the Danes. Both were defeated and killed.

Following their success at York, the Danes once again took to the saddle, riding south into Mercia and spending the winter at Nottingham in the east of the kingdom. There they set themselves up in an old fortress on the north side of the River Trent. In desperation, the Mercian king Burgred appealed to Wessex for aid. His call was answered by Æthelred who, with his younger brother Alfred, led a West Saxon army to Nottingham. A stand-off followed, with neither side making the first move. The stalemate eventually ended with a peace treaty between Burgred and the Danes which saw them depart from Mercia.[37] In 869, they went back to York and stayed for a year before returning to East Anglia for the following winter. The East Anglian king Edmund was defeated in battle and taken prisoner, his heathen captors slaying him so savagely that he was later canonised as a martyr-saint. After his death the Danes took control of his entire kingdom, using it as a secure base for raiding English lands in the west. The raids saw Christian religious sites plundered ruthlessly, their defenceless occupants being slain or enslaved. In eastern Mercia, not far from the East Anglian border, the monastery of Peterborough was burned down and its clergy were slaughtered. There was little that the English could do to prevent or avenge such atrocities. Indeed, with York, Nottingham and East Anglia now in Danish hands it was only a matter of time before other places were similarly overwhelmed. It was abundantly clear that the Great Heathen Army had no intention of going home. Its leaders were not merely seeking to amass plunder but were determined to create their own kingdoms in Britain.

In 870, the Army crossed Mercia and invaded Wessex. During this campaign it was led by two kings – Bagsecg and Halfdan – who seized a West Saxon fortress at Reading. In January of the following year, King Æthelred and his brother Alfred marched on Reading, only to be hurled back by the Danes. Within days, the brothers confronted the enemy again at Ashdown in Berkshire. There the heathen king Bagsecg was cut down as he and Halfdan led half of their army against Æthelred. The other half came against Alfred and was put to flight, leaving five dead Viking jarls in its wake. After this battle the war continued, the next significant clash taking place barely two weeks later at Basing in Hampshire. The shifting tides of fortune made this a Danish victory, but within a couple of months the West Saxon royal brothers were again victorious. It was then early springtime of 871. The year had already witnessed two major battles and there were still many months left of the campaigning season.

Æthelred died in the spring and was buried at Wimborne in Dorset. He had already named Alfred, the last surviving son of Æthelwulf, as the next king of Wessex.

Shires and ealdormen

The great expansion of Wessex in the ninth century had led to a reorganisation of how the kingdom was governed. Royal authority was delegated to senior members of the nobility known as ealdormen, each of whom was responsible for a specific territory or 'shire'. In contemporary charters the rank of ealdorman was usually rendered in Latin as *dux*, from which our modern word 'duke' derives. Below the ealdorman the thegn represented the next tier of authority, his rank denoted by the Latin word *minister* in charters. Of the shires, four original ones divided the heartland of Wessex into four parts: Somerset, Dorset, Wiltshire and Hampshire. This division appears to have been in existence before 850, with each shire taking its name from a royal settlement designated as the centre of administration. Somerset and Dorset were the dependent territories of Somerton and Dorchester respectively, while Wiltshire and Hampshire were similarly answerable to Wilton and Hamwic/Hamtun (present-day Southampton). The eastern provinces – Sussex, Kent and Surrey – were not designated as shires so early but were nevertheless governed by ealdormen appointed by the West Saxon kings. A different system appears to have operated in Mercia, where ealdormen seem to have emerged at local level as leaders of population groups rather than as appointees of the king. Mercia can thus be said to have lagged behind Wessex, being less quick to develop a shire-based system. Ninth-century Mercian kings still ruled what was essentially a collection of peoples or tribes rather than a more centralised realm in which provinces were overseen by royal appointees.[38] Certainly there seems to have been no formal 'shiring' of Mercia until the following century. Moreover, the custom of electing Mercian kings from a pool of eligible candidates hindered the establishment of a single, hereditary dynasty that might have provided stability and consistency. Hence, we see the kingship of Mercia rotating between several royal families, each competing to advance its own fortunes and ambitions. The kingdom's organisational weaknesses were brought into sharp focus by the Viking invasions.

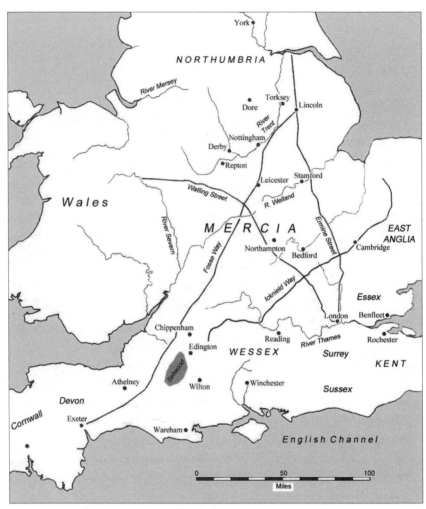

Alfred and the Danes

3

PRINCESS

Alfred was twenty-three years old when he succeeded Æthelred as king of Wessex. He was already a seasoned military commander, having accompanied his brother in several campaigns against the Vikings. The first of these was the expedition to Nottingham in 867, in support of the beleaguered Mercian king Burgred. Alfred was only nineteen at that time – a young English prince riding to war against the fearsome Great Heathen Army. In the following year he married Ealhswith, the daughter of a senior Mercian nobleman. Ealhswith's father, Æthelred Mucel, was a lord of the Gaini, a people who may have been one of the oldest Anglo-Saxon groups in Mercia. As noted in the previous chapter, the Gaini can perhaps be associated with Gainsborough in Lincolnshire – if the name of the town has been correctly interpreted as 'fort of the Gaini'. Little else is known of Æthelred Mucel but he seems to have witnessed a number of West Saxon charters in the late 800s. He might also be the 'Ealdorman Mucel' who appears in some Mercian charters around the middle of the century.[1] A slightly earlier 'Ealdorman Mucel' who witnessed documents from c.810 to the 840s may have been his father.

Whatever her true paternal ancestry, Ealhswith had Mercian royal blood from her maternal forebears, her mother being one of the daughters of King Offa. She had a brother called Æthelwulf, possibly the same man as a Mercian ealdorman of this name who witnessed charters in the 850s.[2] Alfred himself had a family connection with Mercian royalty, his sister Æthelswith being the wife of King Burgred. Ealhswith and Alfred were married in her homeland at a ceremony witnessed by many important people.[3] Afterwards, they moved to Wessex and started a family. Five of their offspring survived the perils of infancy to reach adulthood, the eldest being their firstborn, a daughter to whom they gave the name Æthelflæd. The next in age was a son called Edward, then two more daughters – Æthelgifu and Ælfthryth – and lastly a younger son Æthelweard.

Neither the date nor the place of Æthelflæd's birth is known. As the first child of Alfred and Ealhswith she was probably born within a year or two of her parents' marriage. The year 869 seems a reasonable guess and is unlikely to be wide of the mark. Her birthplace was most likely a royal residence in Wessex, perhaps the palace at Chippenham in Wiltshire, not far from the Mercian border.[4] Chippenham was already associated with important events involving members of Alfred's family, having been the venue for his sister's marriage to Burgred in 853. It would have been a suitable place for Ealhswith to give birth to their first child. Given the troubled times, her husband might not have been at home when the baby arrived. In all likelihood he was away on campaign with his older brother Æthelred, honing his skills as a warrior and commander.

Æthelflæd's birth coincided with a period of profound anxiety among her people. To be West Saxon or Mercian in the late ninth century meant being ever-aware of the Viking menace that prowled beyond the eastern horizon. In the early years of her infancy, Æthelflæd would have been too young to share this fear, too young to understand why her father was rarely at home. She may have been under a year old when he became king. In a less perilous era he might have been able to spend more time with his daughter, watching her learn and grow, but the demands of kingship were too great a burden. Of particular concern was an event that had occurred just before his brother's death: the appearance of a new Viking fleet in the Thames estuary. It was led by Guthrum, a Danish warlord whose soldiers acknowledged him as a king. Guthrum sailed upriver from London to Reading where Halfdan was still ensconced with his own forces. There the two Viking hosts merged together to form a much-enlarged Great Heathen Army. Alfred had been king for barely a month when Guthrum and Halfdan launched a combined assault on Wessex. Although heavily outnumbered, Alfred met them in battle at Wilton in Wiltshire. There he was heavily defeated but managed to avoid being slain. During the remaining months of 871 he confronted the Danes again and again, engaging them in several battles and countless skirmishes. Such incessant warfare must have been exhausting, even for a young king in his early twenties. Little wonder, then, that he eventually sued for peace, presumably by offering his foes a large payment from his treasury. The offer was accepted and the heathen force went away. It left Reading and went to London, remaining in the city over the winter months. The next year, 872, it was on the move again, first to Northumbria then back southward into Mercia. It spent the winter in north-east Mercia, at Torksey in Lincolnshire, where the site of its winter camp has been identified by archaeological finds. It eventually moved south to Repton, an important Mercian settlement containing a royal mausoleum, where it over-wintered. The presence of this large Danish army in Mercia's heartlands brought the downfall of King Burgred who was forced to abandon his throne in 874. He fled into exile, becoming a religious pilgrim and making his way to Rome where other Englishmen had already established a small enclave. He never returned to his homeland and spent the remaining years of his life in the holy city.

Some historians think that the next king of Mercia was a puppet of the Vikings. His name was Ceolwulf but not much more is known about him. In *ASC* he was identified merely as a thegn, not as a king. There he was also described as 'unwise', a reflection of contemporary opinion in Wessex where he may have been thought of as a self-serving turncoat who threw in his lot with heathen enemies. The chroniclers claimed that he swore an oath of loyalty to the Danes and told them to use Mercia in whatever way they wished. He is said to have guaranteed this pledge by handing over hostages from among his own people. Yet we know from numismatic evidence that this so-called 'unwise thegn' was indeed a king, for several coins issued in his name from the Mercian mint at London give him the Latin title *rex*.[5] His name alliterates with those of some of his predecessors, suggesting that he may have belonged to the so-called 'C' dynasty of Mercia which included kings with names like Cenwulf and Cuthred. Indeed, it is possible that he was a descendant of an earlier Ceolwulf who had reigned in the 820s. If so, we have no reason to think of him as a puppet of the Danes. He should be seen rather as a legitimate monarch, elected by the Mercians according to their own customs. It is likely that he ruled with far more independence than the West Saxon chroniclers allowed him. The very fact that he issued coinage under his own name contradicts any notion that he had less power or status than other kings. He was probably the unnamed English leader who won a victory over Welsh enemies in 878, assuming that this battle took place in the Anglo-Welsh borderlands of western Mercia.[6] We are surely seeing a king who acted independently of the Danes rather than as their subordinate or puppet. The West Saxon chroniclers imply that the part of Mercia under Ceolwulf's rule was allocated to him by the leaders of the Great Heathen Army. It is more likely that this was simply the part that still remained in English hands after the fall of King Burgred in 874. A large swathe of eastern Mercia – including the old royal centre at Repton – now lay firmly under Danish control. Ceolwulf's realm must have been confined to the western provinces, even if its precise limits are not known.

Ceolwulf and the Danelaw

Eastern Mercia became part of the Danelaw, a huge area stretching from Essex to York that had been conquered by the Great Heathen Army. The '-law' suffix shows that the population in this area was subject to the legal customs of its new masters. Here, the Danes established themselves in fortresses or fortified towns, each with its own territory.[7] The most important were the so-called 'Five Boroughs': Nottingham, Leicester, Derby, Stamford and Lincoln. Other major strongholds included Northampton, Bedford and Cambridge. King Guthrum, who was swiftly emerging as Alfred's arch-enemy, would eventually settle in East Anglia. To what extent his authority was acknowledged elsewhere is unclear but he may have been recognised as overlord by one or more of the strongholds in eastern Mercia. It is unfortunate that Ceolwulf's relations with Guthrum and other Danelaw leaders can only be viewed through West Saxon eyes. An accurate, unbiased picture is difficult to reconstruct from a chronicle that scorns Ceolwulf as an 'unwise thegn'. It may be fair to acknowledge him as a fully-independent Mercian king who happened to rule a smaller realm than that of his forebears. Like Alfred, he was no doubt prepared to negotiate with Vikings whenever the need arose, making whatever deals were necessary to ensure the survival of his kingdom.

After the fall of King Burgred and the partition of Mercia, the main strength of the Great Heathen Army left Repton. It separated into two divisions, one led by Halfdan and the other by Guthrum. Halfdan crossed into Northumbria and headed to the River Tyne where he wintered with his troops. He took over the surrounding countryside and established a base from which to launch raids against the northern Celtic peoples – the Britons of Strathclyde in the west and the Picts in the east.[8] The other division of the Army, led by Guthrum, went south from Repton to spend the winter of 874–5 at Cambridge. Guthrum shared command with two other kings whose names were Oscytel and Anund. The presence of this force within easy striking distance of the Thames meant that the Danes once again posed a direct threat to Wessex. So, although King Alfred had little need to worry about Halfdan, he would have been anxious about Guthrum's next move.

In the summer of 875, Alfred fought a sea-battle against seven Viking ships. The location is unknown but it was a West Saxon victory and one of the enemy vessels was captured. This brief success was overturned when Guthrum and his associates led their army into Wessex, dodging a clash with local forces and occupying the settlement of Wareham in Dorset. Some months later, in 876, Alfred came with an offer of peace – most likely a substantial payment – and the invaders accepted it. In return, they promised to depart from his kingdom, swearing solemn oaths on a 'sacred ring'. Their words, however, proved false. They simply led their troops out of Wareham under cover of darkness and rode west to the old Roman city of Exeter. Alfred pursued them with his own horsemen but failed to catch up before they sealed the city against him. Then the Danes offered another pledge of peace, sealing it with hostages from their own ranks. This time the agreement held firm and, when autumn came, the heathens departed and returned to eastern Mercia for the winter. There they divided up the land among themselves, founding the Five Boroughs and other major strongholds. It is at this point that the Wessex chroniclers would have us believe that the Danes allocated a separate domain to Ceolwulf, the rest being kept for distribution among themselves. As already noted, this is not necessarily what happened, but it is the only account we possess. Whatever the true course of events, Ceolwulf emerged as ruling the only part of Mercia still under English control, a mere rump of the once-mighty kingdom of Offa's day.

Winter was traditionally the time of year when warriors sheathed their swords and took a break from fighting. Military campaigns in the cold season were rare, for commanders knew that the risk of inclement weather made long journeys an uninviting prospect for their troops. Roads and tracks were likely to be muddy or icy, while night-camps could be bitter for man and horse alike. This was why the Viking armies in Britain tended to look for suitable winter bases as soon as summer passed into autumn. Raiding would normally resume in the spring, when conditions began to improve. A major campaign in winter was therefore an exceptional occurrence, but not entirely unheard of. If planned and executed successfully it could catch an enemy unawares. Alfred was the target of such an onslaught in early January 878, when the Danes broke the latest truce. Coming out of Mercia, an army led by Guthrum struck hard at Wessex, attacking the royal settlement of Chippenham. The location may have been carefully chosen, for Alfred and his family were in residence after celebrating Christmas. We learn from *ASC* that the raiders arrived in secret, presumably under cover of darkness, so perhaps this was an attempt to slay the English king. If so, it failed, for Alfred and his relatives survived. His kingdom, however, was completely overrun. Using Chippenham as a raiding-base, the Vikings now harried the people into submission. Some of the West Saxon nobility, no doubt fearing that the House of Cerdic had fallen, fled to other lands rather than submit to heathen invaders. Alfred himself, accompanied by a small company of nobles and soldiers, withdrew to a remote part of Somerset. He came to the Isle of Athelney, an area of dry ground in a vast fenland of salt marshes. In that inhospitable place, and facing the additional challenge of winter, he and his companions struggled to survive. Asser summed up the king's dire situation:

> He had nothing to live on except what he could forage by frequent raids, either secretly or openly, from the Vikings as well as from the Christians who had submitted to the Vikings' authority.[9]

We can be certain that Alfred's wife and children were with him during this period. It was a grim time for all of them. Whatever mirth they had shared around the fireside at Christmas must have seemed a distant memory. They had been forced to exchange the comforts of the feasting-hall for a life of fear and hardship in the bleak, cold marshlands. Alfred's daughter Æthelflæd was probably around eight years old at the time, still a young girl but old enough to understand that she and her family lay in deadly peril. The experience must have had a profound effect upon her. No longer a carefree princess in a richly-adorned palace, cushioned from the horrors of war, she now lived a far more basic existence in what was essentially a military camp. Every day, she would have seen the anxiety in her father's face as he wondered what the future held in store.

Winter was over and the holy time of Easter had been celebrated when the defence of Wessex resumed. Alfred began by constructing a fort at Athelney, to be used as a base from which to launch counter-attacks against the Danes. The forces available to him at the outset were meagre: he had those warriors who had accompanied him from Chippenham, others who presumably managed to join him afterwards, and local troops led by loyal henchmen such as the ealdorman of Somerset.[10] With this small army, Alfred went out to confront the enemy on numerous occasions, stubbornly demonstrating his refusal to give up his kingdom without a fight. His courage and energy gave hope to his people and, in early May, he rode to the great forest of Selwood in Somerset. There, at a famous monument known as Ecgberht's Stone, the men of Wiltshire, Somerset and Hampshire rallied to his banner. Many of them had not expected their king to rise again after enduring so much danger and hardship. They now saw him standing proud and defiant at the stone and were themselves filled with renewed hope. With enough manpower to once again put a viable army in the field, Alfred marched out for a decisive showdown with the Danes. The great battle took place at Edington in Wiltshire. Asser describes the men of Wessex 'fighting fiercely with a compact shieldwall' and inflicting heavy casualties. Eventually, the Vikings abandoned the battlefield and fled back to their encampment with the West Saxons in pursuit. The demoralised survivors, including King Guthrum himself, could then only watch as Alfred's army assembled in force outside the camp. The ensuing siege went on for two weeks until hunger and despair forced Guthrum to sue for peace. He offered unconditional surrender, making no demands of his own and inviting Alfred to take as many Viking hostages as he wished. Most treaties between Vikings and their foes involved a reciprocal exchange of hostages but, on this occasion, Guthrum set custom aside. He was clearly in desperate straits. Not only did he promise to take the remnant of his army out of Wessex, he even pledged himself to Christianity. He was duly baptised, with Alfred standing as sponsor and welcoming him from the font as an adopted son. Keeping his promise, Guthrum left Wessex and crossed into Mercia, remaining there for a year before leading his warriors back to East Anglia. Although still regarded by the East Anglian Danes as their king, he appears to have abstained from further raiding until the end of his days.

Alfred had saved Wessex from the fate that had befallen eastern Mercia. Had he failed, his kingdom would have become part of the Danelaw. He had also secured his position as king not only of the West Saxons but of all the southern English. The Scandinavian menace did not, however, stay away for long. A new Danish raiding-fleet had established itself in northern Francia, the land of the Franks, berthing its ships along rivers flowing out towards the coasts of Britain. Alfred recognised it as a threat and decided to confront it. In 882, he launched a naval expedition which resulted in the capture of two vessels.[11] Three years later, the same heathen force divided into two parts, one of which sailed to Britain and landed in Kent. The former Roman city of Rochester, seat of one of the oldest Anglo-Saxon bishoprics, was put under siege. It was saved by Alfred, who drove the besiegers back to their ships. Some of them returned to Francia. The rest lingered off the English coast and made peace with Alfred, but it was not long before they started raiding again. Teaming up with East Anglian Vikings they established a joint base at Benfleet in Essex.[12] It was no doubt in response to this flagrant breach of the treaty negotiated with Guthrum that Alfred launched a major raid of his own, leading a fleet from Kent to East Anglia. The Vikings sent thirteen ships to meet him and a savage sea-battle was

fought at the mouth of the River Stour.[13] Although this encounter was won by
Alfred, a swift counter-attack by the heathens negated his victory and he sailed
home to Wessex.

Alfred's military reforms

Embedded within the *Anglo-Saxon Chronicle* in its entry for 893 is an interesting
note on Alfred's military forces:

> The king had divided his levies into two sections, so that there was always
> half at home and half on active service, with the exception of those men
> whose duty it was to man the burhs.

The chronicler is here referring to a system of military service already in place
before the early 890s. It is clear that Alfred had previously reorganised his army
to ensure that Wessex was adequately defended. The levy or *fyrd* of warriors had
traditionally been mustered whenever need arose, to provide the king with
troops for specific campaigns.[14] It comprised the armed retinues of noblemen
who were obliged to bring their forces to supplement the royal warband. Anglo-
Saxon kings had traditionally been able to activate this obligation via a legal
right known as the *trimoda necessitas* or 'three necessities', by which they could
demand men not only for warfare but for building and repairing bridges and
fortresses. In the eighth century, Offa of Mercia had undoubtedly relied on this
threefold obligation for the construction of his dyke.[15]

Alfred's reorganisation of military service came in the wake of his victory at
Edington and turned the Wessex fyrd into something more akin to a standing
army – a permanently mobilised force divided into two parts, each serving in
rotation. One part was available for campaigns and expeditions while the other
defended the kingdom. The campaigning force was mounted on horseback, for
Alfred had seen the effectiveness of mobile armies during his earlier struggles
with Danish raiders. Having seen how the Danes used horses to travel swiftly
across English lands he decided to adopt the same strategy. Those members of
the fyrd designated to stay behind as a defence force did not simply revert to
civilian life but remained in their home districts on active duty as a professional
body of soldiers. They were expected to support local burh garrisons whenever
these were sent forth in pursuit of raiders. Hence, they were not allowed to set
aside their war-gear. They probably had no need to, for they were not labourers

or peasants who had to work the land. Indeed, it seems unlikely that the stereotypical free peasant farmer had ever been represented in Anglo-Saxon armies in significant numbers.[16] Warfare in early medieval Britain, as elsewhere in contemporary western Europe, was an activity reserved for men of a certain status. Peasants, even free ones, were generally excluded from combat roles by law or custom. The lowest social group likely to have fought in Alfred's fyrd was the ceorl or 'churl', a commoner rather than a nobleman but a more prosperous individual than a peasant. Ceorls may have made up a sizeable proportion of the burh garrisons who, like the two divisions of Alfred's fyrd, were permanent military forces. History shows that these reforms were highly successful, enabling the king and his ealdormen to deal quickly with unforeseen crises inside the borders or to launch punitive expeditions into enemy-held territory.

As well as reorganising the fyrd, Alfred initiated a programme for the construction of burhs across his kingdom. Building these fortified settlements was by no means an innovation on his part: it was something that Anglo-Saxon kings had been doing for a long time. In fact, the term 'burh' had become a broad umbrella label for several different types of defensible site. It derived from the Old English verb *beorgan*, meaning 'to protect' or 'to shelter' and was usually bestowed on places that lay within an enclosure. It still survives today as an element in place-names, the most common modern forms being 'borough', 'burgh', 'brough' and 'bury'. In pre-Viking times it was applied to long-abandoned prehistoric earthworks and derelict Roman forts as well as to enclosed settlements established by the Anglo-Saxons themselves. Some burhs had been used by kings as far back as the seventh century. For example, Bede in the early 700s referred to the great fortress of Bebbanburg as having been a royal stronghold in the Anglo-Saxon kingdom of Bernicia a hundred years earlier. The Bernician kings utilised a site that had formerly been a native British fortress, giving it a new name with the suffix '-burg'. This name has since evolved into 'Bamburgh' and the remains of the Anglo-Saxon fortress lie beneath the imposing medieval castle.

Alfred's new burhs were intended to protect Wessex against further Viking onslaughts. The devastation wrought in the period before the victory at Edington had not been forgotten and sharp lessons had been learned on the English side. Alfred had seen how Viking armies used fortifications as raiding-bases, and how they moved swiftly from one to another. His new burhs were designed to level the playing-field by providing the armies of Wessex with similar strongpoints. Careful planning enabled him to create an effective network of fortified settlements that could be used not only for defence but also for launching counter-strikes into Danish territory. They had a range of functions, serving their localities in different ways. Some were built as temporary fortresses for short-term military needs while others were designed as permanent settlements in which soldiers lived alongside civilians in what were essentially fortified towns. Those nearest to the Danelaw would one day become springboards for recovering the lost English lands in the east.

The typical Alfredian burh was an enclosed settlement garrisoned by soldiers who lived alongside a civilian population. In some cases, the burh was established within a former Roman town whose stone walls were still sufficiently intact to provide a ready-made defensive perimeter. Old Roman ramparts sometimes needed major repairs to restore them to effectiveness but they were always stronger than anything the Anglo-Saxons could build from scratch. At non-Roman sites, the new burh would be defended by a perimeter ditch fronting a substantial bank of earth surmounted by a wooden palisade. Such defences tended to be of rectilinear shape like those at Roman settlements, enclosing a street-pattern laid out as a grid. In adopting these designs, Alfred was consciously aiming to give his burhs an air of Roman imperial prestige.

A small number of burhs had been established in Mercia by kings such as Offa in the eighth and early ninth centuries, and these may have inspired the creation of Alfred's network. Traces of what appear to be defences from Offa's time have been identified at the Mercian sites of Hereford, Winchcombe and Tamworth.[17] What made many of Alfred's burhs different was their 'urban' character and their role in a kingdom-wide network that transcended local boundaries. These were not so much fortresses guarding specific districts as embryonic towns serving as economic and administrative hubs for much larger areas. Not since Roman times had Britain seen a similar programme of urbanisation and territorial reorganisation. Even the layout of the new burhs was reminiscent of Roman town planning, with internal streets laid out in a grid pattern radiating from a central crossroads. Many burhs were sited close to Roman highways, mainly because these were still the best surviving roads providing swift routes for armies.

A contemporary list of Alfred's burhs has survived in a document known as the 'Burghal Hidage'. This gives the names of more than thirty sites, adding in each case the amount of land deemed necessary to support the garrison. The unit of land-measurement was the hide, roughly equating to the land sufficient for maintaining one household. For each burh, the hidage figure was based on the length of the perimeter wall. A simple formula was used in the calculation: each 5.5 yards of wall would be manned by four soldiers, and each soldier would need to be provided by one hide. So, for the West Saxon burh at Winchester, the assessment of 2,400 hides indicates a garrison of 2,400 men and allows us to estimate that the wall was 3,300 yards long. At some sites, there is a close match between the actual length of the wall and the corresponding estimate drawn from the Burghal Hidage. Thus, at Winchester, the length of the Roman walls forming the defensive perimeter of the burh is 3,318 yards. This sort of correlation suggests that the document is indeed an official one, a survey drawn up at the West Saxon royal court. The main point of debate is the date of compilation, with some historians suggesting c.879 while others prefer to look beyond Alfred's reign to that of his son Edward in the early 900s.[18]

Wales

Alfred's triumph at the battle of Edington in 878 not only strengthened his position among the southern English; it also enhanced his status further afield, prompting the rulers of other lands to offer their allegiance. By acknowledging him as their overlord and becoming his clients or 'sub-kings' they could obtain his protection, not only against Viking marauders but also against enemies closer to home. Offers of submission are known to have come to him from Wales, a land where various small kingdoms had a long history of competing with one another. In the 870s, the dominant power among the Welsh was Rhodri Mawr ('Rhodri the Great'), king of Gwynedd. Rhodri died in battle in 878, the year of Alfred's victory over Guthrum, at the hands of English foes. Although the identity of his killers is not recorded, they were almost certainly Mercians fighting on behalf of King Ceolwulf.[19] Rhodri's death released the other Welsh kingdoms from subjection to Gwynedd, but his sons attempted to reimpose it. Their aggressive ambitions encouraged two southern Welsh kings – Hyfaidd of Dyfed and Elise of Brycheiniog – to submit to Alfred in the early 880s.[20] Alfred offered military protection in return. He probably saw Rhodri's sons as a threat to his own position, especially as the eldest had already entered into a potentially dangerous alliance with the Danes of York.[21] Elsewhere in southern Wales, the kingdoms of Gwent and Glywysing were being oppressed not by other Welsh powers but by English neighbours in Mercia. At that time, the Mercians were no longer ruled by Ceolwulf but by his successor, a man called Æthelred whom the Welsh knew as 'Edryd Long-Hair'.[22] Asser tells us that Æthelred's military strength and 'tyrannical behaviour' persuaded the kings of Gwent and Glywysing to turn to Wessex for protection, the price being an oath of allegiance to Alfred. Æthelred himself would soon follow the same path, becoming not only Alfred's subordinate but also his closest military ally. In the years that followed, the relationship between these two men would prove crucial in the great struggle against the Vikings.

The Lord of the Mercians

Æthelred's story is closely bound up with the decline and partition of the kingdom of Mercia. His origins are unknown but he was probably a native Mercian rather than an incomer from another English territory. It has been suggested that he sprang from the former royal house of the Hwicce, a people of south-west Mercia who had once had their own kings. The suggestion comes chiefly from Æthelred's patronage of Worcester and Gloucester, two important Hwiccian sites. Another possibility is that he was related in some way to his older namesake Æthelred Mucel, the Mercian ealdorman who had become Alfred's father-in-law.[23] Of the younger Æthelred's early life and rise to power the sources say nothing. He first enters history in a charter of 883 in which he granted privileges to Berkeley Abbey in Gloucestershire, this being done 'with the consent of Alfred and the whole Mercian witan'.[24] A witan was an assembly or council comprising members of the secular and religious elites in an Anglo-Saxon kingdom. It functioned as an advisory body for kings but was not a parliament in the modern sense and had no legislative powers of its own. The grant of 883 exempted Berkeley Abbey from various rents that Æthelred would otherwise have received as ruler of Mercia. In return, the abbey gave up twelve hides of land, these being handed by Æthelred to one of his thegns. In making such a grant he was discharging the responsibilities of a king, even though the charter describes him as an ealdorman. There is little doubt that, on this occasion at least, he regarded himself as Alfred's subordinate, although perhaps this was because Alfred himself was present to witness the grant. A charter from the following year shows Æthelred granting five hides to Æthelwulf, an ealdorman, during a meeting of the Mercian witan at Princes Risborough in Buckinghamshire.[25] Again, the grant includes exemptions from taxes that would normally be paid to the ruler of Mercia but this time there is no mention of Alfred. Instead, we see Æthelred acting alone, without requiring Alfred's consent, even if the charter refrains from calling him a king. The same can be said of another charter – albeit one of unknown date and uncertain reliability – in which Æthelred renewed a Mercian royal grant that had been made by King Burgred.[26]

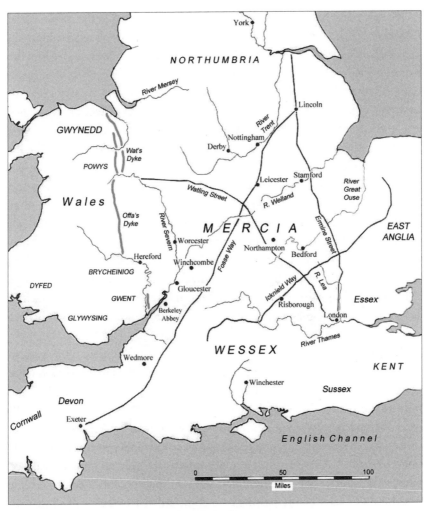

Lord Æthelred's Mercia

We may note that Æthelred is never described as a king in the *Anglo-Saxon Chronicle*. All the surviving versions of *ASC* refer to him simply as an ealdorman or as *myrcna hlaford*, 'Lord of the Mercians'. Charters from Wessex give him the title *subregulus*, a Latin term meaning 'under-kinglet', to reflect his subordinate rank. Their scribes saw him as a vassal of the West Saxon dynasty, or as an ealdorman like the royal officials who governed the shires of Wessex. We do not know whether his own people in Mercia ever called him a king. Perhaps some did. His ambiguous status explains why modern historians often describe his predecessor Ceolwulf as the last true king of the Mercians. Æthelred is seen as a man who wielded similar powers without using a royal title. Chroniclers and charter-scribes showed no ambiguity when writing of Alfred, whom they usually referred to as *rex*, 'king', whether of Wessex or – more ambitiously – of the Anglo-Saxons as a whole. In some quarters Alfred may have been seen as king of Mercia too, even if it was Æthelred who exercised direct authority there. The uncertainty surrounding Æthelred's status continues when we turn to the chronicler Æthelweard, whose late tenth century version of *ASC* describes him as *rex*. Irish sources follow suit and it is possible that Æthelred himself had no objection to being addressed in this way.

Æthelred's Mercia, like Ceolwulf's, must have been confined to the western provinces, for the east lay under the heel of the Great Heathen Army. The sequence of events which led to the transfer of power from Ceolwulf to Æthelred can only be guessed at. If we choose to believe the West Saxon claim that Ceolwulf was a Viking puppet we might surmise that he was ousted by a rebellious Mercian faction who restored the west of the kingdom to fully-independent English rule under Æthelred. Alternatively, we might wonder if Ceolwulf himself managed to extricate a portion of western Mercia from the shadow of the Danelaw, ruling it as his own realm before passing it to Æthelred. This seems a good fit with what we know of Ceolwulf from his coinage, which was minted at London – still apparently a Mercian city at that time. His coins are very similar to Alfred's and clearly came from the same London mint. It is possible that the two kings were collaborating in certain ventures, perhaps in a military alliance as well as in coin-production. A likely context for such a pact is the aftermath of the victory at Edington in 878, which would have given Ceolwulf an opportunity to align himself with a resurgent Wessex and thereby obtain Alfred's protection. According to a list of Mercian kings, Ceolwulf's reign ended in 879 or 880. If he wasn't deposed by an internal revolt he may have died in battle, perhaps in an unrecorded conflict on the Welsh border. Whatever the precise circumstances of his departure, the rulership of English-controlled Mercia eventually came to Æthelred.

In pledging allegiance to Alfred, Æthelred recognised the West Saxon king's overlordship and became a loyal *subregulus*. This relationship was certainly in place by 883, when Alfred witnessed Æthelred's grant to Berkeley Abbey by giving his 'consent' to it. However, dealings between the two men went beyond the usual set of obligations between overlord and vassal. They shared a bond based on mutual trust and common objectives. Both were committed to halting the Viking advance and to wresting back the English territories that had been lost. Their partnership bore fruit in 886 when Alfred – probably with Æthelred's help – took control of London after it had been captured by Vikings. London lay in south-east Mercia and had long been an important place in the kingdom, minting coins for Mercian kings as recently as the reigns of Burgred and Ceolwulf. Anglo-Saxon settlement there was concentrated at Lundenwic, a village that had grown into a flourishing centre of international trade by c.700.[27] Lundenwic lay one mile west of the former Roman city of *Londinium*, which the early Anglo-Saxon settlers called Lundenburh, both sites being in use in the late ninth century Their strategic and economic advantages had, unsurprisingly, attracted the attentions of Scandinavian raiders.

Viking raids on London are recorded in 842 and 851, while heathen forces wintered there in 871 and at nearby Fulham in 879. By 886, the place had fallen into Scandinavian hands again, hence Alfred's campaign to recapture it.[28] He did not, however, attach it to his own kingdom, granting it instead to Lord Æthelred. This gift coincided with two important political developments: a widespread recognition of Alfred as king of all the English and a new marriage alliance between Mercia and Wessex. The first was noted in *ASC*, embedded in an entry for 886 which says of Alfred that 'all the English people submitted to him, except those who were in captivity to the Danes.'[29] Asser's account employs a slightly different wording but essentially echoes the chroniclers: 'All the Angles and Saxons – those who had formerly been scattered everywhere and were not in captivity with the Vikings – turned willingly to King Alfred and submitted themselves to his lordship.'[30] The submission was more than wishful thinking by propagandists at the West Saxon royal court. It was a real event, a major leap forward for the concept of English unity. There are hints that it may have involved a formal pledge of loyalty to Alfred, a solemn oath sworn by every Englishman and Englishwoman.[31] In a legal code issued by him as a revision of earlier laws drawn up by King Ine in the eighth century, one section decreed that 'each man keep carefully his oath and pledge'.[32] The implication is that a particular oath and pledge were being referred to and that these were so well known that further explanation was unnecessary. That they were meant to be sworn by every English person is clear from a later law-code, issued by Alfred's son and successor Edward, which mentions an oath and pledge 'which the whole people has given'.[33] Both Alfred's and Edward's laws refer to the same thing – a national oath of loyalty, sworn by everyone who was English regardless of whether they lived in Wessex or Mercia or Kent or anywhere else outside the Danelaw. It was most likely sworn in 886 or soon after, when Alfred could claim with some justification to be the only English king in lands not yet under Scandinavian control.

Alfred's granting of London to Æthelred was an acknowledgement that the city had historically belonged to Mercia. This was a generous gesture from overlord to client, from a powerful king to a trusted subordinate. Some historians wonder if the transfer of authority involved another, more personal aspect. It has been suggested that London may have been Alfred's wedding-gift to Æthelred, who received the hand of the king's daughter Æthelflæd around this time.[34] The marriage was undoubtedly arranged for political purposes, to strengthen the existing alliance between Alfred and Æthelred and to bind them more closely as kinsmen. It highlighted their respective positions, with the overlord confirming his seniority by becoming father-in-law to the subordinate. Æthelflæd would probably have been fifteen or sixteen years old at the time; her husband was older, perhaps by a considerable margin. He had been witnessing charters and commanding armies for a number of years and must have reached adulthood by c.880 at the latest. It is quite likely that he was the same man as a certain Ealdorman Æthelred who had served the Mercian king Burgred as far back as the early 870s.

The wedding would have been a lavish occasion befitting the high status of bride and groom. Dignitaries from Mercia and Wessex would have attended, their presence amounting to a roll-call of the elite of both kingdoms. Æthelflæd's father and her Mercian mother would have been the most honoured guests, followed by her younger siblings and her husband's relatives. The leading Mercian and West Saxon aristocratic families would also have been represented, together with bishops, abbots, abbesses and other senior clergy from all the lands under Alfred's overlordship. After the wedding, Æthelflæd had to leave her father's kingdom to take up residence in her husband's domain. Her paternal aunt Æthelswith had made a similar move from Wessex to Mercia to become the wife of King Burgred in 853. It was quite common for a cross-border marriage to take a princess far away from her homeland, this having been the case for Judith, daughter of the Frankish king Charles the Bald. Judith was only twelve or thirteen years old when she arrived in Wessex as the new bride of King

Æthelwulf in 856. She was a stranger in a strange land, living among people whose language was different from her own. In Æthelflæd's case, the adjustment to married life in Mercia was somewhat less challenging. She already had close family ties there, being half-Mercian by blood. Throughout her childhood she would have had contact with members of the Mercian elite who visited her father's palaces or who travelled in his entourage. One such individual was Lord Æthelred, her father's closest military ally, whom she almost certainly encountered long before her betrothal to him. Marriage did not therefore cause a major social or cultural upheaval in her life. In any case, the places that she and her husband would use as their principal residences lay in the south-west of their territory, within a day or two's ride of her West Saxon homeland.

Peace with the Danes

Alfred's recapture of London in 886 altered the frontier between the lands under English and Danish rule. The changes were significant enough to warrant a formal treaty between the two sides, to clarify the new boundary and to minimise the risk of further clashes. Negotiations were duly conducted between Alfred and his old adversary Guthrum, at that time still the most senior figure among the Danelaw leadership. The original document setting out the terms of the treaty no longer survives but a copy is preserved in a manuscript from c.1100.[35] It was once widely believed that the terms were drawn up in the wake of Alfred's victory at Edington in 878, with a ceremony at Wedmore in Somerset after Guthrum's baptism seeming to provide a plausible context. The belief in a so-called 'Treaty of Wedmore' persists today, even though a glance at the text shows that 878 is far too early. We are left in no doubt that the new frontier assigned London to the English, a scenario that only makes sense after the campaign of 886. London had previously fallen into Viking hands, having been in a vulnerable position ever since the Great Heathen Army took control of eastern Mercia in the late 870s.[36] It did not return to English rule until its recapture by Alfred. The treaty was surely defining a real boundary that reflected the city's current situation, so 886 is the earliest possible date for it. We know that Guthrum died c.890, which gives a five-year window for the treaty negotiations.

What Alfred and Guthrum drew up was essentially a personal arrangement between two kings, neither of whom could guarantee a lasting truce beyond their own lifetimes. Indeed, Guthrum's track record did not bode well even in the short term. Yet the new treaty was plainly intended to outlive them both. It incorporated a hope that peace would be ensured not only for the current generation but for future ones, 'the living and the unborn'. On the ground, it redrew the border between Mercia and the Danelaw, using the Roman road known as Watling Street to mark the eastern limit of English-held territory. It also sought to regulate future relations between English and Danish people living on either side of the new line. The wergild or 'compensation payment' for an Englishman slain by a Dane was fixed at the same value as that for a Dane slain by an Englishman. This payment would, of course, be greater if the victim was of high social status, but the key point was that each 'nation' would be treated equally under the law. The economic realities of daily life on a fragile frontier were likewise acknowledged by both parties, neither of whom wanted to disrupt opportunities for cross-border trade. Hence, the final part of the treaty made clear that trade should be allowed if permissions were obtained from landowners on either side.

The treaty between Alfred and Guthrum

(The following modern English version of the Old English text is based on Frederick Attenborough's translation.[37])

These are the terms of peace which King Alfred and King Guthrum, and the councillors of all the English nation, and all the people who dwell in East Anglia, have all agreed upon and confirmed with oaths, on their own behalf and for their subjects both the living and the unborn, who are anxious for God's favour and ours.

1. First as to the boundaries between us. Up the Thames, and then up the Lea, and along the Lea to its source, then in a straight line to Bedford, and then up the Ouse to Watling Street.

2. Secondly, if a man is slain, whether he is an Englishman or a Dane, all of us shall place the same value on his life — namely 8 half-marks of pure gold, with the exception of commoners who occupy tributary land, and freedmen of the Danes. These also shall be valued at the same amount — 200 shillings — in either case.

3. If anyone accuses a king's thegn of man-slaying, if he dares to clear himself, he shall do so with the pledges of twelve king's thegns. If anyone accuses a man who belongs to a lower order than that of king's thegn, he shall clear himself with the pledges of eleven of his equals and one king's thegn. And this law shall apply to every suit which involves an amount greater than 4 gold coins. And if he dare not attempt to clear himself, he shall pay three times the amount at which it is valued.

4. Every man shall have knowledge of his warrantor when he buys slaves or horses or oxen.

5. And we all declared, on the day when the oaths were sworn, that neither slaves nor freemen should be allowed to pass over to the Danish army without permission, any more than that any of theirs comes to us. If, however, it happens that any of [the Danes] in order to satisfy their wants, wish to trade with us, or we with them, in cattle and in goods, it shall be allowed on condition that hostages are given as security for peaceful behaviour, and as evidence by which it may be known that no treachery is intended.

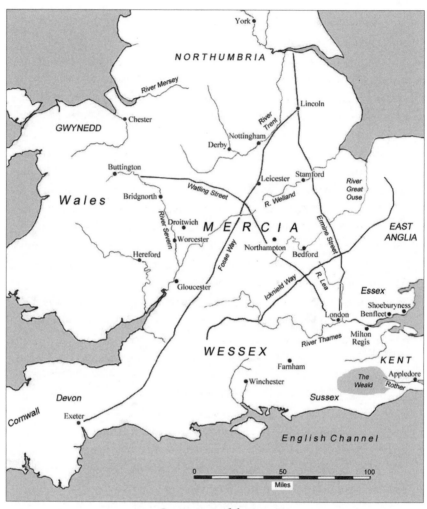

Campaigns of the 890s

4

A NEW MERCIA

Women and power

As the bride of a man who was king in all but name, Æthelflæd would have been expected to take up the traditional role of royal wife. This role incorporated a bundle of duties and responsibilities, together with various rights and privileges. We should keep in mind that Anglo-Saxon wives, like those in other parts of early medieval Europe, were regarded as subordinate to their husbands. The society in which they lived was patriarchal and hierarchical, with political power resting firmly in the hands of a male warrior elite drawn from the landowning classes. Women were nevertheless respected and protected in Anglo-Saxon law. They were allowed to own goods and land, keeping these possessions for themselves even when married. As a group they were neither downtrodden nor servile – the exceptions, of course, being female slaves.[1]

Royal women were inevitably closer to the networks of power than others of their gender. They included not only blood relatives of the king but those who became his kinswomen by marriage. The latter, in most cases, arrived as the human aspect of political alliances arranged between powerful families. Their marriages sealed oaths of loyalty, pledges of peace and guarantees of protection made by one king to another, or by a king to a favoured nobleman. The Old English language had a word for a bride in such transactions: *frithuwebbe*, 'peace-weaver'.[2] Such a woman would already have been familiar with the traditionally female work of weaving and spinning. Now, as a political bride, she was expected to weave the bonds of alliance between her own and her husband's kin. It was not necessarily an easy or simple task, especially if the alliance was resented in some quarters. Her behaviour would be under constant scrutiny, especially from senior females among her husband's relations. She was required to be an expert hostess in the feasting-hall, conducting herself with dignity and courtesy. However, membership of the royal family did not automatically give women a role in running the kingdom. Governance of the realm was regarded as a male preserve, an area in which women had little scope for input. Some Anglo-Saxon queens did witness charters but not, it seems, as a matter of course. This demarcation of rulership was an ancient one, rooted in ancestral custom, and there were few exceptions. Among the kingdoms of the Viking-Age only Mercia bucked the trend in any significant way.

In the charter record we see the wives of Mercian kings from the late eighth century onwards taking a higher profile in matters of royal administration. The change appeared during the reign of King Offa (757–96) and saw queens frequently witnessing land-grants and other matters of royal administration. Offa's wife Cynethryth not only witnessed his charters but had her name on coins issued during his reign.[3] She was evidently a busy woman, simultaneously managing the royal household – a traditional responsibility of the king's wife in early medieval Europe – and raising her children. Her regular appearance as a charter witness was certainly not the norm and it was rare for a queen to have such prominence on so many occasions. This was as much the case in an Anglo-Saxon kingdom as in an Irish, Welsh or Frankish one. Cynethryth's example was followed by all but two of the queens who came after her in the ninth century. Four of the six Mercian royal wives who are known to have existed between her and Æthelflæd made regular appearances in charter witness-lists. The last of the six was Æthelflæd's aunt Æthelswith, wife of King Burgred, who was named in all of her husband's surviving charters. It appears that Æthelswith played an active role in the administration of the realm, witnessing transfers of royal land and other important matters affecting the upper levels of Mercian society.[4] The other three prominent queens were Ælfthryth (wife of King Cenwulf), a second Cynethryth (King Wiglaf's wife) and Sæthryth (Beorhtwulf's wife).

The high profile enjoyed by ninth-century Mercian queens can be contrasted with the situation of their counterparts in contemporary Wessex. There, since the beginning of the ninth century, the king's wife had slipped into the background. Æthelflæd's own mother Ealhswith had come to Wessex from Mercia to marry Alfred, leaving a land where queens took part in governance for a land where they had little or no power. Ealhswith witnessed none of Alfred's charters, except for one that is usually deemed a forgery. Unlike Æthelswith, she was not allowed to be her husband's partner in the public business of kingship. It had not always been so. Older charters from the early 700s show West Saxon queens taking part in the business of the realm as occasional charter-witnesses.[5] In 722, the wife of King Ine had even led a military assault on a rebel fortress. Nonetheless, we see a marked change in the early years of the Viking Age, a diminishing of status for West Saxon queens.

Ironically, the catalyst was a powerful and ambitious woman, one of the four daughters of Offa of Mercia. Her name was Eadburh and her story was told by Asser, who described her as a woman of 'great wickedness'. Offa had given her in marriage to King Beorhtric of Wessex (reigned 786–802) over whom she soon began to exert a malicious influence. Asser claimed that 'she began to behave like a tyrant after the manner of her father', turning her husband against his friends.[6] Her scheming ended when, intending to poison one of Beorhtric's henchmen, she inadvertently poisoned the king himself. Fleeing to Francia, she sought refuge with the mighty Charlemagne, who generously gave her a nunnery and the rank of abbess. Within a few years she was 'publicly caught in debauchery' with an Englishman and thrown out of the Frankish realm, ending her days as a beggar in Italy.

Back in Wessex, this unsavoury episode left such a stain on the royal house that drastic measures were taken to prevent a repeat. Henceforth, the wife of a West Saxon king would no longer sit beside him on her own throne, nor would she be referred to as a queen. She would instead remain in the background, staying out of the official business of the kingdom and keeping a low profile. One outcome of this reduction in status was the absence of the king's wife from charter witness-lists of the 800s. From Ecgberht to Alfred, the women who would otherwise have been present as queens of Wessex are virtually invisible – all except one. The Frankish princess Judith, second wife of King Æthelwulf and stepmother of Alfred, witnessed her husband's charters as an acknowledged queen. She had this status only because her mighty father demanded it.[7] Others had to wait until they were widowed before being allowed to emerge from the shadows as dowager queens. Only then, with their husbands gone, do they seem to have become more prominent in public life. Ealhswith turns up as a charter witness within two years of Alfred's death, no longer in the position of king's wife but with a different status as the widowed mother of the new king.[8] Not until the mid-tenth century did these prohibitions start to be loosened for the wives of living West Saxon monarchs. For most of Æthelflæd's lifetime they were not relaxed and, as Ealhswith's daughter, she would have seen them at close quarters. As soon as she became the spouse of the ruler of Mercia, she would have found her own situation far less restrictive.

Away from the secular world of the royal court, women of high birth could attain positions of power in another way, by devoting themselves to the religious life. Conversion from paganism to Christianity in the sixth and seventh centuries had brought the Anglo-Saxon kingdoms into contact with the Church, itself a powerful institution with a hierarchy of status. The Church offered women an opportunity to become abbesses in charge of monasteries, sharing equal status with abbots and often governing communities of monks as well as of nuns. Abbesses, like abbots and bishops, became important figures in a kingdom. Senior clerics, regardless of gender, replaced the pagan priests and priestesses who had advised the kings of pre-Christian times. They might be called upon to give guidance or counsel, even on secular matters.[9] High rank in a religious community might have been a career option for Æthelflæd herself, had her father not chosen her as the bride of the Lord of Mercia. Her younger sister Æthelgifu did take the clerical path, being appointed as the first abbess of newly built Shaftesbury Abbey in Dorset while still a teenager.

It is not known if any of the politically prominent Mercian queens – such as Offa's wife Cynethryth – were involved in the martial aspects of royal governance. The sparseness of the surviving written record for Mercia prevents us from finding out. In Æthelflæd's case, we know that she not only witnessed her husband's charters but assisted him in building fortifications and planning military campaigns. Unfortunately, due to a lack of information for her predecessors, we cannot be sure if any of them ventured as far as she did into the traditionally male environment of warfare.[10] What we can say with reasonable certainty is that neither she nor they were likely to have actually fought in battle. There is absolutely no evidence that any kingdom of early medieval Europe deployed female soldiers. On the contrary, contemporary sources are unanimous in portraying war as an exclusively male activity. Archaeology reinforces this view with its analysis of female graves where weapons have been found. These objects may have been precious to the deceased but their presence does not imply that women were expected or even permitted to fight in war. Early medieval society typically had a division of roles along lines of gender, age and social class. It is clear that women, young children, the elderly, the clergy, the peasantry and the enslaved were all exempt from military service. These exemptions seem to have been backed up by laws prohibiting non-combatant groups from bearing weapons or other military gear. It goes without saying that in times of peril no prohibition would have deterred valiant individuals, regardless of age or gender, from fighting to defend their families against violent marauders. But the key point is that early medieval soldiering was an occupation reserved for certain classes of men and was effectively barred to everyone else.

Elf-friend

Sometime between her marriage to Æthelred c.886 and the beginning of the next decade, Æthelflæd gave birth to a daughter. This was her only child, as far as we know, and certainly the only one who survived the perils of infancy. We might speculate that Æthelred had hoped to be succeeded as Lord of Mercia by a son, but it was not to be. He and his young wife became the parents of a baby girl whom they named Ælfwynn, which means 'Elf-friend'. She went on to reach adulthood and outlived both parents. According to the twelfth-century chronicler William of Malmesbury, her birth was a grim ordeal for her mother, who thereafter became celibate to avoid repeating the experience. William said that Æthelflæd was 'a woman of great soul who, from the difficulty experienced in her first or rather only labour, ever after refused the embraces of her husband, protesting that it was unbecoming for the daughter of a king to give way to a delight which in time produced such painful consequences.'[11]

William is not a contemporary witness for the Anglo-Saxon period so we should be wary of accepting this as an accurate report. It might be a fictional anecdote, devised by William or by one of his contemporaries in an attempt to show Æthelflæd as morally pure.[12] Depicting her as celibate added an ascetic aspect to her character, putting her on a par with virgin nuns like her younger sister Æthelgifu. We should, however, keep in mind that William was a native of Wessex and a monk of Malmesbury Abbey, a foundation with historic links to the West Saxon royal dynasty. It is possible that he did have access to stories – some based on fact – handed down from the distant past.[13] Whether the tale of Æthelflæd's celibacy has any factual basis, or is simply an invention, is impossible to judge. Some historians have chosen to give it the benefit of the doubt, accepting it as a genuine folk-memory of words actually spoken by Æthelflæd. If they are correct, her decision to stay celibate after Ælfwynn's birth requires explanation. One theory is that she refused to bear any more children because she did not want to bring forth a Mercian son whose ambitions might disrupt the political relationship with Wessex.[14] The problem with this is that it implies tension between her and her husband, who may have longed for a male heir. How could she have justified making such an important dynastic decision by herself, on purely political grounds, without considering Æthelred's wishes? For all we know, he may have been happy to raise a son whom he could train as a loyal ally of West Saxon kings. Did Æthelflæd really mistrust him so much that she feared to bring forth a boy who might one day unravel the crucial alliance with her birth-family? A more plausible suggestion is that she may have been physically unable to bear another child, either because she had been left damaged by Ælfwynn's birth or for some other gynaecological reason.[15] Even in the absence of a definitive explanation, the anecdote reported by William of Malmesbury is not without interest in its own right. As one modern historian has observed, it uniquely depicts 'a ninth-century Englishwoman telling her husband "*I* have decided that *we* are not going to have any more children"'.[16]

Nothing is known of Ælfwynn's childhood before her early teens, when she began to appear on charters as a witness. By then, it is likely that she had already accompanied her parents on numerous journeys around Mercia. Although her father might not have been a king he essentially wielded a king's authority and his entourage was a royal court in all but name. Such courts tended to be peripatetic, moving from place to place on regular tours or 'circuits' of a ruler's domain. So, from a very young age, Ælfwynn would have been familiar with the Mercian settlements favoured by her parents. No doubt she had also visited Wessex in these years to visit her maternal grandparents. We can assume that she received formal schooling.[17] She was the eldest grandchild of King Alfred, himself a passionate believer in education who had instituted a revival of learning in Wessex. Alfred had encouraged scholars and writers to join his court, recruiting them from Mercia and Wales and from even further afield in the Frankish lands. One who answered the summons was Asser, the Welsh monk who became the king's biographer. Another was Wærferth, bishop of Mercian Worcester, whose friendship with Ælfwynn's parents is well-documented in charters. Alfred established a school for young members of the royal household and there his own children were educated.[18] It is likely that Ælfwynn received similar tuition at the Mercian court under her mother's guidance, with Bishop Wærferth among her teachers.

Hæsten

King Guthrum of East Anglia died c.890. Within a couple of years, a new Viking army arrived on the south coast of Britain. This host had been raiding in Frankish territory, moving from one place to another in a quest for plunder. In 892, it had come to the ancient port of Boulogne where it had obtained horses and ships. It then split into two divisions, the smaller led by a Danish warlord called Hæsten. Leading a fleet of eighty vessels, Hæsten crossed the English Channel to make landfall in northern Kent, seizing the settlement of Milton Regis. The other, larger division also landed in Kent, but on the south coast of the old kingdom. It approached the mouth of the River Rother before moving upstream as far as the great forest of Andred, an area known today as The Weald. It then returned to the river-mouth where it occupied a fort at Appledore in the Romney Marshes. Unsurprisingly, news of these landings soon reached the ears of King Alfred. He responded by gathering an army and marching to Kent, setting up camp between the two Viking forces. He hoped to intercept either of them whenever they sent raiding-parties out from their bases. These Vikings were indeed a dangerous presence, not least because they were frequently joined on plundering forays by warbands from the Danelaw. The pledges of peace that had sealed the treaty between Alfred and Guthrum had seemingly been set aside by some sections of the East Anglian army. These adventurers now joined others from Northumbria as allies of the new arrivals from the Continent, participating in combined raids as well as launching expeditions of their own.[19]

While Alfred's encampment in Kent seems to have prevented the heathens at Milton and Appledore from breaking out in full force, they cunningly resorted to sending out small raiding-parties who travelled through woodland to evade the English patrols. Skirmishes broke out constantly. Hæsten eventually agreed to a truce with Alfred in early 893. He offered his two sons for Christian baptism, Alfred standing as godfather for one while Lord Æthelred of Mercia stood for the other. Hæsten also swore an oath of allegiance to Alfred, giving him a number of hostages and receiving gifts in return. He then left Milton and crossed the Thames into Essex, where he proceeded to build a fort at Benfleet. Meanwhile, the Viking force at Appledore evacuated its base *en masse* and went raiding in Wessex, gathering a large amount of plunder. It eventually turned around, intending to join Hæsten at Benfleet, but it was caught by West Saxon pursuers led by Alfred's son Edward. A battle took place at Farnham in Surrey and the raiders were soundly defeated. The survivors fled towards the Thames, crossing the river into Buckinghamshire, closely pursued by English forces. By then, Hæsten had already reneged on his pledge by using the fort at Benfleet as a base for new raiding-expeditions. His army was bolstered by warriors coming back from the defeat at Farnham, these men then being left to garrison Benfleet while he himself went off to raid in Mercia. He was thus far away when Edward and Lord Æthelred arrived at Benfleet with a large English army. The fort was overwhelmed and the defenders were driven off. Everything within was confiscated by the English – not only the material possessions of the Viking warriors but also their women and children. Among the prisoners were Hæsten's wife and his newly baptised sons. Some of the longships moored nearby were also captured; the rest were destroyed. The loot and captives were sent to London.

Hæsten's family were eventually returned by Alfred as a gesture of goodwill in exchange for a new truce. Hæsten then left Benfleet but remained in Essex, setting up a new camp at Shoeburyness near the mouth of the Thames estuary.

As if Hæsten were not enough trouble to deal with, Alfred learned to his dismay that Northumbrian and East Anglian Vikings were attacking Wessex from the sea. One group of raiders laid siege to a fort on the north coast of Devon while another targeted Exeter. Alfred marched west to confront them. When he reached Exeter, the Vikings withdrew to their ships and sailed away. They briefly made landfall again, in Sussex, but their raiding was repulsed by local forces and this ended their expedition. Alfred's latest treaty with Hæsten soon collapsed when the Danish warlord launched a full-scale assault with all his forces, their numbers again boosted by reinforcements from East Anglia and Northumbria. His huge army marched up the Thames valley, pushing deep into Mercian territory as far as the River Severn. Then, tracing the river's course upstream, the raiders pushed north along the western borderlands of Mercia. The English mobilised to halt them. At that time, Alfred was distracted by events in Devon, so the task of dealing with Hæsten fell to three trusted subordinates: Æthelred, the Lord of the Mercians; Æthelhelm, the ealdorman of Wiltshire; and Æthelnoth, the ealdorman of Somerset. A call went out to the burhs of Wiltshire and Somerset, and also to those of south-west Mercia, summoning their garrisons to the fight. The English troops were joined by contingents from Wales – these presumably being sent by kings who had sworn allegiance to Alfred.

Æthelred and his co-commanders led the combined Anglo-Welsh army up the Severn until they encountered Hæsten's forces at Buttington near present-day Welshpool. There the Vikings had made a fortification but it was quickly surrounded and put under siege. English soldiers were deployed in camps on both banks of the river, forming an effective blockade that prevented the raiders from foraging for food. As the siege went on, the hungry Vikings resorted to eating their horses. In the end, after many weeks of hardship, they tried to break out on the eastern side but suffered heavy losses. A remnant managed to flee for safety, making the long journey back to Hæsten's base in Essex. This was not the last we hear of them. Before the end of the year they had re-formed into another large army, supplemented by the usual contingents from Northumbria and East Anglia. On this occasion, Hæsten himself seems to be absent, for his name no longer appears in the sources. Perhaps he was dead, or had decided to leave Britain for new raiding-grounds on the Continent, or had gone back to Scandinavia?[20]

Leaving their ships and families in safe havens in East Anglia, Hæsten's former associates now made a long overland journey to the north-west corner of

Mercia, arriving at the derelict Roman city of Chester. Once more they were pursued by English forces led by Lord Æthelred, who tried to deprive them of provisions by burning the crops in the surrounding fields. Livestock in the immediate vicinity was likewise confiscated, while any Viking warrior found outside the walls was slain. By then, winter was already setting in and so the siege was abandoned. The English troops went back to their own lands, leaving the Vikings still holding the ancient city but with their food stocks severely depleted. Shortage of provisions meant that a prolonged stay in Chester was no longer an option, so they departed and went raiding in Wales. Early in the following year, loaded with plunder, they headed for home. Turning north-east, they avoided hostile territory in western Mercia and instead took a wide detour via Northumbria and East Anglia to come back to Essex through Danish-held lands.

The year 893 had witnessed two major Viking raids on western Mercia, culminating respectively in the Buttington and Chester campaigns. Both had been thwarted by Lord Æthelred, with the help of ealdormen from Wessex and various Welsh allies. Nevertheless, the heathen forces previously led by Hæsten were not yet destroyed. By the autumn of 894, they had regrouped in sufficient numbers to plan a new round of raids. They once again left Essex, sailing up the Thames to reach one of its tributaries, the River Lea. This they navigated for some distance before berthing their ships twenty miles north of London, probably at Hertford. Here they erected a fort, defending it successfully in the summer of the following year when it was attacked by an English force from London. When autumn came, Alfred himself arrived at the head of an army. It was harvest time in the English cornfields around the Lea and the crops had to be protected from raiders, so the king ordered his men to build a fort on either side of the river. This effectively created a blockade that prevented the enemy from sailing downstream to the Thames. As soon as they realised what was happening, the Vikings quickly abandoned their base, leaving their ships behind and sending their families to safety in East Anglia. They then struck overland across Mercia to their former raiding-grounds in the far west of that land. Coming to what is now the county of Shropshire they built a fortification on the River Severn at *Cwatbrycge* ('Quat-bridge'), probably present-day Bridgnorth, spending the winter of 895 there. An English army assembled for the task of dislodging them but, rather surprisingly, no such campaign was required. The Viking host faded away in the following year, dispersing in scattered groups who wandered back to the Danelaw. Some came to Northumbria, or to East Anglia, while others made their way to the eastern coast where ships took them to the Continent. Perhaps they doubted the odds of a successful outcome for their latest venture in the Severn valley? The military situation had certainly changed since the previous decade. Deep raids into West Saxon and Mercian territory now carried a greater risk of failure and destruction. The English armies of the 890s were better organised than before and were led by capable commanders. In addition, a strong network of garrisoned burhs meant that any band of raiders laden with plunder was unlikely to get far without being challenged.

The last of Alfred's wars against Scandinavian foes came in 896, when the south coast of Wessex was attacked from the sea by Danes from Northumbria and East Anglia. Alfred had already ordered the construction of a fleet of his own, comprising vessels that were considerably larger than Viking longships. They had sixty or more oars and were built to the king's own design. Nine were sent to intercept a small fleet of Danish ships that had entered an estuary in Dorset or Hampshire. Forming a blockade to prevent the enemy's escape, the English crews successfully captured a couple of longships and killed those who were aboard. The other Danish vessels lay upstream, having been drawn up out of the water while their crews went plundering inland. Fate then turned against the English, whose heavier craft ran aground on the riverbank. There they became stranded when the tide went out, and they were still stuck when the Danish raiding-parties came back laden with plunder. A fierce battle broke out, with both sides suffering many casualties. When the tide came in, the lighter Viking ships were soon afloat and were able to sail out into the open sea. Two did not get very far, for they had lost many oarsmen in the battle: strong currents cast them up on the shore of Sussex where their crews were taken prisoner. These captives were brought to Winchester where King Alfred ordered that they be hanged. In the end, only one Danish ship managed to limp home to East Anglia.

Worcester

It is not known if Æthelflæd accompanied her husband on his military campaigns in the final decade of the ninth century. As we have already noted, women in early medieval Europe were not normally expected to play an active part in warfare. However, Æthelflæd's dual role as princess of Wessex and consort of the Lord of Mercia gave her a special status. She was nothing less than the living embodiment of an alliance that bound her father's people to those of her husband. As such, she would have been a powerful symbol of

English unity if she had stood alongside Æthelred and his West Saxon co-commanders on the eve of a major battle.[21] Given her later record of leading Mercian armies in person, the suggestion that she may have been present on one or more of her husband's expeditions in the 890s seems credible. On the other hand, she might simply have stayed at home, supervising the Mercian court and deputising for Æthelred in routine matters of justice and administration.

After the remnants of the latest Viking menace melted away in 896, the Lord of Mercia was able to rule his domain in peace – at least for a while, until the next military crisis. The business of governing his domain in peacetime included a range of duties and responsibilities that he expected his wife to share. Æthelflæd accompanied him on many of his journeys, standing beside him during public ceremonies that reinforced the bond with his subjects. One part of her supportive role involved witnessing her husband's grants of land and privileges to churches or to noble Mercian families. Several charters confirming her presence at these formal events have survived, one of which recorded a grant made jointly by husband and wife to the church of Worcester, seat of a Mercian bishopric since c.680.[22] This document tells us that the grant was made by Æthelred and Æthelflæd 'with the consent of King Alfred and of all the witan in the realm of the Mercians'. Alfred's is the first name on the list of witnesses, followed by Æthelred and Æthelflæd, and then three Mercian bishops: Wulfred of Lichfield, Wærferth of Worcester and Deorlaf of Hereford. The charter also says that the Lord of the Mercians and his wife had previously ordered a burh to be constructed at Worcester 'as a protection for all the people and also to raise there the praise of God'. This is their earliest-known burh-building project and may have been completed c.890 when Æthelflæd was about twenty years old.[23]

Whatever the exact date of construction, the former Roman city was intended to be part of a network of garrisoned settlements that would defend Mercia in the way that Alfred's burhs defended Wessex. The choice of location supports the theory that Æthelred's origins were among the Hwicce, for Worcester lay in the heartland of that people and may have been the seat of their former kings. Alternatively, it may have been chosen because it had connections with later Mercian royalty via its bishopric. We may note that the burh was commissioned jointly by Æthelred and Æthelflæd, rather than by the Lord of the Mercians acting alone. Æthelflæd's involvement is hardly surprising, given her personal experience of the Wessex burhs that had been used so effectively by her father.

The rights of the church of Worcester

The charter referred to above, in which Æthelred and Æthelflæd granted privileges to the church of Worcester, was written in Old English. A modern English version is given below, based on Florence Harmer's translation.[24]

To Almighty God, the True Unity and Holy Trinity in Heaven, be praise and glory and thanksgiving for all the benefits that He has bestowed upon us. For whose love in the first place, and for love of St Peter and of the church at Worcester, and also through the entreaty of Bishop Wærferth their friend, Lord Æthelred and Æthelflæd have ordered the burh at Worcester to be constructed for the protection of all the inhabitants, and also that the worship of God may be celebrated therein. And they now declare in the sight of God, in this charter, that of all the rights pertaining to their sovereignty, both in market and in street, within the burh and without, they desire to give half to God and to St Peter and to the lord of the church, that the foundation may be more honourably maintained, and that the community may, in some measure, the more easily be helped, and that their memory may be, for ever, more steadfastly preserved in that place, for as long as obedience to God shall be found in the monastery. And Bishop Wærferth and the community have appointed the following divine offices before the one which is performed daily, both during their lifetime and after their death: that at nocturns and at vespers and at tierce, the psalm 'De profundis' is always to be sung as long as they shall live, and after their death 'Laudate Dominum'; and every Saturday in St Peter's church, thirty psalms and a mass on their behalf are to be sung both during their lifetime and also after their death. And now Æthelred and Æthelflæd declare that they desire with willing heart to give these dues to God and St Peter, with the consent of King Alfred and of all the witan in the realm of the Mercians; but the wagon-shilling and the load-penny at Droitwich are to go to the king as they always have done. But the rest, both the land-tax and fines for fighting and theft and dishonest trading, and the burh-walls shilling, and all those crimes which involve the payment of compensation, the lord of the church is to have half, for the sake of God and of St Peter, in the same way as we have laid down in the case of the marketplace and the streets. And outside the market, the bishop is to be entitled to his land and to all his dues, as was established in times past by the exemptions of our predecessors. And Æthelred and Æthelflæd have done this with the consent of King Alfred and of the Mercian witan whose names are written hereafter. And they entreat of all their successors, in the name of Almighty God, that no man impair this pious gift, which they, for the love of God and St Peter, have given to the church.[25]

The Worcester burh enclosed part of the Roman settlement, utilising its ancient defences on the south and east but extending beyond them on the northern side where archaeologists have identified a timber-reinforced earth rampart. The River Severn protected the western flank and an outer ditch was dug as an additional form of protection on the other three sides. Archaeological evidence gives an idea of the burh's shape and internal layout, the latter being partly preserved in the modern street-plan. The size of the enclosed area is indicated by the ninth-century defences which have been estimated at more than 1,400 metres in length.[26] We thus know that the burh was quite extensive, being large enough to accommodate two medieval parishes in later times. The charter quoted above offers a useful glimpse into the lives of the chief inhabitants, referring to their various rights and responsibilities. It mentions the tolls levied on salt imported from Droitwich, six miles north-east of Worcester, saying that these would be paid to King Alfred. It also refers to the fines imposed on thieves and rogue traders and to the tax for keeping the walls in good repair. Some of the revenue from the market went into the Mercian treasury, but the charter states that Æthelred and Æthelflæd pledged to donate half of this to the church. Their generosity was acknowledged by Bishop Wærferth, who in turn promised that they would be remembered in the prayers of his monks for eternity.

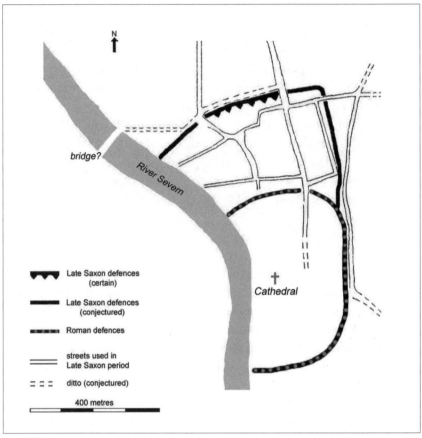

Worcester (after Hill 2001, 150)

Gloucester – the capital

Æthelred and Æthelflæd selected Gloucester, a former Roman city, as the site of another new burh.[27] The Mercian witan assembled there in 896, perhaps to witness the completion of the project. Gloucester's strategic value had been recognised by Roman military commanders as far back as the first century AD when they erected a fort at Kingsholm, half a mile north of the present-day city centre. The fort guarded an important crossing on the River Severn until it was superseded by a larger fortress to the south. This was replaced in the second century by a civilian settlement known to the Romans as *Glevum*. Little is known of its fate in the post-Roman period c.400–500 but it was presumably

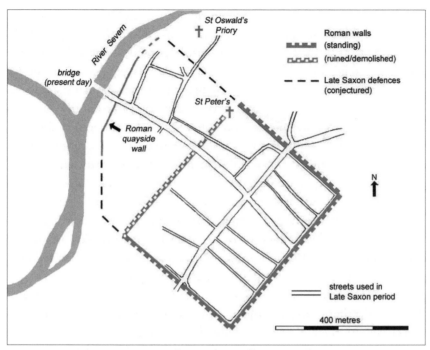

Gloucester (after Heighway 2001, 104)

under the control of native Britons when it was captured by the West Saxon king Ceawlin in 577. It later became part of the kingdom of the Hwicce and, like Worcester, had a close connection with the rulers of that people. A minster church, dedicated to St Peter, had been established c.679 by the Hwiccian king Osric. Its location is unknown but it may have lain within the circuit of the Roman city walls, which were still standing in the late ninth century.[28] Many of the Roman buildings would have been derelict by c.800, their stone having been plundered for the early Anglo-Saxon minster or recycled for other uses. Areas of open ground inside the city were being used as farmland, no doubt originally by local Britons whom the first English settlers displaced in the late sixth century. In 877, Guthrum's army wintered there prior to its attack on Alfred at Chippenham. The old minster may have fallen out of use long before, perhaps as far back as 757 when the monastery attached to it was closed.[29]

The redevelopment of Gloucester by Æthelred and Æthelflæd included a new street layout, part of which is still in use today. As at Worcester, they are likely to have used the design of Alfred's burhs as a template, with Æthelflæd's influence again coming to the fore.[30] On three sides (north-east, south-east and south-west) they seem to have utilised the Roman city walls as a defensive perimeter. Midway along each wall was an ancient gate which they repaired. On the north-west side the Roman wall was either ignored or demolished and the burh was extended beyond it to the bank of the Severn. An ancient bridge across the river was then restored to facilitate trade and communication with lands to the west. The four main Roman streets had run from the gates to a crossroads in the centre and were now cleared of debris to become the main thoroughfares of the burh, with the north-western street being continued down to the river. Lesser streets were laid out as branches and along them were built the houses of traders and craftspeople as well as dwellings for soldiers of the garrison. The military aspect of the settlement was emphasised by the laying of a road along the inner side of the perimeter wall to connect the three surviving gates.

A new minster church was constructed in the north-western corner, outside the Roman perimeter. Like its predecessor, it was dedicated to St Peter and built from Roman stone. It was not a large structure, being a rather modest 120 feet long with a simple rectangular shape, but it became the premier church of Mercia under the special patronage of Æthelred and Æthelflæd.[31] Its foundation coincided with the building of a timber hall at Kingsholm, on the site of an ancient cemetery associated with the first Roman fort. Just as the new minster became the main religious centre for Lord Æthelred and his wife, so did the hall become a favoured residence or palace, perhaps their main centre of government.

Re-designing London

Worcester and Gloucester are the only burhs known to have been founded by Æthelred and Æthelflæd during the lifetime of Alfred the Great. Archaeological evidence suggests that there may have been others. At Hereford and Winchcombe, for example, older defences constructed in the eighth or early ninth century were superseded no later than the early 900s. At both sites the new works can be attributed to Æthelred and Æthelflæd and may have been erected in the 880s or 890s. One Mercian settlement that was certainly turned into a new burh during Alfred's reign was London, but this was the king's own project. Having taken control of the city in 886, he had given it to Lord Æthelred. What the latter received was a refurbished Lundenburh, its Roman walls newly repaired and its internal layout redesigned. This upgrade of the ancient defences was a necessary safeguard against future Viking attacks and was supplemented by the construction of another, smaller burh at Southwark

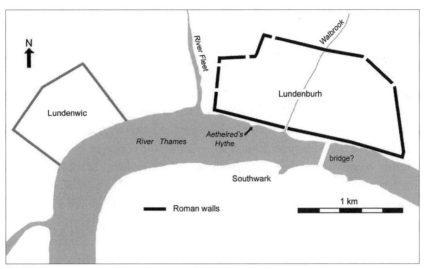

London

on the opposite bank of the Thames. The port of Lundenwic was abandoned, its trading role being taken on by Lundenburh.[32]

Two charters referring to the restoration of London have survived as later copies and allow us to glimpse the economic life of the new burh. The earlier of the two is dated 889 and recorded a grant made jointly by Alfred and Æthelred to Bishop Wærferth of Worcester. It gave the bishop a landholding in London at a place called Hwaetmund's Stone on the bank of the Thames, not far from a wharf known as Æthelred's Hythe. Along with the land came the right to hold a market, from which all profits would go to Wærferth. The later charter was drawn up in 898 during a meeting at Chelsea – an estate four miles upriver – with many of the most senior figures in Wessex and Mercia in attendance. This confirmed Wærferth's previous landholding and granted an adjoining one to Archbishop Plegmund of Canterbury. As well as Alfred, Æthelred and the two bishops, the list of those present at the meeting included Alfred's two older children – Æthelflæd and Edward. It is unlikely that Æthelflæd was there merely as a passive observer. Everything we know about her relationships with her husband, father and brother suggests that she would have taken an active part in the proceedings.[33]

The death of Alfred

Æthelflæd was around twenty-nine years old when her father died on 26 October 899. He had lived fifty or fifty-one years, a fairly respectable span by the measure of the time. Unlike many other early medieval kings he died in his own bed rather than on a bloody field of battle. He was survived by his wife Ealhswith and by five adult children, each of whom received gifts of property in his will. We know of these bequests from a copy of the will preserved in an eleventh-century manuscript written at Winchester. Unsurprisingly, a substantial gift was left to the elder son Edward, who succeeded to the throne of Wessex as the designated heir. Edward is the first named beneficiary and received a swathe of estates stretching from Cornwall to Kent. As the new king he also inherited extensive royal heartlands that passed by default from one West Saxon monarch to the next. The younger son, Æthelweard, was the second beneficiary, receiving a generous bundle of estates. After him came the three daughters, in order of age. To Æthelflæd, the eldest, Alfred bequeathed 'the estate at Wellow', this being the only gift she received. Her middle and youngest sisters – Æthelgifu and Ælfthryth – received two and three estates respectively. The precise location of Æthelflæd's estate is unknown, for there was more than one Wellow in her father's kingdom. East Wellow in Hampshire was a royal estate in the eleventh century but there is also a West Wellow in the same county, another Wellow in Somerset and one on the Isle of Wight.[34] Ælfthryth's inheritance also included an estate called Wellow, presumably not the same one that her older sister received. Two different places bearing the same name are surely meant, unless Alfred intended that his oldest and youngest daughters should share one landholding between them.

We might wonder why Æthelflæd, the king's firstborn child, received only one estate. The answer may lie in her status as wife of the Lord of Mercia, her marriage having brought her a share of revenues and other benefits from Æthelred's landholdings. Some of these Mercian lands would have been royal estates that he had acquired as the successor of kings. Perhaps Alfred bequeathed only one Wessex property to Æthelflæd because she already had an adequate income in Mercia? Elsewhere in the will, he made cash bequests to all his children, giving each son 500 pounds and each daughter 100 pounds. To the Lord of the Mercians, his steadfast ally in the recent Viking wars, he gave a special gift: a sword with a value equivalent to 100 Byzantine gold coins.

Alfred's legacy

Æthelflæd's father is known to history as Alfred the Great and is the only English monarch to have this epithet. It was not bestowed by contemporaries who had known him in life, nor by anyone living in the reigns of his immediate successors, but by people of a much later age. It first appeared in the 1500s in the writings of English historians and became more widely known in the following centuries. The epithet was an acknowledgement of Alfred's popularity during the Middle Ages and beyond into early modern times. He was revered as a paragon of wisdom and heroism – a virtuous warrior-king who had saved his people from pagan Vikings. By the 1700s he was being promoted as a symbol of ancient English freedoms that the Norman Conquest had supposedly destroyed. Later, in the nineteenth century, Victorian historians credited his ship-building projects with laying the foundation of the British navy. Yet none of this veneration tells the real story of his achievements. For that, we must go back to the Anglo-Saxon sources, to the writings of the ninth, tenth and eleventh centuries that documented the key events of his reign. It is clear from these texts that he was not at that time regarded as the greatest of early English kings. Instead, he was ranked no higher than his grandson Athelstan or great-grandson Edgar, both of whom ruled more territory than he had done. Nevertheless, there is no doubt that his victories over the Danes were being recognised by c.1000 as a crucial element in the foundation of England. An observer at that time would have been in no doubt that the survival of Wessex and its royal dynasty was due in no small part to Alfred. Although the task of turning the 'kingdom of the Anglo-Saxons' into the larger kingdom of England was credited to later kings, the part played by Alfred at the beginning of this process was never forgotten. It was rightly acknowledged by those who eventually saw fit to give him the label 'Great'.

The first decade of the tenth century

KINSMEN

In 899, Alfred was succeeded as king of Wessex by his eldest son Edward, known to later generations as 'Edward the Elder'. The succession had been signalled in a charter, written in the previous year, which gave Edward the title *rex*.[1] His right to rule was immediately challenged by his cousin Æthelwold, apparently the only surviving son of Alfred's brother and predecessor Æthelred. Æthelwold had a strong claim on the kingship, being the oldest living *atheling* – a prince deemed eligible to rule. In an age when kingship did not automatically pass from father to son, an adult brother or nephew could step forward as a potential candidate. Æthelwold's father had been older than Edward's, giving Æthelwold a claim to seniority. His challenge, when it came, was hardly unexpected, for tensions had been simmering for many years. It was no secret that Alfred had been grooming Edward as his successor, granting him enough land to form a strong power-base and allowing him to command armies on campaign. Æthelwold could not mount a viable challenge while Alfred was alive but, as soon as the king was dead, he made his move. Leading a band of followers he seized the estates of Wimborne and Christchurch in Dorset. The choice of Wimborne was significant: its minster church housed the tomb of his father. Accompanying Æthelwold was a woman of high birth whom he had taken from a monastery. Her name is not recorded but the *Anglo-Saxon Chronicle* described her as a nun whom he had kidnapped, a tale that might owe more to propaganda than to truth. It is just as likely that she went with him willingly, hoping to become his wife if his bid for the throne was successful. She may even have been coerced into the religious life by people who had a vested interest in keeping her and Æthelwold apart.[2]

Edward's response was decisive. He led an army to Badbury Rings, an ancient hillfort to the west of Wimborne. Æthelwold refused to march out to meet him, defiantly stating that he would stay put whether alive or dead. He remained at Wimborne, together with his associates and his female companion. Then, under cover of darkness, he rode off and escaped, ungallantly leaving the lady to be arrested. He eventually reached Northumbria, the territory of the Danish rulers of York. There he was proclaimed king, receiving oaths of allegiance from the Scandinavian forces who dwelt in the city. It is usually assumed that his new kingship was that of Northumbria itself, but it is possible that the Danes also regarded him as a king of Wessex to rival Alfred's son.[3] This would not have been altogether surprising, for the fugitive prince was clearly a person of interest to the northern division of what had once been the Great Heathen Army. Northumbrian Vikings had recently co-operated with their East Anglian brethren in raids on Wessex, without much success, but Æthelwold's arrival at York may have offered new possibilities for intervention. For the moment, the renegade made no move against Edward and instead bided his time. Coins bearing his name were issued from the mint at York and – in spite of his Christian heritage – the West Saxons nicknamed him 'King of the Pagans'.[4]

With his cousin far away in the north Edward was at last able to begin his reign. No more challengers stepped forward and, within a year of his father's passing, he was formally crowned at Kingston-upon-Thames. The ceremony took place on 8 June 900 and was a suitably grand occasion, attended by the chief dignitaries of the realm. Archbishop Plegmund of Canterbury oversaw the spiritual aspects and may have chosen the venue.[5] Kingston lay on the border between Wessex and Mercia and had symbolic significance for those who supported the idea of a union of the two. It had not been used as a royal inauguration site before, but had a connection with the West Saxon dynasty as the place where King Ecgberht – Edward's paternal great-grandfather – had held an important meeting with one of Plegmund's predecessors in 838. An object now known as the 'Coronation Stone' stands today outside Kingston's Guildhall. It bears the names of seven Anglo-Saxon monarchs, starting with Edward and ending with his great-grandson Æthelred the Unready. The inscriptions are modern but reflect a traditional belief that the stone was used in royal inaugurations. It was not always in its present location, having been retrieved from the ruins of an old chapel in the eighteenth century. In fact, its alleged connection with early English monarchs may date from this time, having been influenced by an erroneous belief that the place-name Kingston means 'king's stone'. The name actually means 'king's farmstead' and refers to a royal landholding of the early Anglo-Saxon period. Nevertheless, a number of Edward's successors did indeed follow him in choosing Kingston as a coronation venue, even if the exact location of the ceremonies remains uncertain.

It is likely that Edward saw himself – and was seen by contemporaries – as not merely the new king of Wessex but as king of all the English.[6] Alfred had adopted the title 'king of the Anglo-Saxons' in his charters and Edward continued the same usage. He shared his father's vision of a single, unified English kingdom ruled by the West Saxon dynasty. Alfred had been quick to recognise that the key to turning this vision into reality lay in the fusion of Wessex and Mercia. Only by merging the two main kingdoms of the south and midlands could the foundations of something greater be established. Alfred had gained the unwavering allegiance of Æthelred, the Lord of the Mercians, strengthening this crucial relationship by giving the hand of his daughter Æthelflæd in marriage. Mercian military muscle had been a vital component of Alfred's campaigns against the Vikings in the 890s and, after his death in 899, the survival of his vision of English unity depended upon the same alliance. For Edward, the continuing co-operation of his sister and her husband was therefore essential if he was to give substance to his own claim of authority as a new 'king of the Anglo-Saxons'.

As things turned out, Edward had no need to worry about the Mercian situation. From the outset, he was able to completely rely on Æthelred's loyalty and support. To what extent this was sustained by bonds of kinship forged by the political marriage is hard to say. At the time of Edward's coronation, the two men had been brothers-in-law for some fifteen years and had played key roles in Alfred's campaigns. They presumably got on quite well. Æthelflæd, too, seems to have been happy to acknowledge Edward as her liege-lord in some sense. Whether she and Æthelred were fully on board with the idea of subsuming Mercia into a larger realm dominated by Wessex is less certain. In the short term, at least, they appear to have felt that it was in everyone's interests to maintain the alliance.

Shrewsbury and Much Wenlock

In 901, Æthelred and Æthelflæd met with the Mercian witan at a place called *Scrobbesburh* on the upper reaches of the River Severn. The same occasion also saw them granting ten hides of land to the monastery of Much Wenlock, an ancient ecclesiastical site fifteen miles to the south-east. The monastery had been founded in 680 by Merewalh, king of the Magonsæte people of western Mercia. Merewalh was a son of the famous Mercian king Penda but, unlike his father, he was a devout Christian. His three daughters entered holy orders and were subsequently elevated to sainthood. Mildburh, the eldest, was a nun at Much Wenlock and ended her days as its abbess, dying there in 715. Her tomb became a place of veneration and pilgrimage, while her story was embellished with tales of miracles and special powers. As a prominent Mercian royal saint it is no surprise to find her cult centre receiving gifts from Æthelred and Æthelflæd. As well as the land-grant, they gave the monastery a valuable chalice in commemoration of Mildburh. These gifts were recorded in a charter, a document that has additional interest beyond what it says about Much Wenlock. It also contains the earliest reference to Scrobbesburh, present-day Shrewsbury, the county town of Shropshire.

It is likely that Shrewsbury was one of the burhs established by Æthelred and Æthelflæd. It is equally likely that the reason for the Mercian witan's assembling there in 901 was to witness the burh's completion.[7] *Scrobbesburh* is an Old English name meaning 'fort in the scrub' or perhaps 'Scrobb's fort'. It was partially rendered into Latin by the scribe of the Wenlock charter as *civitas scrobbensis*. The defences of the tenth-century burh have yet to be found but evidence of activity from the time includes pottery, cultivated grains and butchery waste.[8] An obvious location for the burh is the prominent hill in the present-day town centre, where Norman lords erected a castle in the late eleventh century. This hill and the core of the modern town are encircled by a loop of the Severn on all sides except the north-east. Such a natural defensive situation was recognised long before the Viking Age, for the hill guarded two fords – those marked today by the 'English' and 'Welsh' bridges. It has been suggested that the hill might be the site of Pengwern, a major centre of power in the British kingdom of Powys. Pengwern apparently flourished in the sixth and seventh centuries, before the rise of Anglo-Saxon Mercia, but its location has long been a mystery. If it lay at Shrewsbury it may have been superseded by an early Mercian stronghold, perhaps an original Scrobbesburh that preceded the burh of c.900. As yet, however, there is no archaeological or literary evidence for a fortified settlement at Shrewsbury before the Viking Age.[9]

A typical feature of the 'Alfredian' burhs in Wessex was the siting of a minster – an important church – within the fortified area. The same template was borrowed by Alfred's daughter and son-in-law when they undertook their own burh-building programme in Mercia. In some cases, an existing church was incorporated into the plans, as at Worcester where a seventh-century priory already stood within the circuit of the Roman defences. At Shrewsbury, the old church of St Alkmund's, standing on the hill in the centre of the town, claims to have been founded by Æthelflæd. Tradition states that she retrieved the bones of Alkmund from their original resting-place in Derby and brought them to Shrewsbury. Alkmund was an Anglo-Saxon royal saint, a prince of Northumbria

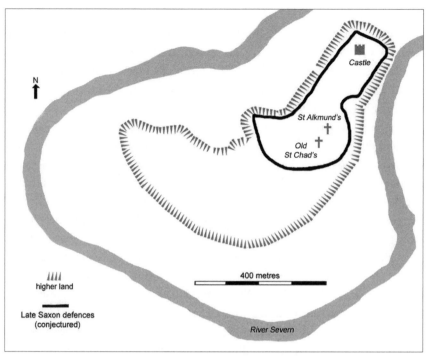

Shrewsbury (after Hill 2001, 152)

who had fled into exile in the late 700s. After seeking refuge with a king of Mercia he was tracked down by his Northumbrian rivals and murdered, his body being laid to rest at Derby. The place subsequently became a major Viking stronghold, one of the so-called 'Five Boroughs' of the Danelaw. As we shall see in a later chapter, Derby was captured by Æthelflæd in 917, sixteen years after the meeting of the Mercian witan at Shrewsbury. It is possible that St Alkmund's church in Shrewsbury was built *after* the Derby campaign and was not the original church of the burh. An older church may have served the inhabitants between c.901 and 917, perhaps the predecessor of Old St Chad's lying to the south of the castle. Old St Chad's, a medieval structure of which only a portion now remains, is presumed to have been founded in Anglo-Saxon times. Local tradition attributes its founding to King Offa of Mercia, a belief supported by the discovery in 1889 of what may be a shroud-pin or stylus from the eighth century. When the church was being demolished c.1790, observers reported seeing fragments of Anglo-Saxon sculpture in the walls, but these no longer survive so their antiquity cannot be verified. A plausible interpretation of the Shrewsbury data would see the tenth-century burh as the successor of an earlier

Mercian royal settlement that already had a minster church. This church may then have been superseded by another minster, one built primarily to house the relics of St Alkmund if these were indeed brought from Derby by Æthelflæd in 917. The burh itself certainly flourished during the tenth century and beyond, acquiring a mint in the 920s and eventually becoming the chief town of the county of Shropshire.

At Much Wenlock, the Anglo-Saxon monastery lies under the ruins of Wenlock Priory, a Norman foundation of the twelfth century. Archaeological excavations have revealed little conclusive evidence of pre-Norman activity and, although traces of a small rectangular building found in 1901 were initially dated to the seventh century, their true age is unconfirmed.[10] It is thought that the monastery founded by King Merewalh may have been attacked by Vikings during raids on Mercia in the 870s before being refounded by Æthelred and Æthelflæd some thirty years later. In the eleventh century, the monastery was rebuilt by Earl Leofric of Mercia and his wife Godgifu ('Lady Godiva') whose foundation was the final Anglo-Saxon settlement on the site. The present-day parish church of Much Wenlock, located in the town centre, was established by monks from the priory and has stonework from the 1100s. Its dedication is to the Holy Trinity but its own traditions claim that its site has been used since Anglo-Saxon times, either as a place of worship for monks from the nearby monastery or as a nunnery founded by St Mildburh herself. As with the priory, the pre-Norman history of the parish church has so far proved elusive.

Foster-son

Æthelflæd's brother King Edward was married three times. His first wife is not named in contemporary texts but William of Malmesbury, writing 200 years later, calls her Ecgwynn. William probably had access to sources that are no longer available to today's historians and, in giving a name to Edward's first wife, he might be reporting authentic tradition. He describes her as a woman of noble birth but says nothing specific about her origins. He also cites a rumour that she was Edward's concubine but this might be a spurious tradition. It is more likely that she and Edward were legitimately married and that her background was aristocratic. Their union would have been sanctioned by King Alfred and might even have been arranged by him to seal a political relationship with Ecgwynn's family. Around the year 894, Ecgwynn bore a son who was given the name Athelstan, perhaps in memory of Alfred's eldest brother who had died some forty years earlier.[11] The child was no more than five or six years old when, according to yet another tradition related by William of Malmesbury, his paternal grandfather presented him with lavish gifts: a scarlet cloak, a gem-studded belt and a sword in a gilded scabbard. William adds that these trappings of kingship were accompanied by a ritual in which Alfred ceremonially 'knighted' Athelstan. While we should be wary of accepting the story at face value, it is possible that William's source was genuine and that Athelstan was in some sense earmarked by his grandfather as a future king.

William goes on to say that Alfred wished for his grandson to be educated in Mercia at the court of Æthelred and Æthelflæd. No other source refers to this alleged period of fosterage but William's testimony finds support in a lost charter of Athelstan cited in another, much later charter of 1304. The earlier charter reputedly dealt with privileges granted by Athelstan to St Oswald's church in Gloucester in 925, the year of his coronation as king of Wessex. It referred to his 'pact of paternal piety' with Æthelred, Lord of the Mercians, who had died fourteen years earlier. The implication is that he regarded Æthelred as his foster-father. Although neither William of Malmesbury nor the charter of 1304 are contemporary witnesses, they do seem to be independent of one another. Together they suggest that Athelstan was fostered in Mercia with his aunt and her husband, a scenario accepted by most modern historians.[12] This fits well enough with a picture of upheaval and family rivalry in Athelstan's early years. By 900, his mother was no longer at the royal court and his father had taken a new wife, a lady called Ælfflæd. She was the daughter of Ealdorman Æthelhelm, probably the West Saxon nobleman of this name who, in alliance with Lord Æthelred, had led the men of Wiltshire in a campaign against Hæsten. What happened to Ecgwynn is unknown but we can probably assume that she died. It is possible, though perhaps less likely, that she was simply cast aside to make way for a new wife. Ælfflæd bore Edward two sons and six daughters. The new princes – Ælfweard and Edwin – became æthelings or candidates for kingship alongside their older half-brother. Their mother seems to have been successful in advancing their positions at the royal court.[13] In 901, when Athelstan was six or seven years old, he and Ælfweard were present on two occasions when their father granted land to the royal minster church of Winchester.[14] Although Ælfweard can only have been a small child at the time – perhaps only two or three years old – he preceded Athelstan on the list of witnesses in both charters. The implication is that Edward's firstborn son was being sidelined in favour of his younger half-siblings. According to William of Malmesbury, the decision to send Athelstan to be educated in Mercia was made by Alfred. If William is correct, the decision must have been made before Alfred's death in October 899 when Athelstan would have been around five or six years old. The young prince duly arrived at the Mercian court where, in William's words, he was 'brought up with great care by his aunt and the eminent ealdorman'.[15] Æthelflæd and Æthelred already had a child of their own – their daughter Ælfwynn – but they now welcomed their nephew as a foster-son.

Athelstan's upbringing in Mercia included – as Alfred had wished – a formal education. No doubt this would have followed a curriculum similar to the one his father had experienced in Wessex, learning how to read and write in both Latin and Old English.[16] Edward had been taught by tutors based at the royal court, receiving an education alongside other children of high birth – his own siblings as well as sons and daughters of the West Saxon nobility. Some of the teachers were men, others were women, but all would have come from ecclesiastical backgrounds. Edward learned not only the Psalms and other religious works but also the lore and poetry of his people. It is likely that his eldest son was exposed to a similar mix of Latin and English literature under the watchful gaze of Æthelflæd and Æthelred. William of Malmesbury refers to the young Athelstan's fear of strict Mercian tutors who wielded the cane, but this is surely a detail invented by William himself.

In addition to a formal education, Athelstan would have learned how to hunt – an activity closely associated with the royal and aristocratic elites – riding with the hounds in the company of his foster-parents. It is reasonable to assume that his cousin Ælfwynn rode beside him on these occasions. She was his senior by six or more years and was no doubt nearing the end of her schooldays when he arrived in Mercia. Hunting, of course, was regarded as an ideal training-ground for the sons of the military aristocracy. It gave a novice warrior valuable experience in the use of spears and other weapons, as well as introducing him to other skills such as horsemanship. William was probably making an assumption when he stated that Athelstan learned about weapons and tactics in Mercia but on this point he was surely correct.[17] The Mercian court in the early tenth century was as good a place as any for gaining experience of the military life.

Kin-strife

In 902, Edward's renegade cousin Æthelwold brought a war-fleet from his adoptive kingdom of Northumbria to the coast of Essex. The former kingdom of the East Saxons had formerly been part of the 'Greater Wessex' established by Æthelwold's great-grandfather Ecgberht in the early ninth century, but it lay now in the shadow of Danish East Anglia. The population was predominantly English but may have felt little in common with a West Saxon king in distant Winchester. Perhaps Æthelwold hoped that the local nobility would support him? He was certainly successful in persuading the neighbouring East Anglian Danes to join him on a raid into English Mercia, a venture that penetrated as far west as the upper Thames. He and his allies then crossed the river into Wessex, using an ancient ford guarded by the burh at Cricklade. All the countryside southward as far as Braydon Forest was harried mercilessly before the raiders headed back home.[18] Although Edward set off in pursuit he failed to catch up and instead launched a counter-raid on East Anglia. His troops ravaged a broad swathe of territory in Cambridgeshire and Norfolk before being ordered to gather for the homeward march. The order was ignored by the men of Kent who, despite the king summoning them seven times, chose to stay behind and continue plundering. In the second week of December, the Kentishmen were attacked by Æthelwold and his Viking allies at a place called The Holme – probably the Cambridgeshire village of this name, seven miles south of Peterborough. The ensuing battle saw the defeat of the Kentish force and the slaughter of its leaders who included two ealdormen, an abbot and a royal thegn. However, although the Vikings were victorious they, too, lost many prominent commanders: King Eohric or Erik, probably the ruler of East Anglia; Beorhtsige, the son of an English prince; several Scandinavian jarls; and Æthelwold himself. The most puzzling of these casualties is Beorhtsige whom the chronicler describes as 'son of the ætheling Beornoth'. Alliteration of initial B in the names of father and son has prompted speculation that they belonged to the so-called 'B dynasty' of Mercian kings. Beorhtsige is also possibly the same man as the Beorhtsige who witnessed one of King Alfred's charters in 898.[19] If so, and if he really was the son of a Mercian ætheling, he had presumably switched his allegiance to Æthelwold in the hope of fulfilling a thwarted personal ambition. Perhaps he hoped to gain the kingship of Mercia, wresting power out of Lord Æthelred's hands, if Æthelwold's cause proved successful? Alternatively, both Beorhtsige and his father might simply have belonged to the old royal houses of Essex or East Anglia.

Æthelwold's demise ended the most serious dynastic challenge to Edward's authority. Although the attempted *coup d'état* had fizzled out in a battle that Edward's forces had lost, the military result turned out to be irrelevant. More significant were the political repercussions: Æthelwold was dead and the throne of Wessex now lay more securely with Alfred's heirs. A couple of interesting observations can be made about the campaign of 902. First, it is curious to note the apparent insubordination of the Kentishmen in ignoring a royal command. Their determination to continue raiding looks at first glance like a rejection of Edward's authority. Refusing to retreat from enemy territory might seem courageous and heroic at best, foolhardy and insubordinate at worst. There may have been disagreement on the English side over whether the campaign should continue, with a cautious Edward hoping perhaps to avoid a decisive showdown with Æthelwold. It would be useful to know if, and to what extent, the defeat of the Kentishmen affected Edward's future relationship with their homeland. Perhaps his eventual third marriage, to the daughter of a Kentish ealdorman slain at The Holme, was a deliberate attempt to heal old wounds?[20]

Our second observation is equally important in a political sense, if not more so. It concerns the absence of any record of Mercian involvement in the war of 902. We hear no mention of Æthelred or Æthelflæd, nor any reference to Mercian troops joining Edward's army for the counter-strike on East Anglia. Nor are the Mercians cited as defending their own land during Æthelwold's earlier raid towards the upper Thames, even though his army passed through Mercian Oxfordshire. It is possible, of course, that local Mercian forces were simply overwhelmed before being able to mount an effective response and hence played no further part in that campaign. Another possibility is that overall command of forces in south-east Mercia lay with Edward, not with Æthelred. We should also keep in mind that the historical record is incomplete, not only because of the loss of documents but also because the narrative offered by *ASC* and other contemporary texts is so selective. Even if Æthelred and Æthelflæd had played a role in the war there is no certainty that this would have been mentioned. Besides, as we shall see below, Mercia's rulers may have been too distracted by events in the north of their territory to assist King Edward in the south.

Ingimund

For Æthelflæd, the year 902 witnessed not only the death of her rebellious cousin Æthelwold but also the passing of her mother. Described by contemporaries as 'the true and dear lady of the English', Ealhswith died on 5 December, a week before the Battle of the Holme. Her final days may have been spent at St Mary's Abbey in Winchester, a nunnery that she herself had founded in widowhood. She was laid to rest in the same city, at the New Minster built by her son Edward. This new royal church, originally planned by her husband Alfred, stood close to the seventh-century Old Minster which it had replaced as the main spiritual home of the dynasty.

The same year witnessed a major setback for the Vikings in Ireland. An alliance of native Irish kings captured the Norse stronghold of Dublin, toppling its royal dynasty and forcing large numbers of Scandinavian colonists to leave. Contemporary Irish chroniclers reported the city's recapture by native forces, noting that 'the heathens were driven from Ireland . . . and they abandoned a good number of their ships and escaped half dead after they had been wounded and broken'.[21] Groups of Norse refugees from Dublin and other places sailed away to establish new colonies. Some may have settled in the Hebridean islands off the west coast of Scotland, or further south along the shores of Continental Europe. Others made landfall along Northumbria's western coasts, creating a string of settlements running from the Solway Firth down to the Mersey estuary. Several groups came to Wales and one of these, led by a certain Ingimund, put ashore on the Isle of Anglesey. It then seized a place that the Welsh Annals called Maes Osfeilion, probably Maes Rosmelion in the east of the island.[22] Anglesey belonged to the kingdom of Gwynedd whose ruler, King Cadel ap Rhodri, responded to the Norse newcomers by leading an army against them. In the ensuing battle the Welsh were victorious and, although Ingimund survived, he decided that he and his people should move on. So they took to sea once more, this time sailing along the North Welsh coast towards the estuary of the River Dee in north-west Mercia. The chief place in that area was Chester, the ancient Roman city that had been briefly occupied by Danes in 893.

According to the *Fragmentary Annals of Ireland*, Ingimund landed near Chester and sought an audience with Æthelflæd, who was in the vicinity at that time. *FAI* goes on to say ' that the 'queen of the Saxons' was not accompanied by her husband Lord Æthelred, who had been struck down by illness. Ingimund asked for land on which he and his folk could settle, claiming that he had grown tired of the raiding life. Æthelflæd was no stranger to negotiations between English and Scandinavian leaders, having seen her father use diplomacy with the Danes as an alternative to war. She now took a similar path, agreeing to Ingimund's request and giving him a sizeable portion of territory on the Wirral peninsula between the Dee and Mersey estuaries. It was no small gift, for the peninsula had good havens for seaborne trade and, although the soil was not of the best quality, some areas were suitable for cultivation. A link to the mainland on the south-east side gave access to the Roman road network and to overland trade routes that criss-crossed Mercia.

If Ingimund really had wanted to retire from war and raiding he had found a suitable place to do so. He and his people established a colony in Wirral and, for a while, they lived in harmony with their English neighbours. Such, at least, is the tale related by the Irish annalist. The story is certainly plausible, even if not all of it can be verified. Its first part is corroborated by the Welsh Annals, which tell of Ingimund's settlement in Anglesey, his defeat by Cadel and his subsequent departure from the island. Archaeological evidence for Norse settlement on Anglesey in the early tenth century provides further support for the Welsh annalists' account.[23] The second part of the Irish story is likewise consistent with what we know of the history of Wirral in this period. A large number of place-names in the northern and western parts of the peninsula are indeed of Norse origin, leaving us in no doubt that this was an area of intensive Scandinavian settlement. It is likely that Norse-speakers became the dominant group in the population by c.930.[24] Their presence fits well with the tale of negotiation and land-giving related by *FAI*. Similar arrangements between local rulers and Viking leaders occurred elsewhere in early medieval Europe, with the former gaining protection for vulnerable or strategic districts while the latter obtained land without having to fight for it. To Æthelflæd, her resettlement of Ingimund's people in Wirral may have seemed a useful way of deterring raids by other Scandinavian groups.[25]

Her strategy unravelled when Ingimund broke his pledge. The Norse colony in Wirral was only a few years old when, according to *FAI*, it rose in revolt. The nearby fortress-city of Chester was too much of a temptation for Ingimund and he desired to take it for himself. At a secret meeting with other Vikings – described by the Irish annalist as 'chieftains of the Norsemen and Danes' – he made plans for an assault. The Danish involvement suggests an alliance between the Wirral Norse and adventurers from southern Northumbria or the East Mercian Danelaw. Meanwhile, Æthelflæd learned of the revolt and responded swiftly, mustering a large force 'from the adjoining regions' and installing it at Chester. When Ingimund's Vikings arrived outside the walls, the defenders sent a message to Æthelflæd and Æthelred, seeking advice on what to do next. The order came back: go out and meet the enemy in battle, but leave the gate open and place a unit of horsemen just inside and out of sight; during the battle, pretend to flee back through the gate, so that any pursuers can be trapped and slaughtered by the cavalry. The feigned retreat worked well. Many Vikings took the bait and were slain inside the city.

However, despite their casualties the attackers remained in sufficient numbers to begin a siege. They decided to dig a tunnel under the walls, supporting it with timbers. At this point, the English resorted to subterfuge. Æthelflæd and her husband were aware that Ingimund's army included young Irish warriors who were in fosterage with the Vikings. Secret messages were sent to these men, urging them to turn against the heathens by helping to lure them into a trap. The Mercian rulers had devised a plan whereby the Irish fosterlings would pretend to be in contact with traitors inside Chester who wanted to make a deal with the Danish troops in Ingimund's army. A meeting would then be arranged with the Danes 'in a place where it would be convenient to kill them'. The Irishmen agreed to play their part in the deception and the Danes were slaughtered, having put aside their weapons in a traditional gesture of peace. This further depleted the besieging force but left the majority Norse contingent unscathed. The Norsemen, clustering in the tunnel beneath the walls, were targeted by a barrage of rocks and wooden beams thrown from above. They tried to prevent the tunnel from collapsing by supporting it with sturdy timbers but finally gave up when boiling beer and hives full of bees came hurtling down on their heads. They then departed, having failed to capture the city. Ingimund's fate is unknown but, if he was not among the casualties, he presumably returned to the colony in Wirral.

Æthelflæd plays a major role in the story and whoever wrote it was plainly sympathetic to her. To what extent it preserves a kernel of real history is, however, a matter of debate. The doubts and scepticism surrounding *FAI* have already been noted but it is worth recalling them here. One major issue is that the detailed account of the siege of Chester looks like a saga-narrative of the type produced by storytellers rather than by chroniclers. We would be naïve to swallow it wholesale, at face value, without exercising appropriate caution. On the other hand, there is no reason to reject it outright. At its core is a plausible sequence of events: Viking refugees from Ireland were given land for a new colony in north-west Mercia; they rose up against their hosts and tried to seize a former Roman city; their assault was repulsed and they withdrew to their colony. This appears to be a logical continuation of the same group's unsuccessful attempt to colonise Anglesey as reported in the Welsh Annals. Modern historians seem more willing to give credence to the Welsh account than to its Irish sequel, yet both appear to be drawing on the same pool of information and are clearly independent of one another. If it is reasonable to accept Ingimund's abortive adventure on Anglesey as a real event, then the treaty with Æthelflæd and the siege of Chester might also be historical. *FAI*'s tale of bees and tunnels and secret meetings should probably be set aside as storytelling but the core narrative could be authentic.

The story has another chapter, or rather a prequel. This is told not by a Welsh or Irish text but by the Mercian Register which says that Chester was 'restored' in 907. The restoration, usually seen as Æthelflæd's work, turned the decrepit Roman fortress into a burh along the lines of Gloucester and Worcester. The task was a challenging one, not least because Chester's size made it the largest burh-building project that Æthelflæd would ever tackle. The Roman walls, originally raised to a height of nearly five metres, were still substantially intact in the early 900s. Within their circuit lay an area of 26 hectares (65 acres) comprising a patchwork of streets and buildings in various states of disrepair. Some structures had collapsed into heaps of rubble which disrupted the straight alignment of the Roman street-pattern. With no easy means of clearing away such obstacles, the few post-Roman inhabitants had to wend their way around them. How many people lived or worked in Chester before the restoration of 907 is unknown but the number is likely to have been quite small. Archaeology has shown that here, as at Gloucester and Worcester, areas of open ground were being used for cultivation and grazing. At Chester, some of this agricultural land may have belonged to one or more Anglo-Saxon churches that are supposed to have existed before c.900. Tradition asserts that one early church, originally dedicated to St Peter, stood in the north-east quarter of the Roman fortress on a site now occupied by Chester Cathedral. It is said to have been rededicated to the Mercian royal saint Werburgh after her relics were brought from Hanbury in Staffordshire in 875.[26] The date seems somewhat dubious, given the occupation of Chester by heathen Danes in 893, and a later date after the foundation of the burh may be preferable. If the relocation of Werburgh's bones occurred in or after 907, it can probably be attributed to Æthelflæd as part of her policy of promoting the cults of Mercian saints. Archaeological excavations at Chester Cathedral have identified what may be pre-Norman stonework but whether this is as old as the early 900s is uncertain. The site nevertheless remains a strong candidate for the church that Æthelflæd would have designated as a minster for the inhabitants of her new burh. Another possibly ancient church is present-day St Peter's in the city centre, on the site of the Roman headquarters building. According to its own traditions it was founded by Æthelflæd, a claim that may or may not be authentic. One church that was certainly in existence by c.975 is St John the Baptist, lying just outside the south-east corner of the Roman walls. It claims to be Chester's oldest church and may have served an early Anglo-Saxon settlement that developed in the years when the Roman fortress lay derelict.

The precise layout of the interior of the Chester burh is not fully understood but Æthelflæd was working to a template devised by her father in Wessex and

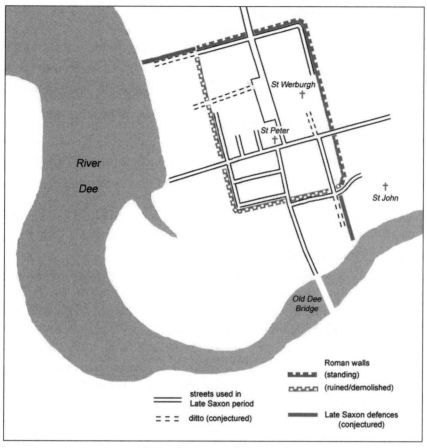

Chester (after Ward 2001, 163)

already employed by her and her husband at Gloucester and Worcester. At Gloucester, one side of the Roman walls had been demolished to extend the burh down to the River Severn. It is likely that something similar was done at Chester, where the southern wall of the legionary fortress looked towards the River Dee.[27] This rampart was probably removed so that the burh could include the riverbank and its moorings. The line of the eastern wall would then have been extended to the river, by a substantial wooden fence, thus ensuring protection by man-made defences on three sides and by water on the fourth. The western wall may have been similarly disregarded to extend the burh on that side to the Dee, thus letting the water provide protection on the west as well as on the south.[28] A nearby ford, the lowest foot-crossing on the river, had been replaced in Roman times by a wooden bridge mounted on stone supports.

This had collapsed in the Anglo-Saxon period and seems to have been replaced by a ferry that was presumably still running at the beginning of the tenth century. A new bridge, the precursor of today's Old Dee Bridge, was eventually built slightly upstream of the Roman one. It was in existence before 1086 but is not thought to be Æthelflæd's creation, despite a suggestion that it should be attributed to her.[29]

Chester's importance to Æthelflæd was demonstrated by her founding of a mint which issued coins bearing the name of her brother Edward on one side and a tower on the other. The tower presumably represents the Chester burh but the design was ultimately derived from Late Roman coins depicting the gateways of major cities. It is likely that Æthelflæd was here invoking the memory of Imperial Rome to add prestige to a resurgent Mercia. By c.930, the Chester mint was one of the most important in Britain, many of its coins being produced by citizens with Scandinavian names.[30]

It is likely that Chester was restored before Ingimund's siege and that the burh was the place described as being under attack in *FAI*, even though the Irish annalist assigned the siege to 906 rather than to 907 or later.[31] The Irish tale speaks of Ingimund's desire to possess 'the wealthy city and the choice lands around it', a description that fits the prosperous burh far better than the semi-derelict Roman site that preceded it. Æthelflæd's alleged presence in the area prior to the Norse assault might even have been due to her overseeing the final stages of the restoration in 907. Her reasons for turning Chester into a burh are not hard to find. It was the largest settlement in north-west Mercia and an obvious choice as a regional centre of power. It had been important to past Mercian kings but lay far from Lord Æthelred's core territory in the south-west and, by c.900, was essentially adrift in a vulnerable borderland. Attaching Chester to Æthelred's domains must have required a military campaign to clear the surrounding region of marauders and other hostile elements, whether these were of Scandinavian, Welsh or English origin.

Before Ingimund's arrival c.902, the main concern was probably the neighbouring Welsh kingdom of Gwynedd, a historic enemy of Mercia. Æthelred had clashed with Gwynedd's forces in the 870s and these were probably still regarded as a threat thirty years later. Securing Chester may have been high on his and his wife's list of priorities as the tenth century dawned, especially after its brief occupation by Danish raiders in 893. By restoring it with new defences and a permanent garrison, Æthelflæd was guarding against future incursions from whichever direction they might come. The Norse colonists in Wirral were a potential menace in 907, as Ingimund's actions would soon demonstrate. Indeed, there is a hint in *FAI* that they mounted a second attack on Chester after the failure of the first. However, other information suggests that their relationship with the rest of Mercia after Ingimund's siege was one of co-operation and assimilation. Chester moneyers with Scandinavian names have already been mentioned and there is evidence that a Norse or Norse-Danish community formed part of the burh's population in the tenth century. We do not know if any of the Wirral colonists relocated there but it is possible that they did. Æthelflæd may have negotiated a new treaty with Ingimund or with his heirs, securing their allegiance in exchange for landholdings and trading privileges in Chester.

Lord Æthelred's illness

The story of Ingimund in *FAI* says that he asked Æthelflæd for land on which he and his followers could settle. We are told that the reason why Æthelred was not present was due to his being incapacitated by an illness from which he would eventually die. Nowhere is the nature of this ailment explained, nor do we know when it began to afflict him. If *FAI*'s chronology is correct, his health was in decline as early as 902. He was evidently well enough to attend a gathering of King Edward's court in 904 where, alongside his wife and daughter, he witnessed the renewal of a land-grant. However, this is his last known appearance in a charter.[32] His health may have continued to deteriorate as time went on, to the extent that he was unable to govern his realm effectively, leaving his wife to increasingly take his responsibilities upon herself.

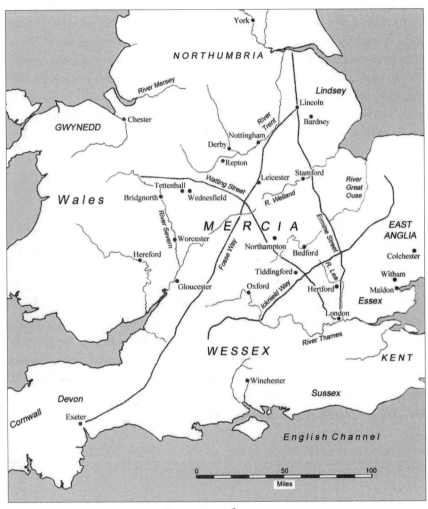

Campaigns of 909–10

6

LOSSES AND GAINS

In 906, the year before Æthelflæd's restoration of Chester, a peace treaty was concluded between King Edward and the Danes. The venue was Tiddingford in Buckinghamshire, a village where the River Ouzel is crossed by an ancient trackway running east–west. The 'A' text of the *Anglo-Saxon Chronicle* says that the treaty was confirmed by the Danes of East Anglia and Northumbria, to whom those of the Five Boroughs in eastern Mercia should probably be added, and that it happened 'just as King Edward decreed'. This seems to imply that the terms were dictated by the English king. However, the 'E' manuscript of *ASC* has a slightly different wording, saying that the treaty came about 'by necessity', suggesting that either Edward or the Danes – or both – felt a pressing need to make peace. Many years had passed since Alfred's treaty with Guthrum had defined the boundary between English and Danish territory, and perhaps both sides now felt that a new agreement was overdue. Some parts of the original frontier may have become less meaningful to people living along it, especially if the line had shifted or blurred. It had been transgressed by Æthelwold and his heathen allies in 902, and again in the same year when Edward launched reprisals on East Anglia. As well as being trampled underfoot during such campaigns, the frontier may have been rendered obsolete by changes in land-ownership. For example, if an estate on the Danish side was sold to an Englishman whose allegiance lay with Lord Æthelred or with King Edward, on which side of the political divide did it now lie? The choice of Tiddingford as a venue for negotiations was appropriate, for it lay close to the Watling Street boundary in a suitably neutral position. It is possible, of course, that Edward felt an urgent need to seek peace because he feared that the Northumbrian and East Anglian Danes were threatening a new war. More specifically, he may have been concerned about the arrival of Norse refugees from Ireland on the shores of western Northumbria. At Tiddingford he may have sought an assurance from the Northumbrian Danes that they would not form an alliance with the new arrivals.[1]

The invasion of Northumbria

The treaty of Tiddingford held for about three years. It collapsed in 909 when a combined force of Mercians and West Saxons invaded Northumbria and 'severely harried the northern army, destroying both people and every kind of cattle; they killed many Danes and spent five weeks in their territory'.[2] The *Anglo-Saxon Chronicle* says that Edward sent the English army, with no mention of his leading it in person, so it is possible that its commander was Lord Æthelred – unless he was too ill to travel at the time. It is not known who broke the peace but perhaps Edward and Æthelred were unhappy with the Northumbrian leaders over something they had done or had failed to do. Eventually a new truce was agreed and the English army went home. However, in the following year the Northumbrians invaded Mercia and plundered it mercilessly, 'rejecting with scorn whatever peace King Edward and his councillors offered them'. The chronicler Æthelweard stated that the Northumbrians also broke their peace with Æthelred 'who then ruled the Northumbrian and Mercian areas'.[3] This implies an otherwise unknown period of Mercian hegemony over the Danes of York, presumably a brief one if it had been imposed as a result of the English raid in the previous year.[4] Any such dominance evaporated when the Northumbrians invaded Mercia in what looks like an act of revenge. They ravaged southward as far as the River Avon on the West Saxon border before turning back north towards the Severn. Knowing that King Edward was at that time in Kent they assumed that he would not be able to respond. He nevertheless sent troops to intercept them and, on 5 August 910, a combined army of West Saxons and Mercians caught up with the raiders as they headed back to Northumbria with their loot. A great battle was fought at Tettenhall near present-day Wolverhampton where the Danes were slaughtered in great numbers.[5] According to Æthelweard, they were caught while marching eastward after crossing the River Severn at *Cantabrycge*. The latter name is almost certainly an error for *Cwatbrycge*, an Old English name thought to refer to Bridgnorth in Shropshire.[6] Æthelweard says that the site of the battle was Woden's Field, a name now borne by the village of Wednesfield, four miles east of Tettenhall.[7] Faced with two alternative locations for the battlefield we can perhaps accept the uncertainty and, in the words of one historian, envisage the fighting taking place 'at Tettenhall or Wednesfield or at both places or near both'.[8]

Danish losses in the battle included two kings, named in *ASC* as Halfdan and Eowils, who may have ruled jointly at York. A third Danish casualty, King Ivarr, was mentioned by Æthelweard. This trio of names is interesting as it suggests Northumbrian co-operation with the displaced Scandinavian leadership of Dublin. 'Eowils' is thought to be an English rendering of Audgisl, the name of a Viking who had raided northern Britain in the late 860s and early 870s. In Irish sources, the earlier Audgisl was often in the company of a Halfdan and an Ivarr, all of whom were connected to the Norse dynasty of Dublin. Their namesakes who died at Tettenhall in 910 might have belonged to a later, York-based generation of the same family.[9] The battle also claimed other prominent Vikings, among them two jarls, in a casualty toll that may have left the raiding army leaderless. Not without reason should the English victory be acknowledged as one of the most important events of the Viking Age. Edward himself seems not to have been present, instead delegating command to trusted subordinates. While one or more ealdormen from Wessex may have led the West Saxon contingent, the senior English commander was surely Lord Æthelred of Mercia, upon whose territory the battle was fought. If he was at that time laid low by sickness, his wife Æthelflæd may have taken command in his stead, perhaps even leading the army in person. An alternative scenario is that Æthelred's illness began in 910 as a direct consequence of wounds received at Tettenhall. This challenges the idea that he was already an invalid and contradicts the Irish tradition – stated in the *Fragmentary Annals* – that his malady appeared as far back as c.902. If he was in good health up to 910, and if the Irish account is to be believed, his wife's dealings with Ingimund could hardly have taken place before that year. However, this alternative chronology would still leave unexplained Æthelred's absence from the post-904 charter record. The simplest interpretation is probably that he was indeed seriously unwell, and frequently laid low by poor health, long before the Tettenhall campaign.[10]

Oswald

In 909, the year when Mercians and West Saxons attacked Northumbria, the bones of St Oswald were retrieved from the Danelaw. Oswald had been a seventh-century king of Bernicia, the northern part of the Anglo-Saxon kingdom of Northumbria in pre-Viking times. His reign had not been long, commencing in 634 and ending with his death on 5 August 642, but in that time he had earned renown for Christian piety and for success in war. He eventually fell in battle against the pagan Mercian king Penda at a place named by Bede as *Maserfelth*, the location of which is unknown.[11] Penda celebrated Oswald's demise by dismembering his body and attaching the head and limbs to wooden stakes on the battlefield. This gruesome treatment turned Oswald into a Christian martyr and royal saint. His head and arms were eventually retrieved from Maserfelth by his younger brother, King Oswiu, during an expedition into Penda's territory c.650. Later, sometime between 679 and 697, Oswald's niece Osthryth unearthed more remains after a tip-off from a man who lived near the battlefield. Osthryth was queen of Mercia, having become the wife of Æthelred, one of Penda's Christian sons. Loading her uncle's remains on a cart she took them to the monastery of Bardney in Lindsey, the north-eastern province of the old Mercian kingdom, and asked the brethren to enshrine them. As patriotic Mercians, the monks were at first reluctant to welcome the bones of an enemy king, even one who had been so devoutly Christian in life, but they relented after a divine miracle confirmed Oswald's sanctity. His cult thereafter gained devotees far and wide, not least in Mercia where King Offa endowed the shrine at Bardney with rich gifts in the eighth century.[12]

When the Mercian kingdom collapsed under the Viking onslaught of the 870s, the monks of Bardney abandoned their monastery in terror. The surrounding lands became part of the Danelaw, leaving Oswald's relics vulnerable to dishonour by heathen marauders. In 909, they were brought to a safer location in western Mercia, to the minster church of St Peter at Gloucester, to be interred in a new shrine. A brief notice in the Mercian Register reported that 'the body of St Oswald was brought from Bardney into Mercia' but did not say who was responsible. According to William of Malmesbury, the transfer was the work of Æthelred and Æthelflæd whom he believed to have had all of Mercia under their rule at that time. On this last point he was surely mistaken, for the eastern provinces of the kingdom were still under Danish control. We are left to ponder the logistical aspects of the transfer and the extent, if any, of Edward's involvement. One school of thought sees the Mercian rulers ordering a daring foray into enemy territory to retrieve the bones.[13] Another sees the transfer taking place during the English invasion of Northumbria which happened in the same year. A third scenario sees the bones being retrieved in a time of truce, with the Danes guaranteeing safe passage to English territory. Such a guarantee could feasibly have been given between the invasion of Northumbria and the Tettenhall campaign, in the months when Æthelred's overlordship was supposedly acknowledged by the Northumbrian Danes. We might wonder if the English soldiers who fought at Tettenhall on 5 August 910 felt that Oswald was watching over them as they battled heathen foes on the anniversary of his martyrdom.[14]

Relics of saints conferred special prestige on the churches where they were enshrined, turning them into cult-centres that attracted pilgrims and wealthy patrons. In exchange for gifts of land for the clergy and precious objects for the Mass, patrons could claim a link with the saint and thus enhance their own prestige. This is what seems to have happened at Gloucester when Oswald's relics arrived there in 909. As an English royal martyr who had died at the hands of pagans he was an appropriate saint for the Viking Age. It apparently mattered little that the Godless enemies who had mutilated his corpse were Englishmen from the very land where his bones now resided. He went from being a victim of the Mercians in the seventh century to one of their most revered saints in the tenth. Not only did Æthelred and Æthelflæd bring him to their principal religious foundation, they rededicated it in his honour as the minster church of St Oswald. The tomb-shrine containing his relics no longer survives among the ruins of the later priory that occupies the site but it is presumed to have stood in a crypt built onto the eastern end of the tenth-century church. Archaeology has revealed that the crypt was a square-shaped structure supported by columns, a design probably inspired by the crypt at Repton which once held the tombs of Mercian kings and queens.

Oswald's cult flourished in western Mercia under the patronage of Æthelred and Æthelflæd. Of the churches in this region now bearing his name some may have received their dedications in the early 900s, soon after his arrival at Gloucester.[15] It is unlikely that there were any such dedications before 910. The only area of Mercia where he may have been venerated earlier was Lindsey, especially at churches connected with the Bardney monastery.[16] After Edward's son Athelstan succeeded to the kingships of Wessex and Mercia in 924–5, he showed special devotion to Oswald, perhaps because of an interest acquired during his fosterage at the Mercian court. Athelstan may have been responsible for creating the idea that the West Saxon royal family was descended from the pious Northumbrian king.[17]

Bremesbyrig

Under its entry for 910, the 'A' text of *ASC* gives an account of the Northumbrian invasion of Mercia and the battle of Tettenhall. An entry for the same year in the Mercian Register says that Æthelflæd built a burh at *Bremesbyrig*. There is no mention of Lord Æthelred, even though he still lived, so he was presumably too ill to accompany her on this venture. It is often regarded as the second burh-building project undertaken solely by Æthelflæd rather than jointly with her husband, the first being Chester in 907. Unfortunately, the location of

Bremesbyrig is utterly lost. One suggestion is that it might have formed part of a defensive network in south-west Mercia that also included Worcester and Gloucester.[18] Another theory looks further north, to Bromborough in Wirral where an important Anglo-Saxon estate existed in the tenth century. A superficial similarity between the names Bromborough and Bremesbyrig has been noted in this context.[19] Bromborough's frontier position certainly makes it a plausible site for a fortified settlement in the early 900s: it lay just within the English part of the Wirral peninsula, nudging the southern edge of the Norse colony. Moreover, it overlooks the Mersey estuary and has considerable strategic value. Yet nothing resembling a tenth-century burh has been found there. Nor do early forms of the name closely resemble Bremesbyrig or contain the latter's intermediate -s-. It is likely that the popular identification of Bromborough as the site of the lost battle of Brunanburh – a major English victory in 937 – has influenced the idea that it was also the site of Æthelflæd's burh.[20]

On etymological grounds a better candidate for Bremesbyrig is Bromsberrow in Gloucestershire, a village roughly ten miles north-west of Gloucester. One objection to Bromsberrow is that a burh in this vicinity might have been unnecessary, given that one already existed twenty miles to the north-west at Hereford. Archaeological evidence shows that the Hereford burh was built before c.850, being substantially improved in the late ninth or early tenth century. Its redevelopment is usually attributed to Æthelred and Æthelflæd in the 890s, or to Æthelflæd alone in the early 900s.[21] In a wider strategic context, Hereford links up with Gloucester and Worcester to form a defensive triangle protecting south-west Mercia. It seems unlikely that Æthelflæd would have placed an additional burh in the centre of this triangle in 910. In any case, since Bromsberrow is not close to a Roman road or to a major river it is hard to see what advantage a fortification there would have had.[22] So, although it is true that the name Bromsberrow could have developed from Bremesbyrig, in the same way that Bromsgrove in Worcestershire was once Bremesgrave, the root of -berrow seems to be berg ('mound or tumulus') rather than burh/byrig ('fort'). Nor does anything in the present-day village indicate the presence of a tenth-century fortification. Although the summit of a nearby hill shows traces of a narrow ditch of unknown date these remains do not look substantial enough for a burh.[23]

Unsurprisingly, Bromsgrove has also been put forward as a possible candidate for Bremesbyrig but here again the second part of the place-name weakens the argument. The oldest documented forms are Bremesgraf (c.804) and Bremesgrave (1086), neither of which suggests an intermediate name ending in –burh/byrig.

With no strong candidates emerging we should probably accept that the location of Æthelflæd's burh is unlikely to be found. Place-name similarities alone are not going to solve the mystery. Our inability to locate Bremesbyrig on a modern map suggests that it failed to develop into a permanent settlement or that it was only ever intended as a temporary fortress. Wherever it lay, it was presumably built during or after a military campaign in which Æthelflæd extended Lord Æthelred's authority into lands that had been part of pre-Viking Mercia.

Widowhood

In 911, when Æthelflæd was about forty years old, her husband died. The cause of his passing is not stated in the *Anglo-Saxon Chronicle* but the *Fragmentary Annals of Ireland* claimed that he succumbed to the illness that had incapacitated him for much of the preceding decade. Although his age at death is not known we can hazard a guess that he was in his fifties. A place of burial awaited him at St Oswald's in Gloucester, the minster church that he and his wife had founded together. He was almost certainly laid to rest in the crypt on the eastern side, close to the tomb-shrine that held the royal martyr's bones.

What happened next is the most remarkable episode in Æthelflæd's story. As the widow of a powerful ruler – a man who was a king in all but name – she might have been expected to give up her involvement in government, politics and warfare. Wives of dead kings usually withdrew from the hub of royal power to take up new roles, often retiring to an estate or becoming abbesses. Æthelflæd's mother Ealhswith had chosen the latter course, taking up residence in a monastery after King Alfred's death. It would have been quite appropriate for Æthelflæd to have followed a similar path. She was, after all, well known as a patron of churches and saints. Comfortable retirement was also an option, to an estate in Mercia or Wessex, perhaps to the one her father had bequeathed her in his will. However, she opted neither for retirement nor for the religious life, choosing instead to succeed her husband as ruler of Mercia.

This was a significant step for a woman to take. It had profound historical significance, for no English territory had accepted a female ruler since Queen Seaxburh of Wessex in the seventh century. The extent of Seaxburh's authority is unknown and there is some doubt as to whether she held much real power at all. Æthelflæd, on the other hand, certainly exercised the full authority of a ruling queen. Her succession after Lord Æthelred's death was clearly what her subjects wanted. Some of them might even have regarded her as their queen, but there is no evidence that she ever used this title. As far as we can tell from the documentary record, she preferred to call herself *myrcna hlæfdige*, 'Lady of the Mercians'. Despite being a princess of Wessex and the niece of a former queen of Mercia she appears to have been content with this non-regal status. It was a pragmatic choice, for it maintained the idea that there was only one royal dynasty among the English at that time. It would indeed have been surprising if she had openly declared herself to be a new queen of the Mercians while her brother was being addressed as king of the Anglo-Saxons. The title *myrcna hlæfdige* was not only the female equivalent of *myrcna hlaford*, the title borne by her husband, but also a mark of continuity. It signalled that the close bond with Wessex would be preserved and that the transition from male to female rule in Mercia would be seamless.

There is no hint that anyone challenged Æthelflæd's right to rule. If any male representatives of the old Mercian royal families were alive they appear to have stayed in the background. It has been suggested that the mysterious Beorhtsige who fell alongside the West Saxon rebel Æthelwold at the battle of the Holme was one such prince.[24] If the identification is correct, his death may have removed a potential challenger to Æthelflæd. The apparent absence of rivals in 911 implies that none was left, or that any Mercian æthelings who still lived were content to accept the situation or were unable to press their claims. We know too little of Æthelred's background to wonder if he had brothers or nephews who might have made a bid for power after his death. What we do know is that he had no son to take his place. His only child was Ælfwynn, a daughter, who was by then in her early twenties. His foster-son Athelstan was a credible successor but was still only a teenager in 911. In any case, an alternative plan for Athelstan's future may already have been mapped out. It is interesting to note in this context that the Mercians themselves would one day choose him as their king.

The process by which Æthelflæd became Mercia's new ruler is hidden from view. We do not know if the title *myrcna hlæfdige* was coined by herself or by others, or if it was freshly created in 911 rather than having been her unofficial title before Æthelred's death. It is possible that she had been known as the Lady of the Mercians since c.902, especially if her husband had been periodically inactive in the ensuing decade. Her title might then have been formalised after his death when she was inaugurated as his successor. Rulership of an Anglo-Saxon kingdom was usually confirmed by the witan, the assembly of the elite, without whose approval a candidate had no legitimacy. We might wonder if the Mercian witan was unanimous in agreeing to Æthelflæd's succession or if there were dissenting voices who argued against it. History shows that a majority was in favour of pledging allegiance to a woman who had already proven herself more than capable of taking on the responsibility. We could also speculate that Æthelred himself, in his final days, had nominated his wife to succeed him. It can probably be assumed that this would have been acceptable to King Edward, who would otherwise have intervened. With his sister holding power in Mercia he perhaps felt reassured that his interests and ambitions would continue to be served.

Although Edward appears to have allowed the Mercians to deal with the succession themselves, he did make his presence felt as soon as the matter was settled. In a curious epilogue, he annexed the south-eastern part of his sister's domain. In the words of the *Anglo-Saxon Chronicle*: 'King Edward took over London and Oxford and all the lands which belonged to them.' At first glance this looks like an aggressive land-grab in which the Thames Valley and surrounding areas were transferred from Mercian to West Saxon control. Looking back to the previous century we may recall that Alfred had captured London from the Vikings in 886, reconstituting it as a burh and trading centre. It had formerly been Mercian, so Alfred had given it to Æthelred. Edward's annexation of the city in 911 reversed Alfred's gift but there is no hint that this was opposed by Æthelflæd. Perhaps the reversal had been agreed previously between all parties, with the original gift meant as a temporary arrangement, a personal gesture from Alfred to Æthelred that would expire on the latter's death?[25]

Reconquest

Alfred's treaty with Guthrum, which can be dated to the years between 886 and 890, was an acknowledgment that large portions of English territory had fallen under Scandinavian control. It is hard to believe that Alfred envisaged the loss of these lands as permanent. His vision of Anglo-Saxon unity under one monarch does not sit well with passive acceptance of Danish rule in eastern Mercia, East Anglia and Northumbria. There can be little doubt that he looked to the future, to a time when these lost territories reverted to English rule. The hard campaigning that would be needed to achieve this goal was entrusted to his heirs, initially to his two eldest children – Edward and Æthelflæd – and to his Mercian son-in-law Æthelred. In the twelve years after Alfred's death, these three continued his policy of dealing with the Vikings using a combination of force and diplomacy. As in Alfred's time, treaty negotiations rarely brought lasting peace. In Mercia, an agreement with the Wirral Norse had collapsed in violence beneath the walls of Chester. Similar treaty-breaking by the Danes of York was the likely trigger for an English invasion of Northumbria in 909. Elsewhere, the rulers of Wessex and Mercia had consolidated their hold over vulnerable frontier areas by placing burhs in strategic locations. The next step was to take back the lost eastern lands. In 911, Lord Æthelred's death removed an experienced commander from the scene, but his widow had already shown herself to be a capable replacement. English policy towards the Danelaw became increasingly aggressive as King Edward and his sister began the process of reconquest that their father had bequeathed to them.

The task was a daunting one. Taking back the conquered areas required the capture of strong fortresses that had been garrisoned by Danish armies for forty years. Staunch resistance was inevitable. It would be a prolonged struggle with no guarantee of victory. Both Edward and Æthelflæd knew that a key element in their plans was the burh-building programme. As well as providing a defensive network against predatory raids, the burhs offered a platform for reconquest. However, the planning, design and construction of these sites was expensive and time-consuming. If a new burh was to be used as a springboard for military campaigns in the Danelaw it had to be placed in a forward position near the frontier. This meant that its garrison would necessarily bear the brunt of any counter-strike by the enemy. One such fortress was erected by Edward in the late autumn of 911 at Hertford in south-east Mercia, on the north bank of the River Lea. It overlooked an important crossing and guarded one of the main routes to London, hence its purpose was twofold: to protect London from the Danes while providing a forward base for English offensives.

Meanwhile, Æthelflæd saw a need to impose her rule on areas of western Mercia lying beyond her core domains in the lower Severn valley. In some of these districts the old allegiances formerly given to Mercian kings had probably collapsed in the upheavals of the 870s. In others, key settlements may have been seized by Viking adventurers or by rebellious Mercian nobles. Only by leading her army into such 'debatable lands' could Æthelflæd attach them to her realm and thus secure her western and northern borders. On the latter frontier, especially, the Scandinavian threat was ever-present. Since the expulsion of the Norsemen from Ireland a scatter of new colonies had sprung up along the western coast of Northumbria. The colonists posed a potentially serious threat to north-west Mercia, either in alliance with the Danes of York or on their own account. So, too, did the Wirral Norse who had already caused problems for Æthelflæd. Another source of anxiety was Wales, a land with which Mercia shared a land border 160 miles in length. Æthelflæd's father had previously accepted the allegiance of several Welsh kings, but their successors were not bound by the same oaths and were therefore unpredictable. As well as being fully capable of launching raids on Mercia they might be tempted to collaborate with Viking armies. Memories of the war of 909–10, when Northumbrian Danes had penetrated deep into the Severn heartlands, were no doubt still fresh in Æthelflæd's mind. It was partly to guard against any repeat of the onslaught, and partly to counter the threat from Wales, that she strengthened her hold on her western border in the early years of her widowhood.

Bridgnorth

An entry in the Mercian Register states that Æthelflæd built a burh at a place called *Brycge*, 'The Bridge', in 912. More than 200 years later, the twelfth-century chronicler John of Worcester described this burh as lying on the west bank of the River Severn. Modern historians identify it as a forerunner of the Shropshire town of Bridgnorth, a place recorded as *Brig* in a document from John's own time. The identification seems secure, for Bridgnorth occupies a strong position beside an ancient crossing of the river. The Old English name Brycge shows that a bridge stood there in Anglo-Saxon times, replacing what must once have been an important ford. In the early twelfth century, the crossing's strategic value was noticed by the Normans who erected a motte-and-bailey castle on a hill overlooking the bridge. The castle is thought to mark the site of Æthelflæd's burh, even though no trace of an Anglo-Saxon settlement has yet been found. The lack of evidence has prompted a search for alternative locations, one of which is the village of Quatford two miles to the south. The element 'Quat' in the village-name also appears in *Cwatbrycge*, the name of a place where a Viking army camped while raiding along the Severn in 895.[26] Danesford, lying roughly midway between Quatford and Bridgnorth, is sometimes pointed out as the place where these raiders crossed the river. At Quatford, the suggestively named Camp Hill has been proposed as an alternative location for both the Danish camp and the tenth-century burh, although traces of a Norman motte-and-bailey castle are the only ancient features now visible. Setting Quatford aside, we find *Cwatbrycge* and *Brycge* being seen by most historians as early names for Bridgnorth.[27] If the identification is correct, Æthelflæd's burh of 912 would have been built on an encampment used by Vikings seventeen earlier, both sites eventually being subsumed beneath Bridgnorth Castle. The second element of Bridgnorth's name was added in the thirteenth century, either to distinguish the original bridge from another erected to the south or to describe the adjacent settlement as being in the northern part of an estate or district. The curious term 'Quat' or 'Cwat' seems to be an old name for this part of the upper Severn valley, appearing not only as the first element in Quatford but on its own as the village-name Quatt and in the parish name Quatt Malvern.

Despite a lack of tenth-century evidence from the site of Bridgnorth Castle this is still the likeliest place to look for the burh.[28] The castle was built in 1101 as a major stronghold on the Welsh Marches, its size reflecting its importance to local Anglo-Norman lords. A massive ruined tower, now leaning precariously after bombardment during the English Civil War, is still a prominent landmark. Clear evidence of pre-Norman defences has yet to be identified but this is hardly

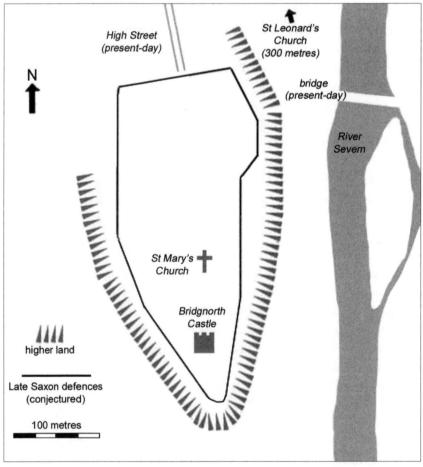

Bridgnorth

surprising given that the castle's enormous bulk would have destroyed earlier levels. The most we can probably say is that the burh may have had a footprint similar to that of the castle and its outer bailey. If so, the enclosed area would have measured some 5.7 hectares (14 acres). Since Bridgnorth did not develop into a town in the Late Anglo-Saxon period its burh should perhaps be seen primarily as a military strongpoint rather than as a fortified settlement for soldiers and civilians.[29] The tenth-century garrison might nonetheless have been served by a church situated outside the defences, possibly a precursor of present-day St Leonard's, which is reputed to have Anglo-Saxon stonework in its fabric.

Scergeat

The burh at Brycge was built in 912. It was one of two fortresses founded by Æthelflæd in that year. Both are mentioned in the same entry in the Mercian Register:

> Here, on the eve of the Invention of the Holy Cross, Æthelflæd the Lady
> of the Mercians came to Scergeat and built the burh there, and the same
> year that at Brycge.

We have noted the case for identifying Brycge as Bridgnorth, but where was Scergeat? Taking the Mercian Register's word order at face value, we can assume that Scergeat was the earlier of the two. Æthelflæd's arrival there is precisely dated to 2 May, the day before the Invention of the Holy Cross – a holy day that falls on 3 May each year. The 'invention' refers to the alleged discovery of the True Cross by St Helena, mother of the fourth-century Roman emperor Constantine the Great. How quickly Scergeat was built is not known but Brycge was presumably founded later in the summer, or at least before autumn passed into winter. Some historians believe that Æthelflæd's founding of two burhs in one year implies that they were built in the same geographical area during a single military campaign. Hence, it has been proposed that Scergeat lay somewhere along the Severn, either upstream or downstream of Bridgnorth.[30] An alternative view sees no need to place Scergeat and Brycge in the same region. This leaves us to wonder where Scergeat lay, for its location remains elusive. The name means something like 'boundary gap' or 'boundary route', suggesting that the burh lay on a frontier near a well-known point of access. The gap was presumably a natural one, like a pass through a range of hills or a tract of open country between dense woodlands, unless it was an artificial break in a linear earthwork such as Offa's Dyke.[31] The boundary might have been recent – like the Danelaw frontier of Alfred's time – or ancient like the River Mersey.

The fact that the name Scergeat has seemingly disappeared might mean that the burh eventually acquired a different name. Alternatively, it might simply have failed to develop into a thriving settlement and was therefore abandoned. Another possibility is that it was never intended to be permanent but was merely a temporary fortification to fulfil a short-term military objective. It may have been built during, or at the end of, a campaign to recapture Mercian territory from Scandinavian or Welsh enemies. Had the name survived it might now appear on modern maps as Shergate, Shargate or Shiregate, or in a more altered form where the first element is now Shaw or some other word beginning with Sh-. A detailed case has been made for Shrawardine in Shropshire, the site of a crossing of the River Severn and a plausible location for a tenth-century fortress.[32]

Another possible candidate for Scergeat, although without a similar-sounding modern name, is Whitchurch in Shropshire. Local tradition claims that the parish church, located on a hill in the town centre, was founded by Æthelflæd in 912.[33] The name of the town is not actually ancient, having been created in Norman times when the church was rebuilt in white stone. Before the 1100s the name was Westun ('west settlement'), reflecting a frontier location on the western edge of Mercia. In an earlier age it had been the site of a Roman fort and civilian settlement called *Mediolanum* (Latin: 'middle of the plain'), guarding a road running south from Chester to the important city of Wroxeter near Shrewsbury. Archaeologists have identified the defences of *Mediolanum* in the vicinity of Castle Hill, potentially also the likeliest location for an Anglo-Saxon settlement. Despite the hill's name there is no certainty that it was the site of Whitchurch Castle, a Norman stronghold known to have been in existence by c.1150. The hill may have acquired its 'castle' designation from the Roman fort or, more speculatively, from an Anglo-Saxon burh. The Norman 'white church' that gave the town its name is believed to have replaced an older church that perhaps reused Roman stonework. Its site is occupied today by St Alkmund's parish church, the dedication commemorating one of the Mercian saints whose cults were promoted by Æthelflæd.

Essex

In 912, while Æthelflæd was bolstering the defences of Mercia, her brother Edward was pursuing a similar policy on his own borders. In the summer of that year he led an army into Essex, probably via his new burh at Hertford, which guarded a crossing of the River Lea. Until that time, the Lea had marked the eastern limit of English-held territory, having formed part of the Anglo-Danish boundary agreed by Alfred and Guthrum. Although we have no record of hostilities during Edward's campaign of 912 we can assume that his intention was to end Danish control in areas along the route of his march eastward. Moving towards the coast, he eventually reached the estuary of the River Blackwater, setting up camp at the former East Saxon port of Maldon. There he remained while his soldiers constructed a fort of earth and timber at Witham, seven miles to the north. Witham lay on the Roman highway between London and Colchester and was a key strategic point. Colchester itself, once an important Roman city, had long been a Viking stronghold. Although it lies today within the county of Essex it was part of Danish East Anglia in 912 and any attempt to recapture it would have involved a major assault. Edward's fortifying of Witham implies that he already had Colchester in his sights, but he did not attack it yet. He was prepared to wait until the time was right. In the meantime, his efforts to loosen Scandinavian influence on Essex bore fruit. The *Anglo-Saxon Chronicle* states that 'a good number of people who had earlier been under Danish domination submitted to him'.[34] If the Danes of East Anglia felt anxious about what was happening they seemingly took no significant action to thwart it. Nevertheless, Edward knew from past experience that they would launch a reprisal at some point. It may have been to guard against such an eventuality that he ordered a second fortress to be built at Hertford, this time on the southern bank of the Lea to guard the London side of the river-crossing.

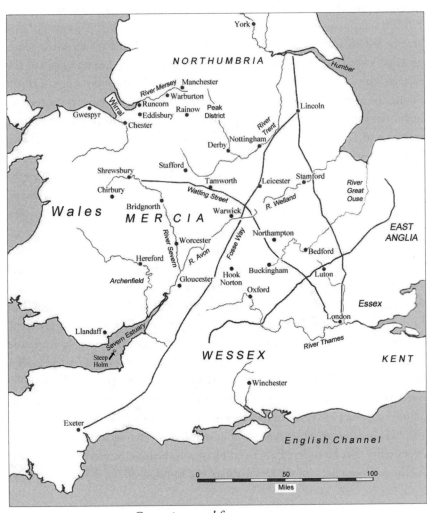

Campaigns and fortresses, 913–15

FRONTIERLANDS

In the spring of 913, shortly after Easter, the Danes of Northampton and Leicester joined forces to mount a raid on English territory. According to the *Anglo-Saxon Chronicle* they broke a peace-treaty, presumably their latest truce with King Edward. Riding west out of the Danelaw they raided across northern Oxfordshire before meeting stiff resistance near the village of Hook Norton. A battle was fought and many English soldiers were slain.[1] Then the Danes turned back east with their plunder. On their homeward journey they met another band of raiders who were riding towards Luton, perhaps from the Danish stronghold at Bedford. These two groups combined to form a larger force which was then attacked and defeated by an English army that not only recovered the loot but also captured a great number of horses and weapons. Nothing more is heard of this brief campaign. The chief protagonists on either side were unnamed by the chroniclers and we are left to muse on the broader context.

Hook Norton was a significant place in this period, a royal estate covering a much larger area than the present-day village. It may have been centred on Tadmarton Camp, an Iron Age hillfort on a ridge a couple of miles to the northeast. The hillfort was an obvious defensive position for the English forces in 913. It lay on an ancient east–west trackway that the Danes were no doubt using at the time as an easy route to the lower reaches of the River Severn. Previous Viking raids had targeted the same part of the Severn and perhaps it was the ultimate objective on this occasion too. However, although the area around Hook Norton lay in southern Mercia it is unlikely to have been under Æthelflæd's control at this time. It may have been a dependent territory of Oxford, where a burh and its hinterland had been transferred to King Edward's rule after Lord Æthelred's death in 911. We can probably assume that the Englishmen slain in the battle of Hook Norton were Mercians who answered to Edward rather than to Æthelflæd. The same can be said of those men who routed the Danish force as it moved towards Luton. So, although the two battles took place in Mercia, the English troops who took part were essentially fighting for the king of Wessex.

Tamworth

With the completion of the burh at Bridgnorth, and perhaps also the one at Scergeat, Æthelflæd may have felt that her western border was better secured and protected. Whichever foes might launch an assault – whether Scandinavian or Welsh – the garrisoned settlements that she and her husband had established were an effective line of defence. She now turned her attention to her long frontier with the Danelaw and to the recapture of Mercian lands in the east. Her brother had already made considerable progress in the south, marching an army into Essex and stamping his authority on areas that had previously answered to Viking lords. His new burhs at Hertford and Witham signalled a statement of intent to the Danes, challenging their hold on lands that they had occupied for forty years or more. Æthelflæd now undertook similarly assertive moves on her own eastern border.

> Here, with God's help, Æthelflæd the Lady of the Mercians went with all the Mercians to Tamworth and built the burh there in early summer . . .[2]

So says the Mercian Register in its entry for 913. Tamworth, once a major centre of Mercian royal power, had probably been in Danish hands since the 870s.[3] Æthelflæd came there with 'all the Mercians' – with her army, in other words – to bring it under her control. It was a useful addition to her realm. Even today, when the shape of the ancient landscape lies beneath a cloak of urbanisation, the natural advantages that first attracted the early Mercian kings can still be discerned. The heart of modern Tamworth occupies a strategic position on slightly elevated ground at the confluence of two rivers – the Tame and the Anker. The place-name derives from Old English *Tomworthig*, meaning 'meadow beside the River Tame', but the earliest royal settlement was known as *Tomtun*, 'Tame village'. The English-speaking people who first colonised the surrounding district in the fifth and sixth centuries were Angles rather than Saxons. It is thought that they came from older settlements near the Humber estuary, reaching the Tame via the great valley of the River Trent.[4] The colonists called themselves *Tomsæte*, 'Tame-dwellers'. Their lands probably included not only the valley of the Tame itself but those of its tributaries, encompassing a territory that stretched across Staffordshire and Warwickshire into Leicestershire.[5]

Charters from the ninth century suggest that the Tomsæte preserved their separate identity long after their lands had become the heart of the kingdom of Mercia. Later Mercian tradition identified the founder of Tomtun as King Creoda, grandfather of the famous Penda. Creoda's kindred were the Iclingas, the main Mercian royal dynasty, who seem to have sprung from the leaders of the Tomsæte.[6] Penda himself is believed to have had his principal centre of power at Tomtun and a contemporary charter refers to his son Æthelred's *vicus* ('village') there.[7] In the eighth century we find the names Tomtun and Tomworthig being used interchangeably in charters during the reign of Æthelbald (716–57). Later in the same century, according to a charter of uncertain provenance, the renowned King Offa had a palace at *Tamuuorthige*. Although the document in question might be a later forgery, the remains of what may have been a large timber hall – perhaps a royal dwelling – have been discovered at Tamworth.[8] It is also possible that Offa's palace and its associated buildings were the focus of an early burh, a fortified settlement preceding Æthelflæd's by more than a hundred years. This might explain why there appear to be two distinct phases of fortification in the Anglo-Saxon period, the earlier being represented archaeologically by traces of a simple perimeter ditch. The later phase is probably to be associated with Æthelflæd and comprised a bank of turf, clay and gravel piled in front of a more substantial ditch, behind which stood a timber palisade mounted on a turf rampart which was up to eight metres wide in places. A wooden walkway ran along the top of the rampart, connecting gate-towers on the northern, eastern and western sides. To the south no defences were needed because the River Anker provided adequate protection.[9] An indication of the scale of the tenth-century burh can be gained from the size of its enclosed area which has been estimated at 23 hectares (57 acres). The three sides of its perimeter defences were subsequently retraced by the walls of the medieval town, which also preserved part of the internal street layout. Unlike Chester and Gloucester, Tamworth had no Roman street-grid to serve as a template so the layout was inevitably less formal. One street came in through a gate in the western rampart and ran to the centre where the kings of Mercia had probably had their palace in the seventh and eighth centuries. Æthelflæd had a palace of her own within the burh, perhaps on the same spot. It would have been a large and impressive structure – a timber hall of no less grandeur than its predecessors. Although local tradition imagines it sitting on the great mound now occupied by Tamworth Castle, a location near

St Editha's Church seems more likely. This is where some archaeologists also locate the older palace of the kings.

Daily life in tenth-century Tamworth is indicated by a number of discoveries. One of the most interesting is a watermill located just outside the burh's south-east corner, on the north bank of the River Anker.[10] It was served by water from the river running along an artificial mill-leat. Archaeologists have found grains of barley, fragments of broken millstones and a wooden paddle from a horizontal waterwheel. Elsewhere in Tamworth, shards of pottery dating from the tenth or eleventh centuries have also been unearthed. Taking all the various 'domestic' finds together, we may note that – despite their small number – they reflect the economic vitality of the burh during the tenth century and beyond.

Æthelflæd's Tamworth would have had a minster church, most probably on the site now occupied by St Editha's parish church in the town centre. St Editha's is a medieval building with stonework dating back to the 1100s. Its dedication takes it back to the Viking Age, for Editha or Edith is reputed to have been Æthelflæd's niece, a daughter of King Edward of Wessex by his first wife Ecgwynn. A tradition circulating in the twelfth century tells of her marriage in 926 to Sihtric, king of Anglo-Danish Northumbria, as part of a political agreement negotiated by her brother Athelstan.[11] Other traditions identify Tamworth's saint as an earlier Editha who lived in the seventh, eighth or ninth centuries, or as a tenth-century namesake who died in 983. We are clearly dealing with a mysterious figure whose true identity is unknown.[12] The original Anglo-Saxon church presumed to lie beneath St Editha's may have been founded in the seventh century during the first phase of Mercian Christianity, when St Chad and his fellow-missionaries were preaching the faith. It is said to have been destroyed by Danes in 874, after which it may have lain derelict before being refounded by Æthelflæd in 913. Her church was also the target of a Danish attack, in 943, and had to be rebuilt twenty years later. Its dedication in Æthelflæd's time is unknown but it perhaps commemorated one of the Mercian saints whose cults she favoured at other burhs. Alternatively, the original, pre-874 dedication may have been retained and might have commemorated an Edith who was venerated locally.

The Danish raid on Tamworth in 874 engulfed the whole settlement, leaving it ruined and partly abandoned until Æthelflæd restored it nearly forty years later. She was no doubt aware of the site's symbolic value as an ancient centre of Mercian power. Its revival in 913 demonstrated Mercia's resurgence and defiance in the face of Scandinavian aggression. Like Edward's fortress at Witham on the doorstep of East Anglia, the new Tamworth issued a strong challenge to the invaders.

Above. Offa's Dyke near
Montgomery, Wales
[© Barbara Keeling]

Left. Worcester Cathedral
[© Barbara Keeling]

Shrewsbury Castle [© Barbara Keeling]

Wenlock Priory [© Barbara Keeling]

Above. Chester: a surviving section of the Roman fortress wall near Northgate [© Barbara Keeling]

Left. Chester: a sculptured image of St Werburgh on a street that bears her name [© Barbara Keeling]

Earthwork traces of the medieval abbey of Bardney [© Tim Clarkson]

Ruins of St Oswald's Priory, Gloucester [© Barbara Keeling]

Bridgnorth Castle, Shropshire [© Barbara Keeling]

Stafford: the foundations of St Bertelin's Chapel, marked in outline beside St Mary's Church
[© Barbara Keeling]

View of Eddisbury Hillfort from the north-west, Delamere, 1987 [© Professor N.J. Higham. Cheshire Archaeology Planning Advisory Service Aerial Photographs]

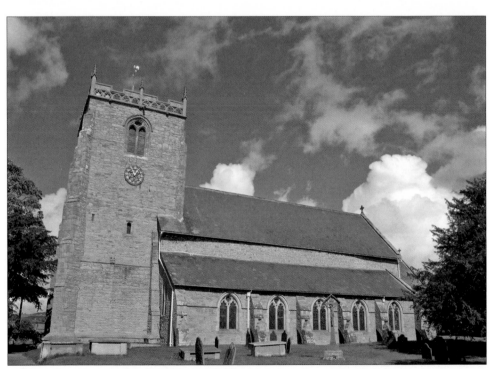

Chirbury: St Michael's Church [© Barbara Keeling]

Above. Bridge abutment on the remains of Castle Rock, Runcorn [© Barbara Keeling]

Left. Æthelflæd depicted in a mural on Holyhead Road, Wednesbury [© Barbara Keeling]

TRAVELLERS AND SETTLERS
CROSSED LANDS AND SEAS
MELDING FOLKLORE
AND TRADITION
A MIGRANT POPULATION
MADE MERCIA THEIR HOME

Statue of Æthelflæd erected near Tamworth Castle in 1913 [© Barbara Keeling]

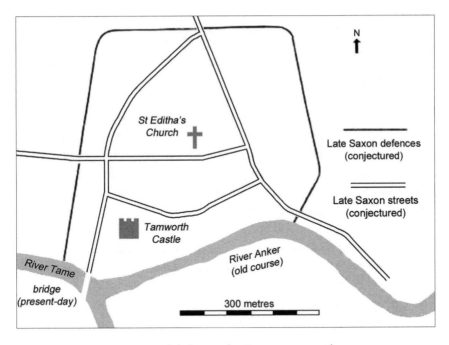

Tamworth (above, after Bassett 2008, 192)
Stafford (below, after Carver 2010b, 21)

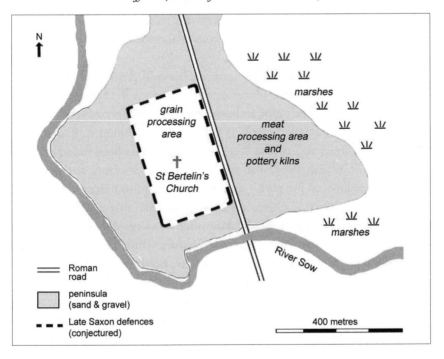

Stafford

After noting the restoration of Tamworth in the early summer of 913, the Mercian Register goes on to say that Æthelflæd founded another burh shortly afterwards, before the feast-day of Lammas (1 August), *æt Stæfforda*, 'at Stafford'. The location was a peninsula of sand and gravel overlooking a crossing-place on the River Sow, one of the tributaries of the Trent. The Old English place-name means 'Staithe Ford', the staithe in question probably being firm ground where small boats could be moored. Extensive marshes gave the peninsula an island-like appearance with natural defensive capabilities on all sides except the north. Archaeological evidence suggests that the Romans had a small settlement here, most likely for agriculture and grain-storage, but the area appears to have been abandoned after their departure. Clear evidence of post-Roman or early Anglo-Saxon activity is then lacking but, according to legend, a Mercian saint called Beorhthelm established a hermitage on the peninsula in the early 700s. Beorhthelm, otherwise known as 'Bertelin', is said to have been a prince who retreated from secular life after his wife and child were slain by wolves. From his hermitage he reputedly converted many of his fellow-Mercians to Christianity, hence his local veneration. The legend asserts that he died at Ilam, thirty miles to the north-east, where his body was enshrined, his hermitage thereafter becoming a monastery. Needless to say, the entire legend is regarded as spurious.[13] It is likely that Beorhthelm's connection with Stafford does not pre-date the founding of Æthelflæd's burh.

The exact position of the burh is uncertain but its defences probably formed a rectilinear shape within the footprint of the later medieval town. Archaeo-logical excavations in the 1970s and 1980s revealed evidence of tenth-century activity, the most notable finds being sherds of a distinctive, Roman-style pottery now known as 'Stafford Ware'. This pottery has been found at other burhs founded by Æthelflæd, such as Chester and Shrewsbury, and may have been an innovation on her part – a conscious attempt to imitate the material culture of the Romans. Other discoveries indicate that grain-processing, breadmaking and butchery were all taking place on a large scale, suggesting that the burh was used as a provisioning centre for armies embarking on campaign.[14] The spiritual needs of the inhabitants would have been met by a minster church which Æthelflæd evidently dedicated to Beorhthelm. Post-holes for a timber building have been found beneath St Bertelin's, a demolished medieval chapel that once stood beside the parish church of St Mary. This building is thought to have been built in the ninth or tenth century and may be Æthelflæd's minster.

The absence of any clear signs of earlier Anglo-Saxon activity implies that hers was the first church on the site.[15]

Raiders from Brittany

In 914, a Viking fleet carrying 'a great pirate host' left its havens in Brittany and sailed towards the Irish Sea. Its leaders were Ottar and Hroald, two jarls of uncertain background and ancestry. They entered the Severn estuary and began raiding the south coast of Wales before attacking the Mercian frontier district of Archenfield. The latter takes its name from Ergyng, a Welsh kingdom annexed to Mercia before c.800, part of which now lies within the English county of Herefordshire. One of the raids captured a Welsh bishop, Cyfeiliog of Llandaff, who was held prisoner on the Viking ships until a ransom of forty pounds was handed over by King Edward. The raiders then launched more raids on Archenfield but were met by Mercian forces mustered from the burh-garrisons of Hereford, Gloucester and elsewhere. Jarl Hroald was killed, as was a brother of Jarl Ottar, and the Vikings were driven off with great loss. They fled to an 'enclosure' – perhaps an ancient earthwork – which was then besieged until they surrendered. After agreeing terms, they promised to depart from all lands under Edward's authority, confirming their oath by offering hostages from among their own ranks. As on numerous occasions in the past, the peace was soon broken and the raiding resumed. This time, the targets lay on the opposite side of the Severn estuary, on the northern coast of Wessex. Although guarded by West Saxon forces this shoreline was now attacked twice, the raiders creeping ashore under cover of darkness. On both occasions they were repulsed, the survivors being forced to swim back to their ships. Reluctant to launch further raids they soon began to run out of food. They camped on Steep Holm, a small island in the Severn estuary, but hunger forced them to set sail once more. After briefly landing in Dyfed, a kingdom in south-west Wales, they went to Ireland in the autumn and were no longer an immediate concern for the English.

The activities of Ottar and Hroald had affected both Wessex and Mercia and were reported in the *Anglo-Saxon Chronicle*. However, although the chroniclers referred to King Edward's involvement they made no mention of Æthelflæd. This might seem surprising, given that the raiders targeted Mercian territory and were confronted by forces from Mercian burhs. One of the burh contingents came from Gloucester, Æthelflæd's chief centre of power, and would surely have taken its orders from her rather than from her brother. It is possible, of course, that she did indeed take command of the Mercian forces in this campaign and that her role was deliberately ignored by the West Saxon chroniclers who instead gave all the credit to Edward.[16]

Eddisbury

Whatever the nature of Æthelflæd's role in the defence of her south-western borderlands in 914 she was certainly not idle elsewhere. In the early summer of the same year she built a burh at *Eadesbyrig*, a place usually identified as the ancient fort of Castle Ditch on Eddisbury Hill in Cheshire. This lay on the north-west margin of Mercia, eleven miles east of Chester in an area known today as Delamere Forest. Originally built in the pre-Roman Iron Age, Castle Ditch occupies the entire summit of the hill on which it stands. Today, the remains of its inner and outer ramparts are still visible as grass-grown banks of earth. Visitor access is somewhat difficult as the summit is currently worked as farmland but some idea of the topography can be gleaned from aerial photographs. These dramatically illustrate the size of the Iron Age fort and the shape of its defences, which enclosed a summit area of 2.8 hectares (7 acres). A visitor standing at the eastern entrance gains an impressive panorama with views stretching northward to the Mersey valley, eastward to the Peak District hills and southward into Staffordshire. Below the hill on the south side lies a major Roman road running from Chester to Northwich and then on to Manchester and York.

When Æthelflæd arrived in 914 she reused the Iron Age defences, perhaps designating the outer rampart as the burh perimeter while ordering the inner rampart to be reduced in height.[17] Archaeological excavations in the 1930s identified seven phases of activity at the site, of which the penultimate phase was initially seen as Anglo-Saxon. Remains of huts where sherds of 'Dark Age' pottery had been found were believed to be physical evidence of Anglo-Saxon settlement.[18] However, this pottery is now thought to belong to the Iron Age and – to compound the uncertainty – the sherds themselves have been lost. Clear evidence of activity in Late Anglo-Saxon times is nevertheless provided by an oven discovered during excavations in 2010–11. Made of clay, it had been built into the inner rampart and may have baked bread for the tenth-century garrison.[19] Such data is probably too meagre to sway those who doubt that Castle Ditch is the site of Æthelflæd's burh and who prefer to look elsewhere for Eadesbyrig. The existence of another Eddisbury in Cheshire, at Rainow near

Macclesfield in the east of the county, has also been noted. Further doubts have been raised over Castle Ditch because of its position so close to the burh at Chester, only eleven miles away, and because it never developed into a permanent settlement. Its case nevertheless remains strong and it is still regarded as the most plausible candidate.

We may note that the alternative Eddisbury at Rainow has little to recommend it, being situated in a backwater away from major routes and with no obvious site for an Anglo-Saxon fortification.[20] Although it is located in the borderlands between English Mercia and Danish-held territory in the Peak District, other sites in this region offered better options for a commander seeking to construct a burh. Furthermore, the argument that Castle Ditch's proximity to the burh at Chester would have rendered it superfluous can be turned on its head. It would have provided a useful first line of defence against an assault on Chester from the north-west, either by an army marching down from the Mersey crossings or by seaborne raiders making landfall on the river's southern bank.

Notwithstanding the various doubts, Castle Ditch still ticks enough boxes to be regarded as the likely site of Æthelflæd's burh. As well as the name 'Eddisbury', it has other attributes that make it a suitable candidate: pre-existing defences, an elevated position with wide views and proximity to a major Roman road. Finally, we may observe that there were good reasons for Æthelflæd to feel especially worried about her northern frontier in 914. Memories of the Northumbrian invasion of 910 would still have been fresh. There was also the ever-present menace of the Norse settlement in Wirral and similar colonies across the Mersey in southern Lancashire. As we shall see, it was not long before another burh was built in this vulnerable borderland. For the moment, however, the Lady of the Mercians turned her attention back to the eastern marches.

Warwick

In the late summer of 914, Æthelflæd built a burh at Warwick, which at that time was called *Wæringwic* ('dwellings at the weir'). As with her other fortresses, the location had strategic value, being near a major Roman road. In this case the road was the Fosse Way, running north-east to south-west across the southern half of Britain. In Roman times it had connected the cities of Lincoln and Exeter; in the Viking Age it offered a route from Danish north-east Mercia to

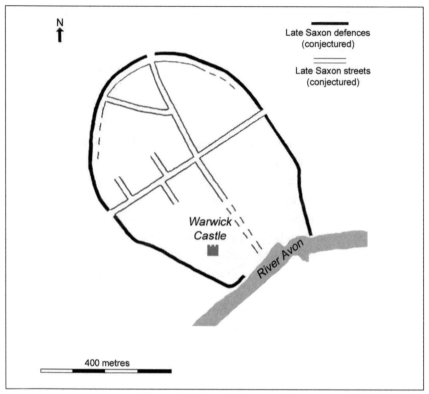

N

Late Saxon defences
(conjectured)

Late Saxon streets
(conjectured)

Warwick
Castle

River Avon

400 metres

Warwick (after Hill 2001, 155)

Wessex. Lincoln was at that time an important Danish stronghold, one of the Five Boroughs, as was Leicester which likewise stood on the Fosse Way. Warwick itself did not stand directly on the same road but lay only five miles to the west. Its natural topography made it an ideal site for a fortress, the most prominent feature being a sandstone hill rising as a cliff above the River Avon and providing a secure defence. In ancient times the river was crossed by a nearby ford which could be watched from the clifftop. Today, the summit of the hill is dominated by the great castle of the Earls of Warwick, originally built in 1068 as a Norman motte-and-bailey stronghold. In the early tenth century, this high vantage point would have offered a wide view southward over the Avon valley. Æthelflæd's burh is thought to have encompassed the summit, including the site of the later castle. Archaeologists have yet to unearth the tenth-century defences but they are believed to have been traced by the medieval town walls, which form an oval encircling the clifftop. The streets of the old town are likewise assumed to reflect those of the burh, with four main thoroughfares running from a central crossroads to gateways in the perimeter wall. A minster church may have been founded before Æthelflæd's time, perhaps as far back as the seventh century, serving the original settlement of Wæringwic.[21] We should note that a small hill on the castle's south-west side, traditionally known as 'Ethelfleda's Mound', has nothing to do with the Lady of the Mercians and is actually a Norman feature.

Norse exiles

Following the collapse of Viking power in Ireland in 902, groups of Norse refugees had been dispersed along the western coasts of Britain, from the Hebrides down to Wales. We have seen how one group, led by Ingimund, colonised the Wirral peninsula in north-west Mercia. Others settled on the shores of Northumbria, in what are now the counties of Lancashire and Cumbria. Many more made their way to the Hebridean isles and to the adjacent coastlands, setting up new colonies and raiding-bases in the territories of the Scots and Picts.[22] It was not long before some of the Norse groups came into conflict with one another. An inevitable flashpoint was the Irish Sea, where competition for trade and plunder was always likely to escalate into bloody clashes. One such encounter took place in 914 when two rival warlords met in a naval battle off the Isle of Man. On the losing side was Bardr Ottarsson, perhaps a son of the Jarl Ottar who had recently raided in the Severn estuary.[23] The victor was Ragnall (Old Norse *Rognvaldr*), a member of the exiled Norse dynasty of Viking Dublin, described in Irish texts as *ua Ímair* ('grandson of Ivarr').

Ragnall's movements after the ejection of his family in 902 cannot be traced with certainty but he seems to have established a power-base on Man or in nearby Galloway. His later career brought him into Æthelflæd's story and will be discussed in the next chapter. For the moment, we may note that his defeat of Bardr Ottarsson marked his debut on the historical stage as a key player in the Irish Sea region. Ottar himself, after abandoning his raids on Welsh and English territory, sailed over to Ireland. It may be that his was the 'great fleet' that appeared in Waterford harbour in 914.[24] The arrival of this force, the biggest display of Norse power in Ireland since the departure of the Dublin dynasty twelve years earlier, announced that the period of exile was over.

Buckingham

The departure of Ottar's Vikings from the Severn estuary allowed King Edward to turn his attention back to the reconquest of the Danelaw. The year 914 was already waning when, in early November, he led an army to Buckingham in south-east Mercia. This old settlement on the River Great Ouse had lain well within English territory in the days of Alfred and Guthrum but a gradual encroachment from the east may have brought it closer to the Anglo-Danish frontier. Edward came with his troops and stayed four weeks, ordering the construction of two fortresses, one to guard each bank of the river. There he also received the submission of a number of Danish leaders. Securing the allegiance of these men was a major achievement, for the *Anglo-Saxon Chronicle* tells us that those who submitted included 'all the jarls and the chief men who owed allegiance to Bedford, besides many of those who owed allegiance to Northampton'.[25] Among the jarls was a certain Thurketel, probably a senior figure among the Bedford Vikings. We can envisage him and his associates attending a formal ceremony in which they swore oaths of allegiance to the English king. As a result, two of the main Scandinavian strongholds in eastern Mercia were severely weakened. One factor in persuading some of the Northampton Danes to submit to Edward may have been his sister's new burh at Warwick, just a day's march west of their fortress. With Warwick on one side and Buckingham on the other, it is possible that they began to feel as if they were being pinned down.[26]

Bedford, Chirbury and Weardbyrig

In the autumn of 915, Edward entered the Danelaw with an army and advanced on Bedford. A year earlier, at Buckingham, Jarl Thurketel and other Danish leaders had transferred their allegiance to him. The majority of those in Bedford now followed suit, in sufficient numbers for Edward to take control of the fortress. He apparently achieved this without a fight, perhaps because the Danes had lost too many soldiers since Thurketel and his henchmen switched sides. The *Anglo-Saxon Chronicle* says of Bedford that 'most of the garrison who had previously occupied it submitted to him', implying that some Danish warriors remained defiant. These presumably departed voluntarily or were expelled by force. Edward stayed at Bedford for several weeks, at the end of which he ordered the construction of a second fortress, this one being built on the south bank of the River Great Ouse facing the erstwhile Danish stronghold.

In the meantime, his sister had been no less busy, establishing three new burhs of her own during 915. The first was at *Cyricbyrig* ('Church-burh'), built *ufan midne winter* ('after midwinter'), probably in January. The place is usually identified as Chirbury in Shropshire, a village near the present-day border between England and Wales. The border here follows the course of Offa's Dyke, the old Mercian frontier, which lies less than two miles to the west. Beyond the edge of the village, some 260 metres south-west of the parish church, lies an earthwork known as King's Orchard or Castle Field. Despite enclosing an area of no more than 0.3 hectares (0.7 acres), it is often assumed to be the site of Æthelflæd's burh.[27] Situated twenty-five feet above a stream it has the appearance of a rectangular settlement or encampment enclosed by earth ramparts. An archaeological excavation in 1958 revealed that these defences are quite insubstantial. There was no hint of a wooden palisade, nor was any trace of human settlement discovered in the interior. Nonetheless, the excavation report claimed that this was still the most plausible location for a Late Anglo-Saxon burh.[28] The lack of archaeological evidence is, however, a significant obstacle and an alternative theory has been put forward. This sees King's Orchard not as a tenth-century fortification but as a 'ringwork' constructed much earlier, perhaps as far back as the pre-Roman Iron Age. Such a feature may have been built to guard an ancient east–west trackway that runs through Chirbury into

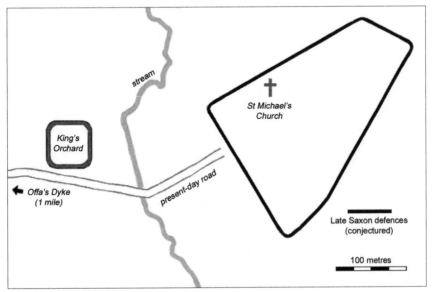

Chirbury (after Stone 2017, 75)

Wales. The importance of this route had been acknowledged by the Anglo-Saxon builders of Offa's Dyke, who left a gap for it to pass through.

If King's Orchard does not mark the site of the tenth-century burh we should probably look towards the centre of Chirbury village where the parish church of St Michael is the main landmark today. Although the oldest parts of the present church date from the 1200s, a stone foundation wall of possible Anglo-Saxon date was found during excavations in the early 2000s.[29] Moreover, the place-name indicates that a church certainly existed in Anglo-Saxon times and this is likely to have occupied the St Michael's site. To Welsh speakers the village is Llanffynhonwen ('church of the white well'), a name suggesting early Christian activity associated with a pre-Christian sacred spring. It is even possible that beneath St Michael's lie the remains of a 'church of the white well' used by local Britons before the first Anglo-Saxon settlers arrived. A tenth-century church serving the inhabitants of Æthelflæd's burh may then have been placed in the same location. We can cautiously imagine the church occupying a central position within the burh, the defences of which may have formed a perimeter of rectilinear shape like those at Stafford, Tamworth and elsewhere. The alignment of this perimeter is presumably reflected in the street-plan of today's village.[30] Chirbury's subsequent history indicates that the burh did not evolve into a medieval town. What we appear to be seeing is a fortress that performed a specific, short-term military role on Mercia's western frontier in the early tenth century. The garrison was probably withdrawn when a change in political circumstances meant that its presence was no longer needed. It was then replaced by a civilian community that continued to worship at the church. By the eleventh century, the burh had been completely superseded by a thriving village and the abandoned defences thereafter slid into disrepair before eventually vanishing altogether. Such a scenario provides a plausible explanation for why no visible remains nor even the basic outline of Æthelflæd's fortification have survived.

The second burh founded by the Lady of the Mercians in 915 was *Weardbyrig* ('Watch-fort' or 'Beacon-fort'). How many weeks or months elapsed between the two projects is unknown but Weardbyrig must have been completed by early September at the latest. On the ninth day of that month, Æthelflæd issued a charter confirming a grant of land at *Fernbeorgen*, a place that we can cautiously identify as Farnborough in Warwickshire.[31] The grant was witnessed by her entourage, among whom were her daughter Ælfwynn, four bishops, an ealdorman and other senior figures from the secular and ecclesiastical elites. The venue was Weardbyrig, here spelled *Weardburg*, so maybe the gathering not only witnessed the granting of estates but also an inauguration ceremony for the new burh.

Unfortunately, we have no idea where Weardbyrig lay. Like the equally mysterious Bremesbyrig and Scergeat, its location remains elusive. One theory, first suggested 200 years ago and still in circulation today, places it at Warburton in Greater Manchester.[32] It is not hard to see how this notion arose, for Warburton stands on the south side of the River Mersey and was historically part of Cheshire. It lay in Mercian territory and was certainly occupied in Anglo-Saxon times, its name being derived from an Old English one. The older of the two churches in the village is dedicated to Werburgh and is assumed to have succeeded an Anglo-Saxon church where this famous Mercian female saint was venerated.[33] Indeed, the first element in the name of the village is actually the personal name Werburgh – although the woman in question is unlikely to have been the saint. Warburton was recorded in the eleventh century as *Warburgtune* and perhaps commemorates an Anglo-Saxon woman who may have owned an estate in the vicinity. She would, of course, have been a namesake of the saint and it is possible that the two became conflated in local tradition. This was sufficiently well-established by c.1100 to attract a community of nuns who dedicated their convent to St Werburgh, the original landowner having presumably been forgotten. Needless to say, any connection between the names Warburton and Weardbyrig is philologically impossible.[34] We must look elsewhere for Æthelflæd's burh.

Even if Warburton is disregarded, it is possible that the Mercian frontier in northern Cheshire might still be the right area. Looking further west, to the coast of North Wales, a case has been made for Gwespyr ('west burh') near Prestatyn. Or perhaps we should consider a different part of the Anglo-Welsh borderlands, such as the western edges of Herefordshire and Shropshire? The Shropshire town of Whitchurch, mentioned above in the context of Scergeat, has been put forward as a possible candidate. Alternatively, we might look further south, to Oxfordshire, where the village of Warborough has a name bearing a superficial resemblance to *Weardbyrig*.[35] The similarity has been noticed by historians but the case is weak, for there is no evidence that the second part of the name Warborough is *byrig* ('fort') rather than *berg* ('mound, tumulus'). Lastly, we might look east to the Danelaw boundary, upon which the Lady of the Mercians had recently established her burh at Warwick. It is in this context that we note the land-grant made at Weardbyrig in early September 915 which dealt with an estate at Fernbeorgen. If the latter has been correctly identified as Farnborough in Warwickshire, it is possible that Weardbyrig lay no great distance away in the same part of Mercia. Wherever it was, its name appears to have disappeared from modern maps. This might mean that it failed to thrive as a settlement, sliding into disuse and obscurity. Yet there is a hint that this was not the case, for a coin from c.930 bears an inscription showing that it was minted at a place called Weardburh. Specialist study of the coin suggests similarities with those issued from Mercian mints at Gloucester, Hereford and Shrewsbury. This has led to a suggestion that Weardburh lay in the same region and that it was Æthelflæd's Weardbyrig, a 'watch-fort' along her western border facing the Welsh kingdoms.[36]

The charter issued at Weardbyrig is the only one in which this place is mentioned. The text survives in a copy written in the thirteenth century, preserved among similar items in the archive of Abingdon Abbey in Oxfordshire. The copy has a date of 9 September 878, which is obviously erroneous as Æthelflæd would have only been a small child at the time. A more accurate date can be estimated from the witness list, which is headed by the Lady of the Mercians herself. The absence of Lord Æthelred implies that he was already dead, indicating a date no earlier than 911. One witness was Abbot Ecgberht whose death in June 916 at the hands of the Welsh was noted in the Mercian Register. This gives a five-year timeframe for the event described in the charter, a window that can be narrowed further if we accept the ninth day of September as a correct date that appeared in the lost original document. We know from the Mercian Register that Weardbyrig was constructed in the summer of 915. We also know that Abbot Ecgberht died in June of the following year, so he must have visited the burh in September 915 when it was newly completed. The ninth day of that month is probably the true date of the charter.

As explained in Chapter 1, some charters purporting to be from the Anglo-Saxon period are forgeries produced in later times. These fakes were intended to justify claims to land-ownership or privileges by providing a spurious antiquity. The situation is complicated by the fact that the majority of authenticated charters do not survive in their original forms but in copies that have been altered or poorly transcribed. This means that, in many cases, historians are unable to agree on which documents are fakes and which are accurate copies. The surviving text of the Weardbyrig charter is generally thought to be an authentic copy, although it plainly contains a number of errors. One obvious mistake is the year 878 instead of 915. Another, although less obvious, is no less significant. It concerns the name 'Ælfwynn' in the witness-list, marked in second place after Æthelflæd. Next to it is written the abbreviation *ep* (for Latin *episcopus*) but the name is feminine and cannot belong to a bishop. Nor is the name an error for 'Aelfwine', the name of the bishop of Lichfield, for he is shown separately as the third witness. The second witness can therefore be identified as Æthelflæd's daughter, Ælfwynn, who would have been in her twenties when she accompanied her mother to the newly built fortress of Weardbyrig.[37]

Runcorn

Cyricbyrig and Weardbyrig were founded by Æthelflæd in 915. The Mercian Register adds that 'in the same year, before midwinter' the burh at *Rumcofan* (Runcorn) was also established. Rumcofan is an Old English name meaning 'at the broad cove' (or 'cover'), where *rum* literally means 'roomy' in the sense of wide or spacious.[38] The burh is thought to have stood on Castle Rock, a small promontory jutting out from the south bank of the River Mersey. This stretch of the river is known as the Runcorn Gap, the gap in question being a natural narrowing of the channel by Castle Rock on one side and a promontory at Widnes on the northern bank. Castle Rock was removed in 1862 when the Mersey was widened to improve navigation but a drawing made before its destruction shows it to have been a triangular feature measuring 1.5 hectares (3.7 acres).[39] Ancient defences were still visible when the drawing was made, these being shown as a rampart running around the edge of the promontory with a ditch where it joined the land. The ditch was six feet wide and would have filled with water when the tide was high. Today, the only surviving part of Castle Rock is a short stub supporting one of the huge stone abutments of the Queen Ethelfleda Viaduct, a Victorian railway bridge carrying the West Coast main line across the Mersey. It is recorded that the remains of Æthelflæd's burh were discovered when the abutment was being built in the 1860s but, unfortunately, nothing was preserved.[40] The railway company was seemingly reluctant to delay construction for the sake of archaeology. It did, however, acknowledge the presence of an ancient fortification by castellating part of the bridge.[41]

Rumcofan was presumably built to guard an important fording-point against hostile forces coming down from Northumbria. Its garrison provided additional protection for Chester, not only as an obstacle to invaders from the north but also as a deterrent to the Wirral colonists or to raiders entering the Mersey estuary from the Irish Sea. Chester lay only sixteen miles to the south-west and

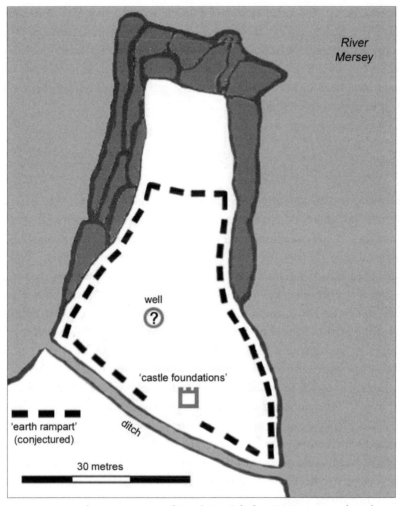

Runcorn: the promontory of Castle Rock (after W. Beaumont (1873)
A History of the Castle of Halton and the Priory or Abbey of Norton, p. 4)
showing the rampart reported by J. H. Hanshall (1823, p. 418)

its inhabitants no doubt felt safer after the founding of Rumcofan. The new burh was only eleven miles west of the earlier one at Eadesbyrig, assuming that this has been correctly identified as Castle Ditch on Eddisbury Hill. It is possible that Eadesbyrig was then deemed redundant, especially if it had been built as a temporary stronghold during a specific military campaign. The Runcorn burh might likewise have been established primarily as a fortress serving a short-term role rather than as a permanent settlement for soldiers and civilians alike.[42] It nevertheless appears to have been given a place of worship, with local tradition asserting that the nearby parish church of All Saints was founded by Æthelflæd in 915. The present church, built in the late 1840s, replaced a medieval structure that had fallen into disrepair. Records show that the older church had been dedicated to St Bertelin (St Beorhthelm) whose cult was one of those promoted by the Lady of the Mercians.[43] Based on the design of Æthelflæd's other burhs, we might wonder if she ordered a second, larger rampart to be constructed to enclose both the church and the promontory fort. This would surely have been the case if she intended Runcorn to be a permanent settlement for soldiers and their families. Indeed, in dedicating the church to Beorhthelm she may have been envisaging that Runcorn would become an additional centre for his cult.

Campaigns and fortresses, 916–18

THE FINAL YEARS

In 912, King Edward had brought an army to Maldon in Essex, staying there while his troops built a fortress at nearby Witham. Four years later, he returned to the same area to build one at Maldon itself, giving it a permanent garrison before returning to Wessex. This new burh, like the one at Witham, was clearly intended to keep a watchful eye on the Danes of East Anglia. Both could potentially be used as launch-points for attacks on the enemy heartlands. They lay at the south-eastern end of a long line of new English strongholds running diagonally from Cheshire to Essex, from the Mersey estuary to the mouth of the Blackwater. This line was now almost complete. To the Scandinavian warlords and settlers living close to the frontier the portents must have looked increasingly ominous. They would have been aware that the Mercian and West Saxon garrisons were not there simply to defend but to attack, like pieces being strategically placed on a chessboard. In the summer of 916, when King Edward completed the burh at Maldon, few folk of Scandinavian stock would have been in any doubt that a great war was looming. For some, this was an opportune moment to leave Britain. One who departed was Thurketel, the Danish jarl who had switched allegiance to Edward in 914. He may have felt that the good times in Britain were over and that the best future for a Viking warrior lay in other lands. Gathering his followers, he took his leave of the English king and sailed over to Francia, never to be heard of again.

Brecenanmere

While Edward was supervising his building project at Maldon, right under the noses of the East Anglian Danes, his sister was occupied with other matters and with different foes. Out on her western frontier she was dealing with Mercia's age-old enemies in Wales. Trouble may have been brewing along this border for some time, with the new burh at Chirbury perhaps being built in response to recent tensions with the Welsh. Things came to a head in 916, on the sixteenth day of June, when an English abbot called Ecgberht was slain with his companions.[1] Who he was and why he was killed are unanswered questions. He was presumably attached to a church or monastery under Æthelflæd's patronage, for he had witnessed her charter issued at Weardbyrig in the previous year. His murder provoked her to exact a swift vengeance. Three days after his death she led an army into south-east Wales and attacked the kingdom of Brycheiniog. Her target was a royal site, an artificial island or 'crannog' on Llangorse Lake in what is now the Brecon Beacons national park. In the Old English language of the tenth century the lake was known as *Brecenanmere* ('Brecon Mere'). It lay roughly a day's march west of the Mercian burh at Hereford where, in all likelihood, Æthelflæd mustered her forces for the campaign.[2] She would have found the crannog an easy target, its small size being barely sufficient to accommodate a tiny garrison. Moreover, although it was nominally defended by water on all sides it was connected to the lakeshore by a wooden causeway some forty metres long.[3] A besieging force could either storm across the causeway to overwhelm the defenders or blockade them from the shore. When Æthelflæd arrived with her army she found that the king of Brycheiniog was not at home. Why he was absent at such a critical moment is unknown but he had not left the crannog deserted. His wife was in residence, together with an entourage which presumably included armed men. The brief account in the Mercian Register does not say whether any fighting took place and the crannog's occupants probably surrendered quickly. Thirty-four of them were taken back to Mercia as captives, among them the king's wife.

Æthelflæd's assault on Brecon Mere was depicted as a reprisal for the slaying of Abbot Ecgberht. A broader context can be imagined, for this was not the first time that the kingdom of Brycheiniog had become entangled with the House of Cerdic. In the 880s, its king Elise ap Tewdwr had felt sufficiently threatened by the powerful realm of Gwynedd to seek protection from Æthelflæd's father Alfred. The price of protection on that occasion was an oath of allegiance and submission to Alfred's overlordship. In the final decade of the ninth century, Brycheiniog was among a number of Welsh kingdoms ravaged by a Viking army that had set up a temporary base at Bridgnorth on the River Severn. Whether Elise was still ruling at that time we cannot say but a certain Tewdwr, possibly his grandson, seems to have been king in the early 930s. Either Tewdwr or his father – a man named in Welsh tradition as Griffi ap Elise – might be the king whose wife was taken captive in 916. Whoever this king was, he may have given allegiance to Edward, renewing the oath sworn by Elise to Alfred. The events of

914, when a Viking fleet entered the Severn estuary, suggest that Edward had political arrangements with one or more kingdoms in southern Wales. In that year he paid a ransom for the Welsh bishop of Llandaff who had been taken captive by the same Vikings. Such a gesture looks like the act of an overlord intervening on behalf of a subordinate kingdom. Alternatively, the king of Brycheiniog in 916 might have previously sworn loyalty to Æthelflæd, preferring submission to Mercia rather than to Wessex. Either way, Æthelflæd's swift and decisive response to Ecgberht's death implies deep anger on her part, regardless of whether the Welsh king was guilty of the slaying by design or omission. There can be little doubt that her seizure of royal hostages represents an imposition – or restoration – of Mercian dominance over Brycheiniog, perhaps in direct opposition to her brother's own interests in Wales.[4]

War in the Southern Danelaw

In the early spring of 917, before the middle of April, King Edward marched an army to Towcester, a former Roman town eleven miles north of Buckingham. There, before Easter, he established a burh by repairing the Roman defences and installing a garrison. Towcester lay directly on Watling Street at the interface between English and Scandinavian territory. Although a Mercian site it was close to Edward's recent zone of activity and had probably been regarded as part of his realm since his acquisition of London and Oxford in 911. This explains why the *Anglo-Saxon Chronicle* attributed the fortifying of Towcester to Edward and not to Æthelflæd. Indeed, the siblings may have agreed that the Mercian-Danish borderlands east of the Fosse Way would be Edward's responsibility while those to the west would be Æthelflæd's.[5] The Towcester fort lay on a road junction from where Danish armies could move south-east towards London or south-west towards Oxford. It therefore offered a first line of defence against the army of Northampton by blocking its raiding-routes.

Within a few weeks, Edward had built another fort, at a place called *Wigingamere* which cannot now be identified. By then, the stage was set for a new round of conflict. In summer, the war began when a large Danish force from Northampton, Leicester and other places 'north from there' advanced on Towcester. The *Anglo-Saxon Chronicle* says that the heathens broke a negotiated peace but it is hard to deny that they acted without provocation. No doubt feeling increasingly hemmed in by English fortresses springing up along their border they launched a pre-emptive strike. They besieged Towcester for a whole day but a stout defence thwarted their attempt to get inside. When English reinforcements arrived, the Danes abandoned the venture and withdrew. They then changed tactics, switching their energies from besieging to raiding. Bands of warriors launched night attacks across the frontier, avoiding the English garrisons and plundering the countryside between Buckingham and Oxford. Cattle and human captives were looted and taken back to the Danelaw. Meanwhile, another area of conflict opened up further east, where a Danish army from Huntingdon and East Anglia advanced to within ten miles of the English garrison at Bedford to build a new fortress of their own at Tempsford. This was meant as a replacement for Huntingdon, which was now evacuated. According to *ASC*, the Danes saw Tempsford as a more advantageous site 'thinking that by operating from there they could in the future dominate a wider area by war and hostility'.[6] In a sense they were playing Edward at his own game, placing a new stronghold close to the frontier as a forthright challenge. They then attacked Bedford but its garrison marched out to inflict heavy losses upon them. A third Danish army, raised in East Anglia and eastern Mercia, came against Edward's new fortress at Wigingamere and placed it under siege. The English defenders withstood the assault for many hours until the Danes finally gave up and withdrew, stealing cattle from the surrounding lands as they went. Edward's next move was to unleash an English counter-offensive using garrisons from his burhs in south-east Mercia. These he sent against Tempsford to put it under siege. Although he seems not to have commanded in person on this occasion, his subordinates performed well and the Danish stronghold was stormed. In the ensuing struggle, the Danes put up a hard fight but many were slain and the rest were taken prisoner. Among their casualties was an unnamed king, perhaps the ruler of East Anglia, together with two jarls – Toglos and Manna – who may have been senior figures at Huntingdon before its abandonment.

Derby

While Edward was campaigning east and south of the Fosse Way his sister was leading her own forces north-west of the ancient road. The Mercian Register described her actions in an entry for 917:

> Here, before Lammas, with God's help Æthelflæd the Lady of the Mercians gained control of the fortress called Derby with all that belonged to it. Four thegns who were dear to her were slain there within the gates.

The feast of Lammas was the first day of August, so we can date this campaign to late July. Derby was one of the Five Boroughs of the Danelaw and had been in Scandinavian hands since the Great Heathen Army's carve-up of Mercia in the 870s. Its recapture by English forces was hugely significant and can perhaps be seen as Æthelflæd's greatest military achievement. It has been suggested that the Danish garrison was under strength at the time because a contingent had joined the assault on Edward's burh at Towcester.[7] This is certainly plausible, for troops from Derby might have been among those at Towcester who were said to have come from places north of Leicester and Northampton. If so, it would then have made good tactical sense for Æthelflæd to attack. Regardless of the strength of the garrison, the Mercian assault turned out to be a bloody affair. Even if the Danes were outnumbered they had no intention of surrendering without a fight. They were defending not only their raiding-base but also their home town, for many of them would have been born and raised there. Some would have been sons of English mothers, or husbands of English women. Their comrades no doubt included full-blood Englishmen who had known only Danish rule and who did not welcome the arrival of an army led by a West Saxon princess.

The details of the Derby campaign are not reported in contemporary sources and can only be reconstructed in outline. One point of uncertainty is the location of the fighting, for the site of the Danish fortress is hard to identify in the present-day city. A strong candidate is the former Roman town of *Derventio*, known today as Little Chester, situated on the east bank of the River Derwent. On the opposite bank, in the modern suburb of Strutt's Park, stood an older Roman site – a fort constructed in the first century AD. This had been superseded by *Derventio*, a small urban settlement with perimeter walls of stone. Sometime in the late third century, *Derventio* was abandoned but its walls may have remained intact for hundreds of years afterwards. They were presumably still standing when the Great Heathen Army arrived in the 860s. At that time there was also an Anglo-Saxon settlement in the vicinity which may have utilised some parts of *Derventio*. It was known as Northworthy ('north enclosure') and probably had a minster church associated with Mercian royalty in which the tomb-shrine of St Alkmund was preserved.[8] Whether the Vikings established themselves at Northworthy or at *Derventio* or built a new stronghold nearby is unknown, but the Roman site with its stone ramparts may have suited their purposes best. Whatever the exact location, they called their settlement *Djúra-bý*, a name rendered in Old English as *Deoraby* and meaning 'deer village', 'oak village' or perhaps 'village on the Derwent'.

Huganus and the Danes

The sixteenth-century *Historie of Cambria* tells a curious story about Æthelflæd's capture of Derby, linking the campaign to her earlier assault on the Welsh kingdom of Brycheiniog in which she had captured the king's wife. It relates how the disgruntled Welsh king, whom it calls 'Huganus', joined the Danes of Derby and fought alongside them when the Lady of the Mercians attacked their fortress. Although the *Historie* claimed to be based on an older Welsh chronicle written in the 1100s, this particular tale looks like imaginative storytelling. It is nevertheless interesting, not least for its ending which shows Huganus choosing death in battle over surrender to a female opponent.

> [Huganus] fled to Derby, and there being peaceably received with fifteen men of war, and two hundred soldiers well appointed, joined himself with [King Edward's] enemies the Danes. When Æthelflæd heard of this, she followed him with a great army, and entered the gates of that town, where Huganus resisted her, and slew four of her chief officers. But Gwyane, lord of the Isle of Ely, her steward, set the gates on fire, and furiously running upon the Welsh he entered the town. Then Huganus being overmatched, and choosing rather to die by the sword than to yield himself to a woman, was slain there.[9]

The capture of Derby in July 917 received no mention in the 'A' text of the *Anglo-Saxon Chronicle*. By contrast, King Edward's activities in the southern Danelaw in the same campaigning season were reported in detail. It is beyond doubt that the Wessex-based compilers of 'A' deliberately ignored Æthelflæd's campaign, preferring to keep the spotlight on her brother. Only in the Mercian Register do we learn of Derby's fall. The West Saxon account of the wars of 917 is therefore skewed and incomplete. It fails to show that this phase of the English reconquest was fought on two fronts, on both sides of the Fosse Way. In concentrating solely on events around Towcester and Tempsford it failed to mention the fall of one of the Five Boroughs. Fortunately, the Mercian Register restored a sense of balance. Viewing the overall picture, it is tempting to assume that Edward and Æthelflæd were co-ordinating their efforts in a strategy that they had devised between them.

The Mercian Register states that not only Derby but also 'all the region which it controlled' now answered to Æthelflæd. We can assume that the region in question was a large swathe of land whose inhabitants had formerly acknowledged Danish rule. Each of the Five Boroughs possessed a similar dependent territory that supported a Scandinavian elite through tribute-payments given mainly as agricultural surpluses. After the summer of 917, such taxes would have gone to Æthelflæd's treasury. Derby and its dependent lands enlarged and enriched her realm, bringing a mixed Anglo-Danish population under her authority. It is likely that around this time she removed the relics of St Alkmund from their original resting-place at Derby to the burh at Shrewsbury.[10] She presumably transferred the bones from eastern to western Mercia as a safeguarding measure, lest a Danish counter-attack put them in jeopardy. While it seems likely that the saint's tomb had not been specifically targeted during the past forty years of heathen rule, there was no guarantee that it would survive a reoccupation. If such fears lay behind the transfer they would not have been groundless: archaeological evidence from Derby suggests that the original Mercian minster was destroyed in the middle decades of the ninth century, presumably by Viking plunderers. A sarcophagus which may have contained the bones of Alkmund did, however, survive. It can be seen today in the city's museum. Of the minster itself no traces remain above ground and the site now lies buried under a modern road.

The campaign of autumn 917

By the end of summer 917, the English had recaptured a considerable amount of territory in eastern Mercia. Two key Danish strongholds – a new fortress at Tempsford and an older one at Derby – had been seized, together with their dependent lands. The campaign of reconquest continued in the autumn with an advance by Edward into East Anglia. Raising soldiers from Kent, Surrey and Essex he marched against the Danish garrison of Colchester. The ancient Roman city was surrounded and besieged until its defences were breached, whereupon the English warriors 'slew all the inhabitants and seized everything inside, except the men who escaped over the wall'.[11] This was another significant loss for the Danes, for Colchester had been one of their main strongholds in south-east Britain since the arrival of the Great Heathen Army in the 860s. It was a setback that their leaders felt compelled to avenge, so a counter-offensive was launched. A large Danish force mustered in East Anglia, supplemented by newly-arrived 'pirates' who were no doubt attracted by the prospect of loot.

It then went southward through Essex to put King Edward's fortress at Maldon under siege before withdrawing when an English relief force appeared. The retreating Danes soon found themselves in deadly peril, for the garrison of Maldon came out to join the pursuit. Battle was joined and the English gained an important victory. Casualties on the Scandinavian side were said to have been high, with the West Saxon chroniclers reporting the deaths of 'many hundreds of them, both pirates and others'.

The focus of English energies now switched back to southern Mercia, where King Edward led an army to Passenham, a settlement roughly midway between Buckingham and Bedford. Here, close to a ford where Watling Street crossed the waters of the Great Ouse, Edward set up camp while sending men nine miles north to upgrade the defences of Towcester with a new wall of stone. At Passenham he received a deputation from the Danes of Northampton, offering the submission of their fortress and its surrounding territory. The chief emissary was Jarl Thurferth who, together with his companions, swore an oath of allegiance to the English king, acknowledging him as 'lord and protector'. Unlike his fellow-jarl Thurketel, who had submitted to Edward three years earlier at Buckingham, Thurferth chose to remain in Britain rather than seek new opportunities abroad. He retained a position of high status under English rule and was allowed to keep his personal estates.[12]

As was customary under the military reforms initiated by Alfred, the English soldiers encamped at Passenham returned home to supervise the harvest. They were replaced by the other half of the fyrd, whom Edward now led to Huntingdon where the recently abandoned Viking fortress was repaired and garrisoned. There the king received the submission of the surrounding district before marching south-east to Colchester which had been damaged during the English siege. While the damage was being repaired, he secured a lasting peace with the Danes of East Anglia. Surprisingly, the *Anglo-Saxon Chronicle* does not describe this as a formal submission, saying only that 'the entire Danish army in East Anglia swore union with him'. The chroniclers quoted the terms of the agreement, observing that the Danes promised Edward 'that they wished all that he wished, protecting all that he protected, by sea and land'. This sounds less like an oath of allegiance than an offer of alliance. Indeed, it has been suggested that Edward was unable to stamp his authority on East Anglia quite as thoroughly as he had managed to do elsewhere.[13] At around the same time, the Danish army of Cambridge also sought peace, but with a separate treaty. This was a straightforward submission to Edward's rule, for we are told that the Cambridge Danes 'independently chose him as lord and protector'.

Danes and Norsemen

The English campaigns in summer and autumn of 917 redrew the political map of southern Britain. Before the onset of winter it was becoming increasingly clear that the era of Scandinavian rule was coming to an end. The Danes seemed incapable of holding onto their territories. Time and again, they had been thwarted by poor leadership and by the lack of a coherent strategy among the various armies. By contrast, their English adversaries were led by two highly effective commanders: King Edward and his sister Æthelflæd. Looking across their frontiers, these two now saw a Danelaw already much reduced. Nevertheless, four of the Five Boroughs of the eastern midlands remained unconquered. Other challenges were looming to the north and west. Even as Mercian and West Saxon soldiers were celebrating victory at Derby, Tempsford and Colchester, the Norsemen were returning to their old power-bases in Ireland. Fifteen years after an alliance of Irish kings had expelled them from Dublin, the tide of fortune was sweeping them back. In the previous chapter we noted the emergence of Ragnall ua Ímair as a major new player in the Irish Sea region, operating perhaps from a base in Galloway or the Isle of Man. His victory over a rival warlord called Bardr Ottarsson off the Manx coast in 914 had marked his entry into the turbulent arena of warfare and politics. As we have seen, Bardr's father was probably the Jarl Ottar who had brought a fleet to Waterford after raiding in the Severn estuary in 914. In 915, a series of raids was launched from Waterford into the Irish hinterland, wreaking havoc across the kingdom of Munster.[14] Two years later, Ragnall and his kinsman Sihtric arrived in Ireland in separate fleets. Ragnall seized control of Waterford and from there led his army to victory over the native Irish. Sihtric likewise defeated the men of Leinster and advanced on Dublin where he was able to re-establish Scandinavian power, setting himself up as king. The eventful year 917 thus ended with Viking power waning in southern Britain but undergoing a revival in Ireland.

Leicester and Stamford

The capture of Derby had demonstrated Æthelflæd's military capabilities, leaving her enemies in no doubt that she was a formidable adversary. The Danes in their remaining fortresses knew that she was more than capable of subjecting them to a similar fate. As the year 917 faded into winter, she and Edward may have met to discuss their plans for the next campaigning season. They wasted little time in resuming the war when the new year dawned. The Mercian Register tells us that the first success of 918 was gained by Æthelflæd herself:

> Here in the early part of the year, with God's help, she peacefully gained control of the fortress at Leicester, and the greater part of the army attached to it were subjugated.[15]

The wording implies that Leicester, one of the Five Boroughs, submitted to the Lady of the Mercians without a fight. Its surrender indicates the strength of her reputation as a war-leader. Behind the chronicler's brief report we glimpse the likely sequence of events: Æthelflæd advanced in force towards Leicester or signalled her intention to do so; the city's Danish leaders, fearful of suffering the fate of their comrades at Derby, decided to capitulate; most of the warbands in the city's dependent territory then followed suit. It is not necessary to interpret the phrase 'by peaceful means' as meaning that Æthelflæd offered some sort of olive branch to the Danes. The imminent threat of siege and slaughter at her hands was probably enough to bring them to the negotiating table.

Leicester, together with its dependent lands, was thus restored to English Mercia. Within the space of twelve months, Æthelflæd had substantially extended the territory under her rule. Two of the Five Boroughs now recognised her authority. The other three, still standing in defiant opposition, represented the last bastions of Scandinavian power in the eastern midlands. If, as suggested earlier in this chapter, Æthelflæd and her brother had agreed to divide their military responsibilities along the Fosse Way, her likely next targets would have been Nottingham and Lincoln, respectively lying north-west and at the northern end of the Roman road. By the same token, Edward would have been responsible for dealing with the fortress at Stamford on the south-east side. That this was indeed the case is implied by the English king's first recorded campaign of 918, in late April or early May. The *Anglo-Saxon Chronicle* tells us that he led his forces to Stamford and ordered a fort to be built on the south bank of the River Welland. On the further bank stood the Danish stronghold, guarding the river's lowest crossing-point. Just as Leicester's inhabitants had submitted to the Lady of the Mercians, so did those of Stamford now submit to the king of Wessex. Leicester's capitulation had been obtained without bloodshed, even if the threat of a Mercian onslaught had swayed the issue. In Stamford's case, the chroniclers do not say that any fighting took place but they do imply that the fortress was besieged or blockaded. We are told that the campaign lasted until the middle of June, suggesting a duration of at least six weeks. The construction of an English fort on the south bank of the Welland indicates that there was no swift surrender of the Danish garrison, and that Edward encountered sufficient defiance to feel that a fortified camp was necessary. By contrast, his sister's military reputation alone seems to have been enough to compel the Danes of Leicester into submission.

Æthelflæd and the North

While Edward was receiving oaths of allegiance at Stamford, his sister was on the verge of another remarkable achievement on a par with her gains at Derby and Leicester. The leaders of Anglo-Danish Northumbria approached her, offering to submit to her authority. As was the case with Leicester, there is no mention of a battle being fought. The Mercian Register suggests that the Northumbrians – whom it calls 'the people of York' – entered into dialogue with Æthelflæd and agreed to accept her overlordship. At that time they appear to have been living in a kingdom without a king, their last Scandinavian monarchs having probably been Eowils and Halfdan who were slain at Tettenhall in 910. Power thereafter seems to have lain in the hands of an Anglo-Danish elite comprising Viking warlords and senior English clerics, the latter being led by Archbishop Hrotheweard of York.[16] What persuaded this group to submit to Æthelflæd is unexplained. We are left to speculate on the possible reasons, with political uncertainty in Northumbria the likeliest.

In 918, York was a prosperous city that had thrived under fifty years of Scandinavian rule, enjoying a lucrative trade benefiting English and Danish citizens alike. It was a prized asset, but one with a vacant throne. As the capital of the erstwhile Anglo-Saxon kingdom of Northumbria it nominally held sway over an extensive territory encompassing all lands north of the Humber and Mersey estuaries as far as Lothian in the east and Galloway in the west. The reality of its situation in 918 was slightly different, for the collapse of English rule after the Danish takeover in 866–7 had seen the loss of old Northumbria's outlying provinces. The far north-western lands around the Solway Firth had been taken over by the Strathclyde Britons. Further east, the province of Bernicia was now ruled as an autonomous realm by a dynasty of English lords based at Bamburgh. As well as fragmentation in the northern borderlands, a string of Norse colonies had been established along Northumbria's western seaboard by exiles from Ireland. To what extent the colonists acknowledged York's authority is uncertain. They may have given allegiance to the new power

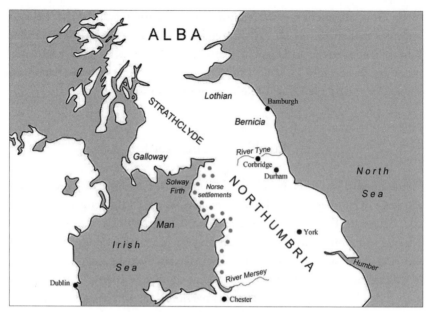

Northern Britain

that had arisen in Ireland in the shape of Ragnall and Sihtric. Indeed, the ambitions of these two posed a serious threat to Northumbria. It is clear from subsequent events that, by 918, they had their eyes fixed on York. Taking all these developments into consideration, it is not difficult to imagine the city's leaders feeling under threat from several directions. An approach to the Lady of the Mercians, offering submission to her authority, may have seemed their best option. If she accepted their offer, they could then claim her protection. It is a measure of the esteem in which she was held by people living outside Mercia that the approach was made to her rather than to her brother.

Northumbria was not the only northern kingdom that had dealings with Æthelflæd at this time. According to the *Fragmentary Annals of Ireland*, she forged an alliance with the Scots of Alba and the Strathclyde Britons to counter the Norse menace:

> Æthelflæd, by her own cleverness, made peace with the men of Alba and with the Britons, so that whenever the same race should come to attack her, they would rise to help her. If it were against them that they came, she would take arms with them. While this continued, the men of Alba and the Britons overcame the settlements of the Norsemen and destroyed and

sacked them. The king of the Norsemen came after that and sacked Strathclyde, and plundered the land. But the enemy was ineffectual against Strathclyde.[17]

The absence of any mention of these events in other texts has inevitably attracted scepticism. Some historians suggest that *FAI*'s account is fiction and that neither the three-way alliance between Mercia, Alba and Strathclyde nor the ensuing raids actually happened. They argue that its authors were so fascinated by Æthelflæd that they were not averse to inventing stories about her. It has also been observed that this would not be the only example of an Irish text promoting an idealised vision of Christian unity in the face of Viking aggression. Against such scepticism we may note that the account is consistent with the political landscape in the second decade of the tenth century. An alliance between rulers who shared common anxieties over the Norse colonies in western Britain would have made good strategic sense. Indeed, it would have been a logical response to the threat posed by Ragnall and Sihtric after their Irish gains in 917.

If we cautiously accept the alliance as historical, what can we say of Æthelflæd's role in forging it through her 'cleverness'? First, we should be in no doubt that her overriding concern was to protect Mercia, in this case its north-western border. The Irish annalist implies that she was expecting a Norse attack on her lands, but that she saw the threat as part of a wider problem affecting other realms further north. There is no hint that the kings of Alba and Strathclyde submitted to her overlordship as the Danes of Derby and Leicester had done and as the Northumbrians were on the verge of doing. Had such a submission by the northern Celtic rulers taken place, we can be fairly confident that the Mercian Register would have recorded it. On this occasion, the treaty was an arrangement between equals seeking mutual co-operation against Norse raids. To some extent, the reciprocal pledges of joint action may have been symbolic or rhetorical, for it is hard to see how forces from Strathclyde and Alba could realistically have come to Mercia's aid, or vice-versa. A more plausible interpretation should therefore be sought. Perhaps the 'peace' forged by Æthelflæd was not so much a military pact with the northern kings as an assurance from them that they would not make common cause with Ragnall and Sihtric? Assigning a specific date is likewise a matter of guesswork. If the focus of negotiations was a shared anxiety about the Norse revival in Ireland, a period from autumn 917 to spring 918 sems feasible. The Northumbrian leaders might then have approached Æthelflæd in May or early June of 918, perhaps not long after her dealings with Alba and Strathclyde. It is possible that their approach was prompted by her treaty with the two Celtic kingdoms, and that the York elite was keen to obtain her protection not only against the grandsons of Ivarr but also against her new friends in the far north.

Æthelflæd's northern allies

The kings of Alba and Strathclyde who are said to have joined Æthelflæd in a military alliance are not named in the *Fragmentary Annals*. Both can be identified nonetheless – one with certainty, the other with a fair measure of confidence. If the alliance was formed in late 917 or early 918 the Scots were at that time ruled by Constantin mac Áeda who had succeeded to the kingship of Alba in 900. His counterpart among the Britons is harder to identify, chiefly because almost no records from Strathclyde have survived. Part of our knowledge of Constantin comes from a text known as the *Chronicle of the Kings of Alba* (hereafter *CKA*) but we possess no equivalent source for the Strathclyde royal dynasty.[18] The entry relating to Constantin in *CKA* does, however, offer a useful starting-point. It tells us that Dyfnwal 'king of the Britons' died during Constantin's reign, which also witnessed the deaths of three Irish kings. *CKA*'s description of the key events of the reign runs in chronological sequence and, since Dyfnwal's death is listed as the first of four, he presumably died before his three Irish peers. From other sources we know that the Irish kings died in 915, 916 and 919, so Dyfnwal's death should be dated to 915 at the latest. He was not therefore alive in 917 or 918. Æthelflæd's ally on the Clyde must have been one of his successors. We can cautiously identify this king as Owain, who was certainly ruling Strathclyde in the 920s and who was probably Dyfnwal's son.[19]

The battle of Corbridge

Under the year 911, the *Fragmentary Annals of Ireland* describe a battle between Scandinavian and English forces in which the latter were led by 'the queen of the Saxons'. Although the annalist did not give this queen a name it is reasonable to assume that Æthelflæd was meant. On the Viking side, the leader was an equally anonymous 'king of the pagans' leading an army of Danes and Norsemen. We are told that the pagans plundered unspecified English lands before being brought to battle where they were defeated with heavy loss. The survivors fled to a forest, carrying their mortally wounded king who eventually died among the trees. His place was taken by a jarl called Ottar who soon found himself in dire straits:

> A huge throng of Saxons came after him, and they surrounded the wood. The Queen commanded them to hack down all of the forest with their swords and battle-axes, and they did so. First they felled the trees, and then all the pagans who were in the wood were killed. The pagans were slaughtered by the Queen like that, so that her fame spread in all directions.[20]

As with other material relating to Æthelflæd in *FAI*, historians are divided on whether this is a report of real events or creative storytelling. One theory is that it preserves a genuine memory of the battle of Corbridge, a historical encounter involving English, Scandinavian and Scottish armies who fought on the banks of the River Tyne in Northumbria. The theory proposes that Æthelflæd despatched a Mercian contingent to fight in the battle alongside other English forces, seeing the tale of the woodland skirmish as an Irish embellishment.[21] A more sceptical interpretation sees the Irish tale as fictional and the Corbridge battle as exclusively northern and of little concern to a Mercian ruler. Although the dangerous Viking warlord Ragnall took part we should question whether his involvement would have given Æthelflæd sufficient cause to send troops. On balance, we can probably assume that no Mercian forces were present and that the story in *FAI* relates to a different encounter. The battle of Corbridge was, however, a significant event, which warrants a closer look.

Our starting-point is the *Annals of Ulster* and its entry for the year 918, which states that Ragnall sailed from his base at Waterford to launch an attack on northern Britain. His objective may have been York where the vacant kingship was a prize worth taking. Advancing across Northumbria he encountered an army of Scots at Corbridge and lost many of his warriors there, among them a Jarl Ottar. This phase of the battle left no clear victor, so the fighting resumed with a Viking onslaught that took a heavy toll of the Scots. Yet the final result was still a stalemate. Another account is given by the *Chronicle of the Kings of Alba*, which does not mention Corbridge and instead places the battle at 'Tyne Moor'. *CKA* assigns the event to the eighteenth year of the reign of Constantin mac Áeda who ruled from 900 to 943. A third source is the *History of Saint Cuthbert*, an eleventh-century text written at Durham, which gives the only

English reference to the battle.[22] It states that the seeds of conflict were sown when Ragnall invaded the lands of Ealdred, a man who was a friend of King Edward 'just as his father Eadwulf had been a friend of King Alfred'.

Ealdred was the ruler of Bernicia in north-east Northumbria where his family had set up an independent English domain in the wake of the Danish takeover of York in the late 860s. His headquarters lay at the coastal fortress of Bamburgh but he was forced to temporarily abandon it when Ragnall landed in northern Britain in 918. After seeking refuge in Alba, Ealdred returned to Bernicia with King Constantin and an army of Scots and together they confronted Ragnall on Tyne Moor.[23] The *History of Saint Cuthbert* says that the battle ended in a Norse victory, contradicting *CKA*'s report of a stalemate. It adds the curious information about Ealdred and his father being 'friends' of Edward and Alfred, implying that the rulers of Bernicia had regarded the kings of Wessex as their liege-lords for two generations. If such a relationship existed, Ragnall's invasion of Ealdred's lands might be interpreted as a challenge to Edward's overlordship. Whether this would have been enough provocation to bring West Saxon or Mercian forces as far north as Corbridge is doubtful. It is also worth noting that it was Constantin, not Edward, who gave refuge to Ealdred. So, although the king of Wessex may have had an interest in the outcome of the battle, neither he nor his sister is likely to have sent their own troops. The woodland skirmish described in *FAI*, if it happened at all, probably took place much further south and can perhaps be connected with Jarl Ottar's raids on south-west Mercia in 914. This Ottar is presumably the henchman of Ragnall mentioned in the Annals of Ulster as a casualty at Corbridge four years later.

The death of Æthelflæd

In June 918, on the twelfth day of the month, the Lady of the Mercians died in her palace at Tamworth. Her body was swiftly conveyed to Gloucester, to be interred alongside her husband's in the minster church that they had founded together.[24] Her age at death is unknown but she was probably around fifty. Nor do we know the cause, although no violence appears to have been involved. Kings and other male rulers in this period lived with the constant risk of succumbing to wounds received in battle, but this would have been an unusual fate for a woman, even for one who had commanded armies in person. Likewise there is no hint that she fell victim to assassins, a fate known to have been suffered by at least one seventh-century Mercian queen. We can probably assume that Æthelflæd died of natural causes, perhaps suddenly and unexpectedly. The site of the church in which she and her husband were interred is marked today by the ruins of St Oswald's Priory. Objects discovered at the site include fragments of ornately carved grave-covers that have been dated to the early tenth century.[25] These are clearly from the graves of important people and it is tempting to associate them with Æthelflæd and Æthelred.

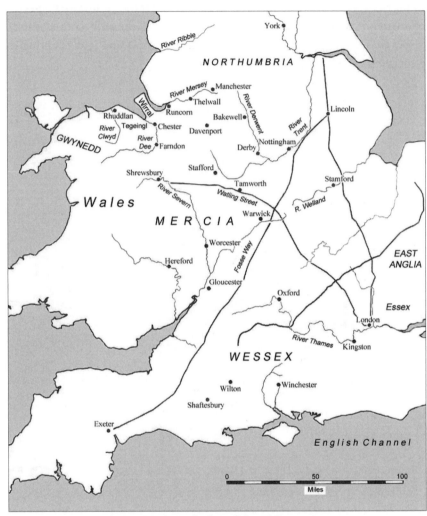

The campaigns of Edward the Elder, 918–24

NIECE AND UNCLE

King Edward was informed of his sister's death while he was campaigning in the Danelaw. What happened next is reported in the *Anglo-Saxon Chronicle*. From the 'A' text we learn that the news reached the king while he was staying in his newly built fort at Stamford:

> During the stay he made there, his sister Æthelflæd died at Tamworth, twelve days before midsummer; thereupon he took over the burh at Tamworth, and all the people of Mercia who had been under allegiance to Æthelflæd turned in submission to him.[1]

Here, a West Saxon chronicler has compressed a series of events that must have taken place over a longer period than this brief report implies. Both compression and brevity were deliberate, the objective being to skip over the political uncertainty created by Æthelflæd's death. A rather different perspective is offered by the Mercian Register in its entry for the same year. After reporting that the Northumbrians had approached Æthelflæd with an offer of submission, the Mercian chronicler added these words:

> But very soon after they had agreed to this she died, twelve days before midsummer at Tamworth, and in the eighth year of her rule over Mercia by rightful lordship. And her body lies in Gloucester in the east chapel of St Peter's church.[2]

This is followed by a separate entry in which Edward's takeover of Mercia happens not in the immediate aftermath of his sister's death but six months later, in early December 918. Again, the chronicler's viewpoint is entirely Mercian and Edward is not mentioned by name. Nor, indeed, is Æthelflæd, the focus being instead on her late husband and their daughter:

Here also was the daughter of Æthelred, Lord of the Mercians, deprived of all authority in Mercia, and she was taken to Wessex three weeks before midwinter. She was called Ælfwynn.[3]

The 'A' text of *ASC* omits any reference to Ælfwynn's 'authority' over the Mercians, implying instead a swift transition of power from Æthelflæd to Edward. It gives the impression that West Saxon rule in Mercia was an inevitable consequence of the death of King Edward's sister. The Mercian Register, on the other hand, leaves us in no doubt that Æthelflæd's authority did not pass directly to her brother but went first to her daughter. Thus, although Ælfwynn was deposed by her uncle before the end of the year, she was for a brief time a new *myrcna hlæfdige*, heiress to a position of power held by her late parents and by generations of Mercian kings before them. Across the entire early medieval period in the British Isles this is the only instance of rulership of a sovereign territory passing from one woman to another.

With the events of June to December 918 being presented so differently in the West Saxon and Mercian versions of *ASC*, a definitive account remains elusive. We are left to weigh the merits of one text against the other, while acknowledging the biases in both. Neither version offers clear answers to questions that now seem important. Was Edward's takeover welcomed or resented by the Mercian elite? Did Æthelflæd herself not envisage the formal union of Wessex and Mercia? These and other matters of controversy and debate will be discussed below. We begin by putting the spotlight on Ælfwynn.

A second *hlæfdige*

Writing in the twelfth century, William of Malmesbury stated that Ælfwynn had no brothers or sisters. If his information is correct, she was the only child of Æthelred and Æthelflæd and may have been conceived early in their marriage, perhaps no later than 890. At the time of her mother's death in 918 she would have been in her late twenties at least, possibly even a year or two over thirty. Her whereabouts in the seven years since her father's death in 911 are unknown except for a single instance of her name appearing in a list of charter-witnesses. The charter confirmed a grant of land and was issued at Weardbyrig, one of Æthelflæd's unidentified burhs, in September 915.[4] Ælfwynn's presence as a witness among other members of the Mercian court shows that, on at least one occasion since her father's death, she accompanied her mother on official business. This document is of further interest in showing Ælfwynn in second place on the witness-list, immediately after her mother and before the bishops, ealdormen and other senior dignitaries. It indicates that Æthelflæd was keen to give her daughter a position of importance among the secular and ecclesiastical elite[5] Furthermore, it raises the possibility that Ælfwynn was being groomed by her mother as the next ruler of Mercia.

Ælfwynn appears to have been unmarried in 915 and still single three years later when Æthelflæd died. Neither the Mercian Register nor the Weardbyrig charter mentions a husband. Had one existed, we would probably know his name. Marriage to the only child of the rulers of Mercia would have given such a man a legitimate claim on their authority after their deaths. Relegating Ælfwynn to a traditional female role, he might then have set himself up as a new Lord of the Mercians. In those circumstances, an individual of high ambition could even have made a bid for the dormant Mercian kingship. None of this would have been acceptable to King Edward nor, we may assume, to his sister. It is even possible that Æthelflæd sought to prevent such an eventuality by keeping her daughter in spinsterhood.[6] In any case, she seems to have envisaged Ælfwynn following in her footsteps as sole ruler of Mercia. An apparently immediate transfer of power from mother to daughter in 918 suggests that this was indeed the case. Such an unprecedented pattern of succession would, however, have required agreement and support from the Mercian witan, whose members would not have accepted a new *myrcna hlæfdige* unless they felt confident in her ability to govern. The Weardbyrig charter shows that Æthelflæd had already begun to give Ælfwynn a higher profile by 915. Other, lost documents may have shown mother and daughter standing side-by-side at similar gatherings of the court. Through such experiences Ælfwynn would have gained knowledge of the business of government. There is no indication that the Mercian witan opposed her accession in 918, yet she could not have obtained her authority if these bishops, ealdormen, abbots and thegns had withheld their support. They would surely have rejected her if she had not been Æthelflæd's designated successor. It is worth recalling that Ælfwynn did indeed hold the position of sole ruler, as her mother had done, albeit it only for a few months, and that she was deposed not from within – by a Mercian revolt – but by a power that came from outside.

The 'A' text of *ASC* depicts Edward's takeover of Mercia as a legitimate process, an expected consequence of his sister's death. It implies that the Mercians were left leaderless until he arrived at Tamworth to receive their submission. Ælfwynn's accession as their new *hlæfdige* is ignored. It had no place in a version of history that sought to justify her uncle's annexation.[7] The corresponding entry in the Mercian Register suggests that the legitimacy of Edward's treatment of Ælfwynn was questioned in her homeland. In telling us that she was 'deprived' of her authority and 'taken' to Wessex, its writer uses the terminology of coercion and abduction. There is more than a hint that physical force was used. The writer also seems keen to emphasise Ælfwynn's status as the daughter of the Lord of Mercians, as if to point out that this meant little to those who deposed her. What we are probably seeing in the wake of Æthelflæd's death is a succession crisis arising from conflicting views of the relationship between Mercia and Wessex. It was a relationship that had not been clearly defined, especially with regard to notions of pan-English unity under the rule of a West Saxon monarch. In Alfred's time, the two realms had been brought closer by dynastic marriage, military co-operation and the willing subordination of Lord Æthelred. This close relationship had continued in Edward's reign, with Æthelflæd providing much of the glue that held it together. However, she was also committed to the preservation of a distinct Mercian identity, promoting the cults of saints who were 'national' not in a pan-English sense but in exclusively Mercian contexts. Moreover, her military campaigns and fort-building programmes appear to have been motivated primarily by a desire to restore lost territories to Mercia rather than to expand her brother's 'kingdom of the Anglo-Saxons'.[8] She had been instrumental in Mercia's revival as a major power, and her death raised the possibility of a reinvigorated Mercian elite seeking to maintain this momentum at the expense of the bond with Wessex. Ælfwynn's views on issues such as Mercian identity and English unity are unknown, but her removal by Edward suggests that he regarded her political aspirations as incompatible with his own. Deposing her was no doubt seen as a high priority at the West Saxon court.

Edward must have been able to count on some support from within Mercia, presumably from one or more factions who saw advantages in submitting to his rule. It is even possible that Ælfwynn did not live up to Mercian expectations, perhaps suffering by comparison with her formidable mother. Æthelflæd had successfully taken on the traditionally masculine roles of rulership and war-leadership and presumably believed her daughter to be of similar calibre. Some among the Mercian warrior nobility might not have shared this belief, preferring to give their allegiance to a proven warlord.[9] Edward's takeover was, to some extent at least, justifiable by ancestry. He was half-Mercian by blood, as much so as his late sister. Moreover, he was certainly no stranger to the Mercians: his son Athelstan had been fostered among them and he himself had ridden to war alongside Lord Æthelred. In any case, his status as Æthelflæd's closest surviving male relative gave him a valid claim to succeed her. Traditionalists among the Mercian elite may have felt that this carried more weight than an otherwise unprecedented female-to-female succession. Others of like mind may have looked not to Edward but to his son Athelstan as a prospective *myrcna hlaford*, or even as a new king of the Mercians. The prince was in his early twenties when his aunt died but it is not known if he was living in Mercia at that time. It is interesting to consider that Edward's arrival at Tamworth might not necessarily have been beneficial to Athelstan, whose candidacy as a future king of Wessex had diminished after Edward's second marriage produced new sons. He was no longer Edward's designated heir, having been passed over in favour of his half-brother Aelfweard. Athelstan's relationship with his cousin Ælfwynn may have been closer than that with his half-siblings in Wessex. Notwithstanding the fact that he was Edward's son, it is possible that he supported Ælfwynn's accession as the new *myrcna hlaefdige*, especially if this was what his aunt had planned for.

Ælfwynn and Ragnall

According to the *Historie of Cambria*, published in 1584, one factor in Edward's removal of Ælfwynn was a fear on his part that she might secretly marry the Viking warlord Ragnall. As with other material in this late and controversial text, we are presented with what looks suspiciously like a fictional tale. The author adopts what we might call a West Saxon viewpoint, asserting that Edward was justified in deposing Ælfwynn because her mother had assigned her to his guardianship.

After the death of Æthelflæd, Edward disinherited her daughter Ælfwynn, and seized the land of Mercia to his own hands. The cause why Edward disinherited this young lady, his niece, whose mother Æthelflæd being his own sister had done so much for him, was (as Castoreus writes) due to Ælfwynn not making the king her uncle (whom her mother had appointed as her guardian and overseer) privy to her doings. She had promised and contracted marriage with Ragnall, king of the Danes, whereupon King Edward, to thwart his enemy, entered the land of Mercia and seized the same to his own hands, and carried also the said lady with him into Wessex.[10]

Ælfwynn, whom we can describe as the second Lady of the Mercians, was removed from power in early December 918. She was taken to Wessex, never to be mentioned again in contemporary chronicles. Her fate is unknown but it is possible that she was sent to a nunnery closely associated with the House of Cerdic. This is the scenario imagined by William of Malmesbury in the twelfth century and is thought to be quite likely. Life as a nun would have precluded marriage, thus removing the risk – to Edward and his heirs – that a future husband of Ælfwynn might lay claim to her erstwhile authority in Mercia.[11] It need not have made much difference if Ælfwynn had lived as a 'lay sister' rather than as a nun in full holy orders. The main reason for placing her in an all-female religious environment would have been to keep her away from potential suitors. As stated above, the Mercian Register's account of her removal contains a hint of coercion. We can probably assume that her entry into a nunnery – if this was indeed what happened – was not voluntary on her part. She had undoubtedly regarded herself, and had been regarded by her subjects, as the legitimate ruler of Mercia. Resentment of her uncle's takeover must surely have gnawed her in those first years of exile. Eventually, no doubt, she would have come to accept her fate. If her place of exile in Wessex was a nunnery it was probably one in which women of the royal kindred were known to have resided in the early tenth century. King Alfred had founded such a house at Shaftesbury in Dorset, appointing his daughter Æthelgifu as its first abbess. Æthelgifu was Æthelflæd's younger sister and Ælfwynn's maternal aunt and, although she may have died before 918, her abbey would have been a suitable home for her exiled niece. Another nunnery had been built at Winchester c.900 by Ælfwynn's maternal grandmother Ealhswith. It was close to the great royal church where both Alfred and Ealhswith lay entombed and would have been an appropriate home for their granddaughter. A third possibility was the abbey of Wilton in Wiltshire, where two of Ælfwynn's younger female cousins are known to have dwelt. It has been suggested that this would have been the most likely residence for Ælfwynn if she had become – or had been forced to become – a royal nun of Wessex.[12] Both of her cousins were eventually buried there, as were their mother and stepmother – King Edward's third and second wives respectively. It is possible that Ælfwynn was laid to rest in the same hallowed place.

Edward and the Mercians

The precise sequence of events from June to December 918 is not easy to reconstruct with certainty. It appears that Ælfwynn's brief period of rule in Mercia commenced soon after her mother's death and was terminated by her uncle before the end of the year. A question remains over where in this six-month span we should place the submission of the Mercians to Edward.

The 'A' text of the *Anglo-Saxon Chronicle* gives the following narrative in its entry for 918:

1. Æthelflæd died at Tamworth on 12 June.
2. Edward came to Tamworth and received the submission of the Mercians.
3. Three Welsh kings submitted to him.
4. He went to Nottingham, occupied the fortress there and installed a garrison of Englishmen and Danes.
5. 'All the people who were settled in Mercia, both Danish and English, submitted to him.'

Reconciling the above with the Mercian Register is not straightforward but it seems that Edward visited Tamworth in June, as soon as he learned of his sister's death, to secure her daughter's allegiance. Ælfwynn would then have been to him what her father had been to Alfred – a subordinate ruler like the *subreguli* of Wales. Edward was presumably still at Tamworth when he received oaths of submission from a trio of Welsh kings, these being identified by the chronicler as Hywel, Clydog and Idwal. All three ruled kingdoms in southern Wales and may have felt nervous about their relationship with Mercia in the post-Æthelflæd era. Seeking Edward's overlordship and protection might have seemed a sensible move. It is possible that they had previously been Æthelflæd's clients but chose not to transfer their allegiance to her daughter.[13] Perhaps they regarded Ælfwynn's military capabilities, as well as her intentions towards Wales, as matters of too much uncertainty? Her uncle, by contrast, not only had a proven reputation in war but had already helped the Welsh during Jarl Ottar's raids in 914.

After leaving Tamworth in June 918, Edward seemingly went back to the Danelaw to resume campaigning. He advanced on Nottingham, one of the two remaining Five Boroughs, and seized control of it. Supplementing the Danish garrison with his own troops he turned it into a mixed Anglo-Scandinavian force. He is then said to have received the submission of 'all the people who were settled in Mercia, both Danish and English'. This can be interpreted as meaning that the remaining Viking armies in eastern Mercia, together with the English living under their rule, pledged allegiance to Edward. Lincoln, the last of the Five Boroughs, is not specifically mentioned by the chronicler but might be included among the places that now submitted.[14] At that moment, the Danish occupation of eastern Mercia effectively came to an end. In early December, Edward travelled west to depose Ælfwynn. It was then that he most likely received the submission of her subjects before imposing direct rule over them. We have no need to imagine that they had already submitted to him six months earlier.

Edward and the North

Æthelflæd's death undoubtedly left some of her projects unfinished. She may have hoped that these would be completed by Ælfwynn, but fate intervened to remove this possibility. It was left to Edward to continue his sister's plans and stratagems, in so far as they were compatible with his own. Some were no longer current or achievable. For example, the offer of submission from Anglo-Danish Northumbria, made to Æthelflæd shortly before her passing, was apparently withdrawn after her death. There is no record of a new offer being presented to Edward. In any case, the Northumbrian situation after 918 was dominated by Ragnall, who had emerged from the battle of Corbridge with a slender victory. He now pressed home his advantage, seizing the vacant Northumbrian kingship. An entry in the *Anglo-Saxon Chronicle* under the year 923 but referring to events in 918 or 919 tells us that he captured York.[15] There he set up his new headquarters, ordering the city's moneyers to produce coins in his name. Although his reign turned out to be brief, lasting only a couple of years until his death in 920 or 921, we have no reason to assume that he was unpopular. Having seen their offer of allegiance to Æthelflæd thwarted by her death, the Northumbrians may have welcomed Ragnall as a worthy substitute. More so, perhaps, than King Edward of Wessex. The rule of a Norse warlord whose connections boosted trade with Dublin may have seemed preferable to the distant overlordship of a southern English king.

Ragnall's arrival at York posed an immediate threat to Mercia. Previous Northumbrian raids are unlikely to have been forgotten, not least the incursion of 910 which had ended on the bloody field of Tettenhall. Edward, in his new role as protector of the Mercians, took steps to guard against this new menace.

In 919, he built a burh at *Thealwæle* (Thelwall) on the south bank of the River Mersey. Here, at a ford ten miles upstream from the one at Runcorn, he installed a garrison of Mercian soldiers. This may have brought to fruition a project originally planned by Æthelflæd. Thelwall's burh looks like a logical next step in her strategy of consolidation and defence along Mercia's north-west frontier. In some sense, then, she may have bequeathed the building of this burh to her brother. The same might be said of Manchester, on the Northumbrian side of the Mersey, which was repaired and garrisoned on Edward's orders during his stay at Thelwall. Unfortunately, the exact locations of these two burhs have not yet been identified. This means that their size and layout cannot be determined, nor can their relationship to earlier or later phases of activity be discerned. In neither case do we know if the burh was a temporary fort serving a short-term military purpose or a permanent one that became the nucleus of a settlement.

At Thelwall, aerial photography and fieldwalking have so far failed to find evidence of tenth-century features.[16] This has led to speculation that the burh lay not in the present-day village of Thelwall but on the opposite side of the river, at Warrington, where an important settlement did exist in the following century. Switching our focus to Warrington would mean accepting that the *Anglo-Saxon Chronicle* misidentified the site of the burh, or that the name *Thealwæle* encompassed land on both sides of the river. The name means 'deep pool at a plank', probably in the sense of 'deep pool with a plank bridge', although the location of these features is unknown.[17] The pool was presumably part of the Mersey but the river's course in this area has been altered so even this assumption cannot be confirmed. The ford guarded by the burh lay on a Roman road from Warrington to Northwich and is almost certainly the one shown on a nineteenth-century map as an 'ancient ford'. A memory of it is preserved in the name Latchford on the south side of the river while a place once known as Old Warps may mark its approximate position on the northern bank. The ford became obsolete when a bridge was built in the thirteenth century.

At Manchester, the obvious candidate for Edward's burh is the Roman fort of *Mamucium* at Castlefield, situated on a sandstone bluff overlooking a ford on the River Medlock. *Mamucium* lay four miles north-east of the Mersey at a major junction of Roman roads, one of which ran from Chester to York via the Mersey crossing at Stretford. No clear evidence of tenth-century activity at *Mamucium* has yet been discovered, prompting considerable uncertainty about the burh's location. Medieval and modern Manchester developed not at Castlefield but half a mile to the north on a promontory between the rivers Irk and Irwell. The old core of the town was the cathedral, itself an ancient foundation that has yielded Anglo-Saxon sculpture. In this area a mysterious earthwork known as the Hanging Ditch has been suggested as a possible Anglo-Saxon boundary feature. However, the chronicle entry suggests repair of an existing fortification rather than construction of a new one, thus leaving the Roman fort as the best candidate. The walls of *Mamucium* were undoubtedly standing in 919, even though the interior may have lain derelict for half a millennium. Æthelflæd had incorporated Roman defences in her burhs at Chester, Worcester and Gloucester and her brother may have done something similar at Manchester. It was once believed that archaeological investigations at *Mamucium* had produced no hint of Late Anglo-Saxon settlement. Although a group of sunken-floored buildings outside the north gate of the Roman fort were identified as early medieval, they were assumed to have been built in the fifth or sixth centuries. Similar sunken buildings from Chester have now been dated to the 900s, so it is possible that those at *Mamucium* might be associated with Edward's burh after all.[18] Medieval Manchester's subsequent growth in the cathedral area some distance away suggests that the Roman fort's reoccupation was temporary rather than permanent. It may have been garrisoned during an otherwise unrecorded military campaign in south-west Northumbria which resulted in the land between Mersey and Ribble becoming part of Edward's domain.[19]

The meeting at Bakewell

In 920, Edward returned to Nottingham to build a new burh on the south bank of the River Trent, opposite the fortress formerly held by the Danes. The *Anglo-Saxon Chronicle* describes what happened next:

> Then he went from there into the Peak District, to Bakewell, and ordered a burh to be built in the neighbourhood and manned. And then the king of the Scots and all the people of the Scots, and Ragnall, and the sons of Eadwulf and all who live in Northumbria, both English and Danish, Norsemen and others, and also the king of the Strathclyde Welsh and all the Strathclyde Welsh, chose him as father and lord.[20]

This is usually interpreted as meaning that Edward convened a formal gathering, attended by various northern rulers, during which he received their oaths of submission. The wording implies that the venue was the newly completed burh at Bakewell, in present-day Derbyshire, a location close to the ancient frontier between Mercia and Northumbria. Some historians have accepted at face value the statement that Edward was chosen as 'father and lord', seeing the event as a ceremony in which his overlordship was acknowledged by the other attendees. Such an interpretation places too much trust in the words of a chronicler who was eager to embellish Edward's achievements. It is hard to see why the rulers of Strathclyde and Alba would submit to a king who had yet to prove that he could impose his authority on their lands.

If we disregard the claim of overlordship as West Saxon propaganda we are left to ponder the real purpose of the meeting. One suggestion is that it was convened to reach agreement on matters of dispute arising from recent shifts in the political landscape. Ragnall's seizure of the Northumbrian kingship may have profoundly unsettled his neighbours, especially those who had fought against him at Corbridge. Edward's takeover of Mercia would likewise have brought the ambitions of the West Saxon dynasty to the doorstep of northern Britain. One of the outcomes of the Bakewell meeting may have been formal recognition of Edward's authority in the south and of Ragnall's at York.[21] Some kind of peace treaty between the Corbridge protagonists might also have been agreed, in the hope of averting a new conflict. Eadwulf's sons, the English rulers of Bernicia, perhaps felt most threatened by Northumbria's new king and may have wanted an assurance that he would not attack their territory. The meeting should probably be seen as an assembly of equals, with no formal submission taking place. It was no doubt similar to the *rígdála* or 'royal meetings' reported in contemporary Irish chronicles. The main business of a *rígdál* appears to have been the settling of disagreements that might otherwise lead to war. Nevertheless, Edward's hosting of such an event at one of his fortresses would have given him a special status among the other attendees, for they had to come to him rather than he to them. This was plainly milked for all it was worth by his propagandists back at Winchester, hence the lofty claim of his superiority as 'father and lord'. Perhaps it was also hoped that the Mercian location might help to make him seem more like a king of Mercia in the eyes of the Mercians themselves. On a different note, we might wonder if the burh at Bakewell had originally been planned by his sister after her capture of Derby, to consolidate her rule in lands that had formerly answered to the Danish stronghold.

The Mercian revolt

In 921, Edward was back in northern Mercia again, this time on the far western frontier. The Mercian Register says that he founded a burh at *Cledemutha*, a place usually identified as Rhuddlan at the mouth of the River Clwyd. In the tenth century, Rhuddlan marked the last crossing-point on the Clwyd before it reached the Irish Sea.[22] Edward's burh seems to have occupied an area of some 8–10 hectares (20–24 acres) on the eastern riverbank, south of the imposing thirteenth-century Rhuddlan Castle. The tenth-century settlement grew into a thriving port that continued to flourish after the Norman Conquest, eventually developing into a substantial medieval town. The footprint and defensive perimeter of Norman Rhuddlan are thought to reflect those of tenth-century Cledemutha, although little is known of the burh's interior layout. As a border stronghold facing the Welsh of Gwynedd and guarding a point of access to the Irish Sea, it had high strategic value and would have strengthened Edward's hold on north-west Mercia. It lay on the western edge of Tegeingl, a territory long disputed between Welsh and Mercian rulers, and may have been built at the end of a successful campaign of conquest in this district.

Also in 921, or perhaps late in the previous year, King Ragnall of Northumbria died. His kinsman Sihtric came over from Dublin to become the new ruler of York. Sihtric's arrival rendered obsolete any treaties agreed by Ragnall, including whatever promises had been made at Bakewell. Sihtric immediately showed his contempt for Edward's pretensions as 'father and lord' by launching a raid into Mercia. His forces penetrated deep into Cheshire, plundering an estate at Davenport near Congleton. Edward's response is not known. He may have been in his southern domains at the time, leaving responsibility for northern defence in the hands of one or more Mercian ealdormen. Uncertainty about the precise sequence of events deprives Sihtric's raid of any wider political context and means that we do not know if it occurred before, during or after Edward's construction of Cledemutha. What we can say is that Sihtric's reign at York was longer and more successful than that of his predecessor. Coins bearing his name were minted at Lincoln, formerly the northernmost of the great Danish strongholds in eastern Mercia. Although Lincoln is often assumed to have submitted to Edward in 918, his authority may have been weaker there than in places such as Nottingham and Derby that lay closer to the Mercian heartlands. Perhaps Lincoln was too far away from his influence, or too close to Anglo-Danish Northumbria?

The coin evidence shows that Lincoln's elite preferred to give allegiance to Sihtric. Nothing suggests that Edward tried to alter the situation. In fact, there is no indication that he was active in Mercia again until 924. In that year, according to William of Malmesbury, the inhabitants of Chester rose against him. William adds that the rebels acted in alliance with Welsh neighbours, perhaps those of Tegeingl whose lands had presumably been conquered by Edward when he built the burh at Rhuddlan. This uprising in north-west Mercia must have profoundly enraged the English king. Æthelflæd had founded a burh at Chester seventeen years earlier and it had proved to be a successful settlement. There is no hint that its inhabitants had ever rebelled against her, but something evidently stirred them to reject her brother. Perhaps they saw him as too 'alien' – the ruler of a far-off southern kingdom who had few links with their city? Or maybe his local representatives were demanding a high tax for the royal treasury?[23] Whatever sparked the revolt, the situation became serious enough to bring Edward north with his army. How long the unrest continued before he quelled it is unknown, but he spent part of the time at Farndon on the River Dee, some seven miles south of Chester. Farndon had an ancient church which – according to later tradition – lay at the centre of an Anglo-Saxon royal estate. Edward died there on 17 July 924, at around fifty years of age. His body was taken back to Wessex, to Winchester's New Minster, to be laid to rest alongside the tombs of his parents.

Athelstan

The 'A' text of the *Anglo-Saxon Chronicle* gives the impression of a smooth transition of power from Edward to his eldest male heir. It makes no mention of Edward's place of death, saying only that he died 'and his son Athelstan succeeded to the kingdom'. Once again, we rely on the Mercian Register for a more detailed account. The succession, it seems, was far from straightforward:

> King Edward died at Farndon-on-Dee in Mercia; and very soon, sixteen days after, his son Ælfweard died at Oxford; they were buried at Winchester. Athelstan was accepted as king by the Mercians and was consecrated at Kingston.[24]

Ælfweard was the eldest son of Edward's second marriage and may have been his father's preferred successor. Although the Mercian Register does not explicitly call him a king he is usually seen as following Edward in the kingship of Wessex. A West Saxon text of the late tenth century says that he was 'crowned with kingly badges' while one twelfth-century writer assigns him a reign of four weeks.[25] Two charters from Edward's reign placed Ælfweard higher than Athelstan in the roll-call of witnesses, implying that the younger prince had leapfrogged his half-brother in their father's affections. Alfred's symbolic anointing of Athelstan as a future king, if it ever really happened, was apparently disregarded in 924.

Drawing together the various pieces of written evidence, we seem to be seeing either a disputed succession to the kingship of Wessex and Mercia or the division of the 'kingdom of the Anglo-Saxons' into its two constituent parts. Ælfweard was probably hailed as king by a faction in Wessex, while Athelstan was likewise elevated to the kingship of Mercia. He was already familiar to the Mercians, having been fostered among them during his youth. It is possible that he was there during the summer of 924, campaigning alongside his father against the Chester rebels and their Welsh allies, and that he was at Farndon when Edward died on 17 July.[26] Had subsequent events unfolded differently, we might now be reading of warfare between the two half-brothers, with one emerging victorious to rule both Wessex and Mercia as a new 'king of the Anglo-Saxons'. Instead, we are told that Ælfweard died within weeks of Edward's passing, leaving Athelstan as sole contender for the combined kingship. The West Saxons eventually joined the Mercians in accepting him as their new monarch. He was formally consecrated as *rex Saxonum et Anglorum* on 4 September 925, at Kingston-upon-Thames in Surrey, a symbolic location on what had once been the frontier between Wessex and Mercia.[27]

Athelstan is often seen as the first king of all the English, for his realm at its greatest extent had a similar footprint to the England we recognise today. His achievements were certainly impressive. In 927, he annexed Northumbria after ejecting its king Guthfrith, a kinsman of Sihtric and Ragnall. In the same year, at the Mercian burh of Hereford, several Welsh kings submitted to him. So, too, did the rulers of Alba, Strathclyde and Bernicia at a separate ceremony in the North. Coins minted in his name described him as *rex totius Britanniae* ('King of all Britain'), an exaggerated claim but one that probably reflected his ambitions accurately enough.[28] Having learned the craft of war-leadership during his fosterage at the Mercian court he was, on the battlefield at least, a worthy successor to Æthelred and Æthelflæd. A remarkably long-range campaign in Alba in 934 bludgeoned the Scottish king Constantin into submission, while a celebrated victory three years later at Brunanburh thwarted a dangerous alliance of Vikings, Scots and Strathclyde Britons. When Athelstan died in 939, he held sway over significantly more territory than any of his forebears. Not for nothing did a contemporary Welsh poem call him *mechteyrn*, 'The Great King'.[29]

Athelstan's coronation in 925 did not completely end the notion of separate Mercian and West Saxon kingships. It did, however, help to solidify the idea of a single 'Kingdom of the Anglo-Saxons' in which Wessex and Mercia were joined together. This kingdom soon evolved into something else, for Athelstan's later charters (928–35) refer to him as 'king of the English'. Behind this title lay a hope that the old political and dynastic divisions were gone and that the English would henceforth be ruled as one people under one king. Turning this into reality took rather longer to achieve, for it is clear that not everyone supported it. Three hundred years of separation between Mercians and West Saxons, or between Mercians and Northumbrians, was not going to be swept aside quickly. Nor was unification an inevitability, even in the final years of Athelstan's reign. It drew closer fifteen years after his death when, in 954, Anglo-Danish Northumbria was annexed to the 'Kingdom of the English'. Yet the old identities remained strong enough to split the kingdom in 957, with separate Mercian and West Saxon kingships appearing for a brief time. Admittedly, this schism was driven as much by dynastic strife as by regional differences, for the two kings in question were nephews of Athelstan. Their names were Eadwig and Edgar, the former ruling Wessex while the latter held Mercia and Northumbria. For a couple of years, their rivalry shattered the vision of English unity. Not until 959, when Eadwig's death left Edgar as sole monarch, was the vision restored. By 975, when Edgar died, the process of unification was almost complete. The kingdom of England can be said to have begun three years later when Edgar's son Æthelred the Unready took the throne after another flurry of dynastic rivalry. Neither Wessex nor Mercia would ever again emerge as separate kingdoms. Throughout the eleventh century the Mercians were governed by ealdormen, then by earls, until the Norman Conquest finally swept the old divisions of Anglo-Saxon England away.[30]

'Queen Ethelfleda': monuments, artworks and texts

10

LEGACY

Remembering Æthelflæd in the chronicles

Æthelflæd's death in 918 was noted by chroniclers not only in Wessex and Mercia but also in Ireland. A brief obituary in the *Annals of Ulster* described her as *famosissima regina Saxonum*, 'the most famous queen of the Saxons'. Neither this nor any other Irish text had mentioned the passing of her father Alfred in 899, nor would they report her brother's death in 924. It seems that, in Ireland at least, Æthelflæd was accorded a special kind of recognition that was denied to her close male relatives.[1] In Wales, too, her departure was considered worthy of mention. An entry in the Welsh Annals, misplaced under the year 917, reported that 'Queen Æthelflæd died'. The Welsh annalists had previously noted the death of 'Alfred, king of the Gewisse' but there is no equivalent notice for Edward. We appear to be seeing a difference in how Æthelflæd and her brother were viewed by contemporary observers in the Celtic West, where she seems to have been regarded as the more significant of the two.

There is no indication that Æthelflæd was held in such high regard by chroniclers in her native Wessex. We have already seen how the 'A' text of the *Anglo-Saxon Chronicle* glossed over her deeds, concentrating instead on her brother's achievements. The conventional view is that this reflected a prevailing attitude at King Edward's court, where anxiety over the relationship between Wessex and Mercia is likely to have been a key concern. While Æthelflæd lived, the historic tensions between the two realms were unlikely to ignite, not least because she maintained the alliance that her husband and her father had forged in the 880s. Nevertheless, she and Æthelred had revived Mercia's military strength to the extent that large-scale wars could now be fought without West Saxon help. Alongside this revival had come a strengthening of Mercian identity, symbolised at a spiritual level by her enthusiastic sponsorship of Mercian saints and their cults. The fact is that when Æthelflæd died in 918 she left Mercia in far better shape than it had been when she had first arrived as Æthelred's bride.[2]

Her death meant that Edward faced the prospect of a newly confident Mercian elite accustomed to pursuing its own objectives independently of his own. As chief architect of this resurgence, Æthelflæd was potentially the most vivid icon for future Mercian ambitions. In the words of one modern historian, 'her reputation could be used with effect by nationalists who hoped to revive the independent kingdom of Mercia'.[3] Hence her role in the English reconquest of the Danelaw was omitted from the 'official' version of the *Anglo-Saxon Chronicle*, leaving Edward to take all the credit. Sidelined in what was to become the standard account of tenth-century English history, Æthelflæd was destined to become a shadowy figure whose achievements would go largely unnoticed.

West Saxon political motives do not provide the only possible explanation for Æthelflæd's solitary mention in *ASC* 'A'. This text was, of course, primarily concerned with events affecting Wessex.[4] Tidings from other lands inevitably received less attention, unless they touched on West Saxon interests. Perhaps we should not be surprised to find little mention of a Mercian ruler leading Mercian armies to recover Mercian territory? Æthelflæd's military activity is sometimes seen as a sub-set of her brother's but this is not necessarily an accurate view. Hers seem rather to have been independent ventures, driven not by an Alfredian vision of pan-English unity but by the ambitions of a reinvigorated Mercian elite seeking to acquire more land. The West Saxon chroniclers might therefore have ignored Æthelflæd because she seemed to be pursuing a Mercian agenda. The omission from *ASC* 'A' of her attack on Llangorse Lake would then be easy to explain as an event that had little relevance to Wessex. It is possible that her conquest of Derby and her burh-building projects were likewise seen as fulfilling Mercian objectives, despite their close fit with Edward's overall strategy.

Away from the West Saxon royal court, Æthelflæd was commemorated more openly. Her name, although apparently unknown in earlier times, was bestowed on a number of high-born girls in the decades after her death. These later Æthelflæds, born to Mercian and West Saxon noble families, were surely named in her honour.[5] Among them was Æthelflæd of Damerham, the second wife of King Edmund who ruled Wessex and Mercia from 939 to 946. Edmund was a nephew of the earlier Æthelflæd but born three years after her death. The first marriage of his son Edgar (reigned 959–75) is presumed to have been to yet another Æthelflæd, the daughter of a Mercian ealdorman. Three more Æthelflæds are named in the will of a West Saxon noblewoman called Wynflæd who owned estates in Wessex in the middle decades of the tenth century. None of these name-sakes had ever met the original Æthelflæd, but they would have been aware of her existence and may have felt honoured to share this connection with her.

A more permanent commemoration of the illustrious *myrcna hlæfdige* was the Mercian Register, a literary monument to her achievements and our chief source for her military campaigns. Other accounts of her deeds may have existed, circulating in a more informal way through oral storytelling or in writings that are now lost. Such information would have been passed down through the years, providing raw material for later writers such as William of Malmesbury. William and several of his contemporaries in the 1100s seem to have been fascinated by Æthelflæd. They saw her through medieval eyes as a rare human being: a female who had successfully taken on the traditionally male responsibilities of generalship and governance. Indeed, this juxtaposition of traditional gender roles was evidently more surprising to them than to the writers of her own time.[6] To William it was a point of curiosity that 'a woman should be able to protect men at home, and to intimidate them abroad'. Being both a native of Wiltshire and a monk at Malmesbury Abbey, his perspective was closely aligned with what we might call a typical West Saxon view. Although he plainly regarded Æthelflæd with a kind of awe, he nevertheless saw her as subordinate to Edward. Thus, she was not so much a ruler of equal status as the king's loyal helper, 'a powerful accession to his party, the delight of his subjects, the dread of his enemies . . . this spirited heroine assisted her brother greatly with her advice . . .'.[7] It has been suggested that William's interest in Æthelflæd was at least partly due to his abbey's support for Matilda, daughter of the Anglo-Norman king Henry I, who claimed the throne of England during a succession crisis in the mid-1100s. William may have regarded Æthelflæd's rule over the Mercians as a useful precedent for Princess Matilda who did indeed become, albeit briefly, a ruler in her own right.[8]

Henry of Huntingdon, another twelfth-century writer, was even more fulsome in his praise of Æthelflæd, whose name he rendered as 'Efleda'. After describing her as 'so powerful that she was sometimes called not only lady or queen, but king also', he offered his own personal tribute in the form of a poem:

Heroic Efleda! Great in martial fame,
A man in valour, woman though in name;
thee warlike hosts, thee Nature too obeyed,
conqueror over both, though born by sex a maid.
Changed be thy name, such honour triumphs bring.
A queen by title, but in deeds a king.
Heroes before the Mercian heroine quailed:
Caesar himself to win such glory failed.[9]

It has been suggested that Æthelflæd's popularity in the twelfth century was due not only to her martial reputation but also to her alleged celibacy. William of Malmesbury cited the tale of her choosing to abstain from sex after her daughter's birth and, regardless of whether the story is true or false, she would have been revered by William and his fellow-monks as a 'chaste queen'.[10]

Remembering Æthelflæd in modern times

Given her success in war against Viking invaders we might have expected to see Æthelflæd hailed today as one of the great heroines of England. Instead, we find that she is barely noticed, at least not in any kind of national sense. England's national heroine is a much earlier female ruler: Boudica, queen of the Iceni tribe of East Anglia in the first century AD. Like Æthelflæd, Boudica led her soldiers against foreign conquerors who had seized the lands of her people. However, in spite of her undoubted bravery, she made no contribution to the foundation of England.[11] She was a native Briton, not an Anglo-Saxon. Although her activities took place in areas that would one day be settled by English-speaking immigrants, her Celtic heritage connects her more closely to Wales – today the last bastion of native British identity. Generations of English schoolchildren have nevertheless learned of Boudica's doomed attempt to halt the Romans, which ended in a crushing defeat. By contrast, few have heard of Æthelflæd and her victories over the Vikings.

Beyond the schoolroom, research by professional and amateur historians alike has served Æthelflæd rather better. The past fifty or sixty years have brought her a measure of scholarly attention via journal articles, conference papers and text-books. Alongside Alfred, Edward, Athelstan and Edgar she is now acknowledged in academic circles as one of the most important figures in the creation of England. Much credit for this must go to Frederick Wainwright whose 1959 article was a trailblazing study and the first major piece of scholarship devoted to her, albeit one that portrayed her as Edward's subordinate.[12] Another significant factor is a growing interest in the history of medieval women, with Æthelflæd being seen as a complex individual who successfully combined the differing roles of ruler, war-leader, wife and mother. The result of all this scholarly interest is that she is now the most well-studied Anglo-Saxon female outside the religious milieu of saints and abbesses.[13] Nevertheless, the audience for academic publications is small and she remains relatively unknown among the general population.

We turn now to literature of a different kind. Æthelflæd has recently featured as a prominent character in works of historical fiction, sometimes as the titular heroine in dramatised biographies. Authors working in this genre typically undertake painstaking research to create an authentic, historically accurate environment for their characters. This undoubtedly adds to the experience for readers and may even encourage them to seek out more information on the real history behind the storyline. One example of a well-researched fictionalised biography of Æthelflæd is Annie Whitehead's *To Be A Queen*, which not only conjures a believable setting but also includes useful historical notes. Like other successful authors in this genre, Whitehead manages to manipulate the boundary between history and invention so that the latter begins to feel almost real.[14] Another fictional portrait of Æthelflæd appears in *The Saxon Stories*, a series of novels by Bernard Cornwell. This has undoubtedly become the most widely known depiction of recent years. The first title in the series, *The Last Kingdom*, tells the story of an Anglo-Saxon nobleman called Uhtred who, as a child, is raised by Danish Vikings. It has given its name to a UK television production which currently attracts a large global audience. In the second season of the TV series we see Æthelflæd – played by the actress Millie Brady – emerging as one of the main characters. A fictional storyline shows her being kidnapped by Vikings and falling in love with a Danish warlord. While this may have little connection with actual history, the show's huge popularity has inevitably sparked interest in the real Æthelflæd and is bringing her some long-overdue attention.[15]

Remembering Æthelflæd in art and folklore

In what was once the kingdom of Mercia, several towns and cities today claim Æthelflæd as their foundress. Some of the claims are supported by contemporary sources such as the Mercian Register, or by archaeological evidence of early tenth-century settlement. Others emerge from local folklore associated with specific sites such as castles and churches. At Tamworth, for example, one local tradition asserts that the great mound of the medieval castle was the site of Æthelflæd's burh. This is an erroneous belief but it can be traced as far back as the 1600s and might be of even greater antiquity.[16] Even today, when the mound has been convincingly identified as a Norman motte, its supposed link with the Lady of the Mercians is still mentioned. A similar tradition exists at Warwick, site of the burh of 914, where a Norman motte in the grounds of the medieval castle is referred to as 'Ethelfleda's Mound'.

In some towns, awareness of Æthelflæd's role in local history originated in Victorian times alongside a general revival of interest in the Anglo-Saxon period. To the Victorians, the story of Alfred the Great resonated with their own ideas about heroism, patriotism and Englishness. This interest in Alfred rescued other Anglo-Saxon kings from obscurity, among them his son Edward, his grandsons Athelstan and Edmund and his great-grandson Edgar. Æthelflæd, too, received a share of the limelight, especially in places that could claim a connection with her.[17] While Alfred attracted attention on a national scale as a pan-English monarch, his daughter was acclaimed at a more local level as ruler of the western midlands. Recognition of her achievements in this region took various forms. In Cheshire, an impressive Victorian structure carrying trains across the River Mersey between Runcorn and Widnes is known locally as 'Ethelfleda Bridge'. The name arose after one of the huge sandstone bridge-supports on the southern side was placed on the site of Æthelflæd's burh of *Rumcofan* during construction in the 1860s. As mentioned in Chapter 7, the railway company gave a nod to the Anglo-Saxon fortification by designing the supports in a castellated style, giving them the appearance of battlemented towers.

A more recent commemoration has been created at Wednesbury, a town situated between Wolverhampton and Birmingham near the source of the River Tame. Local tradition asserts that Æthelflæd erected a burh on the site of an original 'Woden's Fort' from which the modern place-name is presumed to derive.[18] The tradition can be traced as far back as the seventeenth century, when the naturalist and antiquary Robert Plot said of Wednesbury that 'the renowned Ethelfleda, who governed the kingdom of Mercia with so good conduct, fortify'd this Town against the Danes who infested her Nation.'[19] Although there is no contemporary record of a tenth-century settlement at Wednesbury, the possibility that it might be one of Æthelflæd's unrecorded burhs cannot be ruled out. The town is less than nine miles from Tettenhall, site of the great battle of 910, while traces of an ancient fortification were supposedly visible in the early 1800s on the hilltop now occupied by the parish church. More recently, the local tradition received a boost when archaeological excavations on the hill discovered a substantial ditch which might be of Iron Age date.[20] In the 1950s, a public amenity was created near the church and has been known since then as Ethelfleda Memorial Gardens. A plaque informs visitors that a 'fighting platform' associated with Æthelflæd's fort once occupied the site. In 2012, the original brass plaque was stolen, to the profound dismay of local people, but it was replaced by a new granite version in the following year.[21]

Various churches claim to have been founded or endowed by Æthelflæd despite not being mentioned in her charters or in the Mercian Register. The connection is usually inferred from hints such as proximity to one of her burhs, evidence of an Anglo-Saxon church or a dedication to one of the saints whose cults benefited from her patronage. In some cases, as at St Alkmund's in Shrewsbury, the hints are so strong that a genuine connection seems likely. In others, they are less compelling but the possibility of a historical link remains nonetheless. At Churchdown near Gloucester, the former parish church of St Bartholomew's stands on a hill to the south of the village and has stonework dating back to the twelfth century. A belief in Victorian times that the oldest stones were pre-Norman prompted a suggestion that the original church may have been founded by Æthelflæd.[22] Although the stones in question are unlikely to be of Anglo-Saxon date, the possibility of St Bartholomew's having a historical link with Æthelflæd deserves serious consideration. An air of antiquity surrounds the old church, not least because of its position in one corner of an Iron Age hillfort. Furthermore, the parish priests in medieval times were deployed from St Oswald's Priory in Gloucester, the premier church of Æthelflæd and her husband. In 1903, St Bartholomew's was superseded by a new parish church dedicated to St Andrew and located in the centre of Churchdown village. Archaeological excavations at St Andrew's in 2000 discovered artefacts and features that have been dated to the tenth or eleventh centuries. These remains imply the presence of a settlement, probably an agricultural one, in the Late Anglo-Saxon period.[23] Such a place may have been contemporary with an early church on the hill where St Bartholomew's stands today. In the 1930s, the idea of an Æthelflæd connection at Churchdown was visualised in an impressive stained glass window at the new parish church. It shows the Lady of the Mercians in regal pose with a crown and sceptre.

Plaques, information boards and other forms of signage are often displayed at places where an association with Æthelflæd is claimed. The setting might be a church, a castle, a hillfort or an urban street-junction. In some cases, as at the ruined St Oswald's Priory, the information is presented in detail. Elsewhere, it is more concise. The key point is that all these places are publicly acknowledging Æthelflæd as a person of significance in their local histories. This is something that has yet to happen in a national context. Indeed, a line or two of printed text on a signboard in a midland town is, for many people, their first introduction to Æthelflæd. For others it is her image, vividly evoked in public art. One such artwork, an impressive monument next to the great mound of Tamworth Castle, has become so familiar as to be almost iconic. It takes the form of an ashlar column on a granite base, surmounted by the figures of Æthelflæd and

Athelstan. An inscription on the base says that the monument was commissioned in 1913 for millennial celebrations commemorating the foundation of the Tamworth burh. The Lady of the Mercians is here visualised as both military commander and foster-mother, holding a drawn sword while putting a protective arm around her young nephew. It is the best-known of a number of sculptural depictions and frequently appears in publications.[24]

A more recent sculpture, reproduced on the cover of this book, is part of a public artwork on Mersey Road in Runcorn. Created by Philip Bews and Diane Gorvin in 1994, the artwork takes the form of a Viking-style longship with Æthelflæd's head on the prow. She is facing west, gazing in the direction of Castle Rock, the probable site of her burh. Again, a prominent theme is her association with warfare, a longship here serving the same symbolic function as a sword. The metal fencing running along this stretch of Mersey Road forms part of 'Runcorn Promenade' and is divided into a series of illustrated panels, one of which shows Æthelflæd in profile looking out across the river towards a castellated structure on the far bank. Another sculptured head formerly stood on Runcorn's Wigg Island, a conservation area beside the River Mersey. Carved from a rough block of Cheshire stone, this was originally intended to show Æthelflæd keeping watch over the river. It was moved for protection from a nearby construction project and now stands outside the Brindley Theatre in the town centre.

At the opposite end of Mercia, the city of Gloucester unsurprisingly has its own representation of Æthelflæd in public art. A large concrete mural on the side of the Sainsbury's store in Hare Lane depicts the city's history from pre-Roman times to the modern era. Designed by Joyce and Henry Collins, it was unveiled in 1970 and shows Æthelflæd wearing a crown but carrying neither sword nor sceptre. She stands beside a crowned male figure armed with sword and shield who, at first glance, might be mistaken for Lord Æthelred. He is actually Osric, the seventh-century king of the Hwicce who reputedly founded Gloucester Cathedral. Moving east over the Danelaw boundary to Leicester, we find the submission of the city's Viking garrison commemorated by a small bronze statue of Æthelflæd. This was produced by Jack Newport in the late 1970s and can be seen in the courtyard of the Guildhall Museum. It depicts the Lady of the Mercians, with crown and sceptre, standing on a stone base adorned with the name 'Ethelfloeda' in bronze lettering. Turning back to the western midlands, the most recent sculptural representation of Æthelflæd on public display (at the time of writing) is at Wednesbury. Here, she appears as a 'caryatid' supporting an arched gateway at the entrance to the bus station. The arch was erected as part of a redevelopment project in 2004 to commemorate the history of the town, its other side being supported by a male figure representing a worker from the local tube-making industry. Æthelflæd is portrayed without a crown but with both hands clutching the hilt of a long sword, its blade pointing downwards. Not far away, on Holyhead Road, a large metal artwork forms a mural depicting Æthelflæd with spear and shield defiantly facing Viking enemies.

Among other examples of portraits in public art are those produced in stained glass. At Worcester Cathedral we see Æthelflæd standing alongside her husband in a small panel in one of the cloister windows. Both figures wear crowns, with Æthelred holding a spear and shield. The images were designed in the 1930s and belong to a chronological sequence telling the story of English Christianity, the emphasis being on famous people associated with Worcester. Æthelflæd's military aspect is again highlighted: she is shown wearing a breastplate and carrying a sword. In the window of St Andrew's Church at Churchdown, already mentioned above, she is portrayed in less warlike guise holding a sceptre and wearing her near-ubiquitous crown. At Chester Cathedral she is one of a number of early medieval figures in the impressive West Window of 1961. Here, she again appears in regal guise with crown and sceptre. She is accompanied by several saints, among them Werburgh and Oswald whose cults she actively promoted.

Away from public art, Æthelflæd occasionally appears in paintings used as book illustrations. As with the portraits in stone, metal and coloured glass, these usually highlight her war-leadership. In an early twentieth-century compendium of English history her assault on Brecon Mere in 916 is depicted in two monochrome plates reproduced from paintings by the acclaimed military artist Richard Caton Woodville (1856–1927).[25] In one, she is shown directing her troops as they attack the royal crannog; in the other, she speaks to a group of Welsh captives after the attack. From later in the same century comes one of the most striking images of Æthelflæd, a painting by the late Angus McBride (1931–2007) depicting her in the thick of battle. It visualises her as a helmeted rider wielding her sword from the saddle as her soldiers storm the Danish fortress at Derby.[26]

The Mercian shires

The modern counties or shires of the western midlands of England originated in an administrative reorganisation of Mercia undertaken in the tenth century.

Each shire was intended as the dependent territory of a burh which in later times became the county town. The shire was originally expected to provide manpower for the burh's garrison and for related duties such as maintaining the walls and other defences. The number of men required for the garrison was determined by a formula based on the length of the burh walls, this number then being used to calculate how much land – measured in 'hides' – was required for the shire, with each hide expected to provide one soldier. Most of the shires created from these calculations survived until the old county boundaries of England were redrawn in 1974. Until then, there was often a close correlation between medieval wall-lengths in west midland county towns and the size or 'hidage' of their respective counties. The creation of these shires was an extension of a similar process that had already been undertaken in Wessex, where the shires of Hampshire, Wiltshire, Somerset and Dorset were in existence by the late ninth century. This quartet was not only useful in dividing the West Saxon kingdom for military purposes but also helped the king to exercise tighter administrative control, each shire being placed under the authority of a royal ealdorman who acted as the king's representative.

The 'shiring' of western Mercia came later, but how much later is a matter of debate. Arguments have been put forward for various times in the tenth century, with some historians pointing to the aftermath of Edward the Elder's takeover of Mercia in 918 as the likeliest. Others look beyond Edward's reign to that of his son Athelstan (925–39) or to even later decades. It has even been suggested that the shires were the work of Æthelred and Æthelflæd, or of Æthelflæd alone.[27] In favour of such an early date is the fact that every county town in the western midlands began as a burh founded in the period when Æthelflæd and her husband were in power. Supporters of a later date point to the lack of correlation between the shires and ancient Mercian territorial units. The former Hwiccian sub-kingdom, for example, was partitioned between Worcestershire and Gloucestershire. Further north, Shropshire was created by joining the northern half of what had once been the territory of the Magonsæte with the southern half of the former Wrocensæte lands.[28] This apparent disregard for traditional Mercian boundaries has led to the shiring being seen as an initiative designed by Edward or his heirs to bring the western midlands into line with Wessex. It has also been noted that the Tamworth burh, occupying one of the most symbolically important sites in Mercia, never became a shire town. Instead, it sits on the border between Staffordshire and Warwickshire. A period after Æthelflæd's death would indeed seem to provide a plausible context for these administrative changes, with her brother the likely architect.[29] The document known as the Burghal Hidage – a list of mostly West Saxon burhs with corresponding hidage figures – may have been drawn up by Edward's officials as a template for calculating the new Mercian shires. This is not to wholly deny Æthelflæd and her husband a role in the process, even if they did not actually define or name any of today's counties. It is possible that they created 'burh-based administrative units' which can perhaps be envisaged as an intermediate layer of reorganisation between the tribal sub-kingdoms of ancient Mercia and the shires that replaced them.[30]

'Queen Ethelfleda'

The most recognisable modern image of Æthelflæd is the proud, sword-armed figure on top of a stone pillar beside Tamworth Castle. This is the 'spirited heroine' admired by William of Malmesbury and his peers in the 1100s, a woman who overturned traditional gender roles to surpass the achievements of many a king. We have no need to take this image further by picturing her as a female warrior in the literal sense, like a tenth-century Amazon fighting in the melee of battle. It is more accurate to think of her as a general directing her soldiers from the edge of a battlefield. Seeing her girded for war in her monument at Tamworth we are nonetheless reminded of her unique place in early English history as female ruler and military commander. To what extent this uniqueness was due to her personal qualities rather than to opportunities that happened to come her way is difficult to judge. Other highborn women of the Viking Age, if they had been offered the rulership of a kingdom, might have fared as well or better. As far as we know, Æthelflæd is the only woman who exercised such power over a period of years rather than months. She accepted the role willingly, with all the responsibilities that went with it, discharging her duties effectively. Whatever challenges she had to face as a lone female in a political landscape dominated by men she plainly overcame them. Her achievements show beyond doubt that she was the right person in the right place at the right time. She was instrumental in preserving Mercia as a distinct political entity and in making it once again a power to be reckoned with. In so doing she helped to consolidate the 'Kingdom of the Anglo-Saxons', out of which a new kingdom for all the English would emerge fifty years after her death. Alfred, Edward and their male heirs are often regarded as the founders of England but Æthelflæd played a role equal to theirs and deserves similar acclaim. Their reputations perhaps stand taller than hers because we are accustomed to calling them kings. If so, should we not accord her the same status by thinking of her as a queen? It cannot be denied that her bestowing of land and privileges and her command of armies were powers associated with monarchy. Indeed, in what were once the heartlands of her realm she is often commemorated today as 'Queen Ethelfleda'. While it might be argued that we should be wary of describing as queen a woman who may have been content to be addressed as *hlæfdige*, her achievements and her place in history make the regal title seem fitting.

APPENDIX: THE MERCIAN REGISTER ('THE ANNALS OF ÆTHELFLÆD')

902   Here Ealhswith passed away, and the same year was the battle at the Holme between the people of Kent and the Danes.

904   In this year the moon was eclipsed.

905   In this year a comet appeared.

907   In this year Chester was restored.

909   Here the body of St Oswald was brought from Bardney into Mercia.

910   Here the Mercians and West Saxons fought against the host near Tettenhall on 5 August and were victorious. And the same year Æthelflæd built the burh at Bremesbyrig.

911   Æthelred, Lord of the Mercians, passed away.

912   Here, on the eve of the Invention of the Holy Cross, Æthelflæd the Lady of the Mercians came to Scergeat and built the burh there, and the same year that at Brycge.

913   Here, with God's help, Æthelflæd the Lady of the Mercians went with all the Mercians to Tamworth and built the burh there in early summer, and afterwards before Lammas the one at Stafford.

914   Then in this, the next year, [was built the burh] at Eddisbury in the early summer. And later in the same year, late in harvest-time, the one at Warwick.

915   Then in this, the next year, [was built] the burh at Chirbury, and then that at Weardbyrig, and in the same year before midwinter the one at Runcorn.

916   Here the guiltless Abbot Ecgberht was slain before midsummer, on 16 June, with his companions. The same day was the feast of St Cyricus the Martyr. And three days later Æthelflæd sent an army into Wales and broke down Brecenanmere, and there took the king's wife as one of thirty-four people.

917   Here, before Lammas, with God's help Æthelflæd the Lady of the Mercians gained control of the fortress called Derby with all that belonged to it. Four thegns who were dear to her were slain there within the gates.

918   Here in the early part of the year, with God's help, she peacefully gained control of the fortress at Leicester, and the greater part of the army

attached to it were subjugated. The people of York promised – some by pledge, some by oaths – that they were willing to be under her direction. But very soon after they did this she died, twelve days before midsummer, in Tamworth, in the eighth year she held control of Mercia by rightful lordship. And her body lies in Gloucester in the east chapel of St Peter's church.

919   [i.e. late 918] Here also was the daughter of Æthelred, Lord of the Mercians, deprived of all authority in Mercia, and she was taken to Wessex three weeks before midwinter. She was called Ælfwynn.

921   Here King Edward built the burh at Cledemutha.

924   Here King Edward died at Farndon in Mercia. Very soon afterwards his son died at Oxford. Their bodies lie at Winchester. And Athelstan was chosen by the Mercians as king and consecrated at Kingston. And he gave his sister [over the sea to the son of the king of the Old Saxons].

NOTES

Chapter 1

1 The epithet was coined in the late tenth century to distinguish him from his great-grandson and namesake Edward 'the Martyr'.

2 Wormald 1983.

3 See further Downham 2007, xv–xx and Brink 2008.

4 In *Strathclyde and the Anglo-Saxons in the Viking Age*, published in 2014.

5 Swanton 1996, xviii.

6 Swanton 1996, xx.

7 Swanton 1996, xxv.

8 Swanton 1996, xxiii.

9 Swanton 1996, xix n. 35.

10 For an edition and translation of Æthelweard's *Chronicon* see A. Campbell (ed.) *The Chronicle of Æthelweard* (London, 1962).

11 On the authorship of this chronicle, see Darlington and McGurk 1995, 142. On its use of older sources, see Darlington and McGurk 1982.

12 Swanton 1996, xx.

13 On William of Malmesbury's reliability as a historian, see Winterbottom and Thomson 2002.

14 Plummer and Earle 1899, 92.

15 Stafford 2008, 102.

16 Szarmach 1998, 108.

17 For discussion of the Irish annals see S. Mac Airt and G. Mac Niocaill (eds) *The Annals of Ulster to 1131* (Dublin)

18 See Radner 1978 for a modern edition, translation and scholarly analysis of *FAI*.

19 For a useful discussion of the Welsh Annals, see Charles-Edwards 2013, 346–56.

20 An example being the story of Ingimund's arrival in Britain, on which see Chapter 5 below.

21 Among the chronicles used by Lloyd was *Brut y Tywysogion* ('Chronicle of the Princes'), a compilation of annals regarded by today's historians as an important source of early Welsh history.

22 Walker 2000, xv.

23 *Anglo-Saxon Charters*, Charter S.221.

24 Hill 2004, 21.

Chapter 2

1   Yorke 1989, 91.

2   Yorke 1989, 94.

3   *ASC* A, 552, 597, 855.

4   Asser, Chap. 1; *Historia Ecclesiastica Gentis Anglorum* (*HE*) iii, 7. The two eighth-century kings were Cynewulf (Charter S.256) and Cuthred (Charter S.262).

5   For further discussion, see Yorke 1995, 32–64, 171–3.

6   *HE* iv, 12.

7   Higham 2015, 156.

8   The five kings who came after Ine were Æthelheard (reigned 728 to 741), Cuthred (741 to 756), Sigeberht (756 to 757), Cynewulf (757 to 786) and Cyneheard (786).

9   The battle of 710 was noted in *ASC* but with no hint of the result. It was described as an English victory by the twelfth-century chronicler John of Worcester. The later reversal of fortune was recorded as 'the battle of Hehil among the Cornish' in *AC* and as a victory for the Britons. It is usually dated to 722.

10 Brooks 1989, 162.

11 Brooks 1989, 163.

12 Brooks 1989, 170.

13 Brooks 1989, 167.

14 For discussion of the Tribal Hidage, see Higham 1995, 74–111 and Featherstone 2001, 23–34.

15 Brooks 1989, 161.

16 On the Magonsæte, see Pretty 1989.

17 Eagles 1989, 211.

18 Higham 2015, 115.

19 *HE* iv, 13.

20 Fraser 2009, 310.

21 For a useful summary of the Mercian Ascendancy, see the first chapter of Walker 2000.

22 Keynes 1998, 2.

23 *ASC* 779: 'Here Cynewulf and Offa fought near *Benesingtun* and Offa took the town.'

24 Keynes 1998, 2.

25 *ASC* F 793: 'In this year terrible portents appeared in Northumbria and miserably afflicted the inhabitants: these were exceptional flashes of lightning, and fiery dragons were seen flying in the air, and soon followed a great famine, and after that in the same year the harrying of the heathen miserably destroyed God's church in Lindisfarne by rapine and slaughter.' Modern English translation in Garmonsway 1954, 54 and 56.

26 Keynes 1998, 3.

27 *ASC* 825: 'Here was a fight between the Welsh and the men of Devon at Gafulford.' In this context, the 'Welsh' are the Britons of Cornwall.

28 *ASC* A: 'And after Easter of the same year, King Æthelwulf gave his daughter in marriage to King Burgred, as from Wessex to Mercia.'

29 Yorke 1989, 96.

30 But see Keynes 1998, 4 n.14 on why Wiglaf's return is less likely to have been the result of a Mercian uprising against Ecgberht.

31 *ASC* A.

32 On the border dispute, see Stenton 1971, 234–5. On the coins, see Keynes 1998, 6.

33 *ASC* A.

34 Asser, Chap. 8.

35 Asser, Chap. 12.

36 Æthelwulf's will has not survived but we know of it from Asser's *Life* (Chap. 16) and from Alfred's will. See Keynes and Lapidge 1983, 174–5.

37 *ASC* A.

38 Keynes 2001b, 314, 322; Williams 1981. For a different view of pre-Viking Mercia, see Bassett 1996, 148–9. Note also the possibility that ninth-century Mercian ealdormen were royal appointees like those of Wessex (Walker, 2000, 6–8 and 161–3). The supposed dynastic stability of Wessex can, in any case, be questioned (Stafford 1981, 18; Insley 2016).

Chapter 3

1 Keynes 1998, 9 n. 34.

2 Keynes 1998, 9–10.

3 Asser, Chaps 29 and 73–4.

4 Stansbury 1993, 12.

5 The coins in question were discovered as recently as 2015. See J. Naylor and G. Williams, *King Alfred's Coins: the Watlington Viking Hoard* (Oxford, 2017).

6 *AC* 878. On Ceolwulf's possible involvement in the battle, see Charles-Edwards 2001, 101.

7 On the Danelaw, see Hadley 2000 and Abrams 2001.

8 *ASC* A: 'In this year the army went from Repton, and Halfdan went with part of the army into Northumbria, and took winter-quarters on the River Tyne; and the army overran that land, and made frequent raids against the Picts and against the Strathclyde Britons.' Modern English translation based on Garmonsway 1954, 73 and 75.

9 Asser, Chap. 53.

10 Æthelweard; Asser, Chap. 55; Keynes and Lapidge 1983, 248 n. 102.

11 Asser, Chap. 64.

12 Keynes and Lapidge 1983, 252, n. 125.

13 Asser, Chaps 67 and 72.

14 Lavelle 2010, 92–106.

15 On the threefold obligation or 'common burdens' see Abels 1988, 75–7. On its use in pre-Viking Mercia, see Bassett 2007, 55–8.

16 Abels 1988, 65–6.

17 Welch 2001, 158; Bassett 1996, 155–6; Bassett 2001, 5–6; Bassett 2007.

18 On the Burghal Hidage, see Hill and Rumble 1996. Note also that the burh garrisons probably included 'support' personnel as well as the fighting-men who defended the walls (Lavelle 2010, 65).

19 Charles-Edwards 2001, 101.

20 Asser, Chap. 80.

21 Keynes and Lapidge 1983, 263 n. 183.

22 Charles-Edwards 2013, 490–1.

23 Abels 1998, 181; Hill 2008, 91.

24 Charter S.218; Stenton 1971, 260; Walker 2000, 76.

25 Charter S.219; Walker 2000, 77.

26 Charter S.222. On Æthelred's exercising of 'royal' powers, see Walker 2000, 159–60.

27 An earlier date of 883 for the London campaign has also been suggested (see, for example, Keynes 1998, 22–3). On Lundenwic, see Cowie 2001.

28 Keynes 1998, 21–4.

29 Keynes 1998, 24–5.

30 Asser, Chap. 83.

31 Keynes and Lapidge 1983, 38 and 266 n. 200.

32 Attenborough 1922, i; Keynes and Lapidge 1983, 164.

33 Attenborough 1922, 120; Keynes and Lapidge 1983, 306 n. 6.

34 For example, Arman 2017, 82.

35 Cambridge, Corpus Christi College, MS 383.

36 Keynes and Lapidge 1983, 38. On the case for assigning an earlier date to the treaty, see Haslam 2006, 124–7.

37 Attenborough 1922, 99–101.

Chapter 4

1 Stafford 1981, 22. For a comprehensive study of women in Anglo-Saxon society, see Fell 1984.

2 Herbert 1997, 16. See also Dockray-Miller 2000, 43.

3 Stafford 2001, 35.

4 Stafford 1981, 4; Dockray-Miller 2000, 48.

5 Keynes and Lapidge 1983, 235 n. 28.

6 Asser, Chaps 13–14.

7 Stafford 1981, 3.

8 Stafford 1990, 57–9.

9 Herbert 1997, 33.

10 Stafford 2001, 44.

11 William of Malmesbury, *Gesta Regum*, ii, 5.

12 Bailey 2001, 113.

13 Herbert 1997, 24 n. 25.

14 Herbert 1997, 25.

15 Arman 2017, 112.

16 Herbert 1997, 24.

17 Bailey 2001, 114.

18 Keynes and Lapidge 1983, 35–6.

19 *ASC* A.

20 Arman 2017, 111.

21 Arman 2017, 113.

22 Charter S.223. On the antiquity of the Worcester bishopric, see Hooke 1985, 12–13.

23 Walker 2000, 81.

24 Harmer 1914, 54–5.

25 Hooke 1990, 103. This charter is numbered 223 in the Sawyer catalogue. On its religious dimension (e.g. the prayers to be sung for Mercia's rulers), see Thompson 2002, 17–18.

26 On the archaeology of the Worcester burh, see Baker et al. 1992.

27 The term 'capital' in the heading is anachronistic for the period but is used here for convenience. See also Thacker 1982, 209–10.

28 Heighway 2001, 103.

29 For a detailed discussion of the Anglo-Saxon period in Gloucester, see Heighway 1984.

30 Stansbury 1993, 124.

31 For further discussion, see Thompson 2002, 12–25.

32 On London's history in this period, see Vince 1990.

33 The two charters are S.346 of 889 and S.1628 of c.898. For discussion, see Dyson 1990.

34 Keynes and Lapidge 1983, 321 n. 58.

Chapter 5

1 Charter S.350; Keynes 2001a, 48.

2 On this lady see Stafford 2008, 208; Arman 2017, 126. See also Woolf 2001, 99 for a suggestion that she may have been Æthelflæd's sister Æthelgifu who was at that time abbess of Shaftesbury.

3 See Lavelle 2009 for discussion of Æthelwold's revolt.

4 Campbell 2001, 21.

5 Keynes 2001a, 49.

6 Keynes 2001a, 57.

7 Stansbury 1993, 153; Arman 2017, 95.

8 Hookway 2015, 24.

9 Bassett 1991, 18–19. Note also the alternative view that Shrewsbury did not become a burh until later in the tenth century (Baker 2010, 89; Sharp 2013).

10 Cranage 1922; Parsons 2001, 61–2.

11 Foot 2011, 31. But see Insley 2016 for a more sceptical view.

12 Holland 2016, 36. On the charters, see Foot 2011, 206 and Hare 1999, 36–7.

13 Foot 2011, 33.

14 Charters S.365 and S.366; Foot 2011, 37 n. 27.

15 William of Malmesbury, *Gesta Regum*, ii, 6.

16 Asser, Chap. 75.

17 Foot 2011, 36.

18 *ASC* A.

19 Keynes 1998, 39 n. 168; Yorke 2001, 36.

20 Hart 1992, 515.

21 *AU* 902; Downham 2007, 26–7.

22 Griffiths 2001, 179.

23 Downham 2007, 207–8.

24 Harding 2011, 357.

25 Downham 2007, 208. It is worth considering that Æthelflæd may have sold the land to the Norse settlers rather than simply bestowing it as a gift (Quanrud 2015, n. 89).

26 The tradition and the date of 875 were mentioned by Ranulf Hidgen, a monk at St Werburgh's Abbey (the precursor of Chester Cathedral) in the early fourteenth century.

27 On Chester's archaeology in this period, see Ward 2001.

28 Higham 1993, 116.

29 For the belief that the bridge was Æthelflædan, see J. Hemingway, *Panorama of the City of Chester* (Chester, 1836), 31. See E. Jervoise, *The Ancient Bridges of Wales and Western England*, vol. 4 (London, 1936), 25 on the idea that Æthelflæd's burh was served by a ferry.

30 On the Chester coinage and its attribution to Æthelflæd, see Karkov 1995, Lyon 2001, 72–3 and Naismith 2014, 39–41.

31 Wainwright 1948; Charles-Edwards 2013, 502.

32 Charter S.367.

Chapter 6

1 Downham 2007, 86.

2 *ASC* A 909. Modern English translation in Garmonsway 1954, 96. Note a recent suggestion that the 'northern army' referred to by the chroniclers was not a Danish force from York but a Norse one from west of the Pennines (Quanrud 2015, 76–8).

3 Æthelweard, iv, 4.

4 See also Downham 2007, 88–9 for discussion. The notion that Æthelred's overlordship in Northumbria encompassed York has been questioned (Quanrud 2015, 79).

5 MR 910: 'Her Myrce & Westseaxe gefuhton wið þone here neh Teotanheale on .viii. Idus Agustus, & sige hæfdon' ('Here the Mercians and West Saxons fought against the host near Tettenhall on 6 August and were victorious'). The chronicler's date is usually corrected to 5 August.

6 Arman 2017, 257 n. 7.

7 For a detailed investigation of the battle's geographical context, see Horovitz 2017.

8 Smallshire 1978, 23.

9 Dumville 2004, 88–9.

10 Wainwright 1959, 56.

11 *HE* iii, 9. The location of Maserfelth is uncertain (see Thacker 1995, 99).

12 Thacker 2001, 256.

13 See, for example, Arman 2017, 148.

14 Arman 2017, 152.

15 Thacker 1995, 120–1.

16 Thacker 1995, 106.

17 Thacker 1995, 121.

18 Wainwright 1959, 58.

19 For example, Wolfe 2012, 26.

20 The case for identifying Bromborough as Bremesbyrig has been dismissed by Steven Bassett

(2001, 17 n. 59). On the battle of Brunanburh and the case for placing it at Bromborough see Cavill 2011, 344–8.

21 Walker 2000, 100; Bassett 2001, 12; Sharp 2013.

22 Armitage 1912.

23 Conigree Hill, near Bromsberrow, was suggested by Taylor 1893, 90.

24 Campbell 2001, 21–2.

25 See also Walker 2000, 99.

26 On the derivation and meaning of Quat-, see Horovitz 2017, 83–5.

27 Baker and Brookes 2013, 155.

28 Stone 2017, 62.

29 Stone 2017, 69. Bridgnorth is not mentioned in the Domesday Book of 1086.

30 Wainwright 1959, 58; Sharp 2013.

31 Coates 1998, 9. Jane Wolfe (2012, 26) suggested that Scergeat may have guarded the gap between Offa's Dyke and the earlier Wat's Dyke and proposed Old Oswestry hillfort as a candidate.

32 Horovitz 2017, 134–52.

33 Stansbury 1993, 196–7.

34 Modern English translation in Garmonsway 1954, 96.

Chapter 7

1 Blair 1986.

2 MR 913: 'Her Gode forgifendum for Æthelflæd Myrcna hlæfdige mid eallum Myrcum to Tamaweorthige & tha burh thær getimbrede on foreweardne sumor.'

3 Bassett 2011, 16–17.

4 Pollington 2011, 14.

5 Pollington 2011, 16.

6 Pollington 2011, 19.

7 Pollington 2011, 38.

8 Traces of the hall were found near Bolebridge Street in 1968 (Pollington 2011, 41).

9 Sheridan 1973.

10 Rahtz and Sheridan 1971.

11 She was identified as Edith by the thirteenth-century chronicler Roger of Wendover but was left unnamed by William of Malmesbury in the previous century.

12 Thacker 2001, 257–8.

13 Thacker 1985.

14 For the archaeology of Anglo-Saxon Stafford, see Carver 2010a and 2010b, 19–23. On Stafford Ware, see Ford 1999.

15 Carver 2010a.

16 Arman 2017, 196.

17 Stone 2017, 53.

18 Varley 1950.

19 On the clay oven, see Garner 2012, 66 and Stone 2017, 54.

20 Griffiths 2001, 174. See also Higham 1988, 202. For an argument against seeing Castle Ditch as the site of the burh, see Sharp 2013.

21 Bassett 2009.

22 Downham 2007, 28.

23 Downham 2007, 266.

24 *AU*; Downham 2007, 91.

25 *ASC* D. Modern English translation in Garmonsway 1954, 100.

26 Wainwright 1959, 59.

27 For example, Clark 1889, 210.

28 Wainwright 1960.

29 Stone 2017, 71–2.

30 Stone 2017, 75.

31 *Contra* Bailey 2001, 119.

32 Support for Warburton's case was offered by Wolfe 2012, 25.

33 Nevell 2002, 1.

34 Wainwright 1959, 64 n.1; Dodgson 1970, 34–5.

35 Whitchurch: Stansbury 1993, 196–7; Gwespyr: Coates 1998. The case for the Oxfordshire Warborough is weak: see Elmore Jones and Blunt 1958.

36 On the Weardburh coin, see Elmore-Jones and Blunt 1958.

37 Charter S. 225; Sawyer 1968, 127; Keynes 1998, 37 n. 159.

38 Dodgson 1970, 176.

39 Hanshall 1823, 418.

40 Nickson 1887, 6–13.

41 But note that the identification of Castle Rock as the site of the burh has been doubted (Bassett 2001, 17).

42 Higham 1988, 203; Stone 2017, 218.

43 Baggs 1980.

Chapter 8

1 MR 916: 'Her wærð Ecgbriht abbud unscyldig ofslegen foran to middan sumera on .xvi. Kalendas Iulii, þy ilcan dæge wæs Sancte Ciricius tid þæs þroweres, mid his geferum, & þæs ymb .iii. niht sende Æþelflæd fyrde on Wealas & abræc Brecenanmere & þær genam þæs cinges wif feower & ðritiga sume' ('Here the guiltless Abbot Ecgberht was slain before midsummer, on 16 June, with his companions. The same day was the feast of St Cyricus the Martyr. And three days later Æthelflæd sent an army into Wales and broke down Brecenanmere, and there took the king's wife as one of thirty-four people.') Although the chronicler says that Æthelflæd 'sent' an army, her presence as commander is implied by the rest of the text.

2 Stone 2017, 71.

3 On the archaeology of the Llangorse Lake crannog, see Campbell and Lane 1989.

4 Davies 1990, 67–71; Insley 2016.

5 Walker (2000, 100) places the divide between Æthelflæd's and Edward's campaigns on the River Welland.

6 *ASC* A. Modern English translation in Garmonsway 1954, 101.

7 Wainwright 1959, 61 n. 2.

8 Hall 1989, 156–7.

9 Powel, *Historie*, 39. Powel's original text has here been partly modernised. John Castoreus, also known as John of London, was a monk and chronicler active in the early 1300s.

10 Meijns 2010, 476.

11 *ASC* A. Modern English translation in Garmonsway 1954, 102.

12 Abrams 2001, 138.

13 Abrams 2001, 139.

14 Downham 2007, 31.

15 MR: 'Her heo begeat on hire geweald mid Godes fultume on foreweardne gear gesybsumlice þa burh æt Ligraceastre, & se mæsta dæl þæs herges þe ðærto hirde wearð underþeoded.'

16 Woolf 2007, 191.

17 *FAI*, 459 (Translation based on Radner 1978, pp. 182–3).

18 *CKA*, p. 9 of Skene's edition (Translation in Anderson 1922, 444–6).

19 Clarkson 2014, 62.

20 *FAI*, 459 (Translation in Radner 1978, p. 182).

21 Wainwright 1959, 64.

22 On the *History of St Cuthbert*, see T. Johnson-South (ed. and trans.) *Historia de Sancto Cuthberto* (Cambridge, 2002).

23 For discussion, see Clarkson 2014, 69–70.

24 On Æthelflæd's death and burial, see Thompson 2002, 8–25.

25 Heighway 2001, 106.

Chapter 9

1 Modern English translation in Garmonsway 1954, 103.

2 'Ac swiðe hrædlice þæs ðe hi þæs geworden hæfde, heo gefor .xii. nihtun ær middan sumera binnan Tamaweorþige ðy eahtoþan geare þæs ðe heo Myrcna anweald mid riht hlaforddome healdende wæs, & hyre lic lið binnan Gleawcestre on þam east portice Sancte Petres cyrcean.'

3 'Her eac wearð Æþeredes dohtor Myrcna hlafordes ælces anwealdes on Myrcum benumen, & on Westsexe aleded þrim wucum ær middan wintra, seo wæs haten Ælfwyn.'

4 Charter S.225.

5 Bailey 2001, 120.

6 Arman 2017, 208.

7 Stafford 2008, 111.

8 See also Stafford 2008, 113 and Griffiths 2001, 180.

9 Bailey 2001, 117; see also Arman 2017, 209–10 and Foot 2011, 15.

10 Powel, *Historie*, 40. Powel's original text has here been partly modernised.

11 Bailey 2001, 122.

12 Bailey 2001, 125.

13 Charles-Edwards 2013, 504.

14   But see Molyneaux (2015, 28) on the possibility that Lincoln may have remained in Scandinavian hands under the sway of Northumbria.

15   The entry appears in the D and E texts of *ASC*. See Downham 2007, 93–5 on the date of Ragnall's arrival at York.

16   Higham 1988, 207–9.

17   Dodgson 1970, 138.

18   Griffiths 2001, 178.

19   Higham 1988, 212–4.

20   *ASC* 920. See Clarkson 2014, 72–4 for discussion.

21   Davidson 2001, 209.

22   Griffiths 2001, 171.

23   Griffiths 2001, 182.

24   'Her Eadweard cing gefor on Myrcum æt Fearndune, & Ælfweard his sunu swiþe hraþe þæs gefor on Oxnaforda, & heora lic licgað on Wintanceastre, & Æþestan wæs of Myrcum gecoren to cinge & æt Cingestune gehalgod . . .'

25   Foot 2011, 39.

26   Foot 2011, 38.

27   Foot 2011, 74.

28   Molyneaux 2011.

29   The poem in question is *Armes Prydein Vawr* ('The Great Prophecy of Britain'). On the date of composition, see Breeze 1999. See also Bollard and Haycock 2011, 245–62.

30   On the disappearance of Mercian identity, see Insley 2016. In 1007, a royal official called Eadric Streona was described as the ealdorman 'of the kingdom of the Mercians', but he was not an independent ruler.

Chapter 10

1   Wainwright 1959, 65.

2   Dockray-Miller 2000, 56.

3   Wainwright 1959, 68. See also Hollis 1992, 216, on the case for seeing Æthelflæd's Mercia as a threat to Edward's interests.

4   Wolfe 2012, 20.

5   Walker 2000, 119.

6   Fell 1984, 92.

7   William of Malmesbury, *Gesta Regum*, ii, 5.

8   Wolfe 2012, 19.

9   Henry of Huntingdon, Book 5. On Henry's verse, see Szarmach 1998, 125–6.

10   Chance 1986, 610.

11   On Boudica as national heroine, see Frénée-Hutchins 2014.

12   Wainwright 1959; Dockray-Miller 2000, 62.

13   Dockray-Miller 2000, 55.

14   Annie Whitehead, *To Be A Queen* (London, 2013). See also V.M. Whitworth's *The Bone Thief* (London, 2012) for a fictionalised but historically authentic retelling of the retrieval of St Oswald's relics from Bardney.

15   Bernard Cornwell, *The Last Kingdom* (London, 2004).

16   The tradition was mentioned by the seventeenth-century antiquary Sir William Dugdale on page 298 of his *Antiquities of Warwickshire* (1656).

17   On the Victorian interest in Alfred, see Parker 2007. For a comparison of the attention paid to Edward and Æthelflæd in this period, see Higham 2001, 8–9.

18   Hackwood 1902, 8–11 (on the toponym) and 19–20 (on Æthelflæd).

19   *The Natural History of Staffordshire* (Oxford, 1686)

20   Traces of ancient defences were noted in J. Nightingale, *The Beauties of England and Wales*. Vol. 13, part 2 (London, 1813), 19. On the Iron Age ditch see Wallis 2008. See further Hodder 1992 on the archaeology of Wednesbury.

21   *Express & Star* newspaper (online version) 12 July 2013: 'Wednesbury memorial is set in stone after brass plaque theft'.

22   See Smithe 1889, 274, on the stonework. The suggestion of a connection with Æthelflæd is attributed to Reverend William Bazeley (b. 1843), a well-known Gloucestershire antiquary.

23   Nichols 2005, 92.

24   At the time of writing, a new sculpture of Æthelflæd (created by artist Luke Perry) is due to be installed at Tamworth railway station.

25   The paintings appeared in *Hutchinson's Story of the British Nation* (London, 1922).

26   Newark 1989.

27   Stansbury 1993, 194. On the case for a date after c.950, see Molyneaux 2015, 162–4.

28   Walker 2000, 163. Hookway 2015, 36. See also Gelling 1992, 139–42. For a detailed study of the creation of Herefordshire see Waddington 2015.

29   Stenton 1971, 337; Loyn 1984, 133–7. See also Hill 2001, 144–5.

30   The phrase in inverted commas comes from Walker 2000, 164. See also Bassett 1996, 147–57.

BIBLIOGRAPHY

Primary Sources

AC Annales Cambriae (Welsh Annals). J. Morris (ed. and trans.) *Nennius: British History and the Welsh Annals* (Chichester, 1980)

Æthelweard, *Chronicon* A. Campbell (ed.) *The Chronicle of Æthelweard* (London, 1962)

Anglo-Saxon Charters Translations used in this book are from Harmer 1914 and Attenborough 1922. The definitive modern collection is P. Sawyer (ed.) *Anglo-Saxon Charters: an Annotated List and Bibliography* (London, 1968), accessible in electronic form via the online E-Sawyer database (http:// esawyer.org.uk). In the chapter endnotes above, charters are cited by 'Sawyer number' prefixed by S.

ASC Anglo-Saxon Chronicle. Translations used in this book are mainly from Garmonsway 1954 and Swanton 1996.

Asser, *Life of King Alfred* S.D. Keynes and M. Lapidge (eds and trans) *Alfred the Great: Asser's Life of King Alfred and Other Contemporary Sources* (Harmondsworth, 1983)

AU The Annals of Ulster. S. Mac Airt and G. Mac Niocaill (eds) *The Annals of Ulster to 1131* (Dublin)

CKA Chronicle of the Kings of Alba. W.F. Skene (ed.) *Chronicles of the Picts, Chronicles of the Scots, and Other Early Memorials of Scottish History* (Edinburgh, 1867). Selected English translations in A.O. Anderson (ed.) *Early Sources of Scottish History, AD 500 to 1286.* Vol. 1 (Edinburgh, 1922)

FAI Fragmentary Annals of Ireland. J. Radner (ed. and trans.) *The Fragmentary Annals of Ireland* (Dublin, 1978)

Henry of Huntingdon, *Historia Anglorum* D. Greenway (ed.) *Historia Anglorum: History of the English People* (Oxford, 1996)

HE Bede, *Historia Ecclesiastica Gentis Anglorum.* J. McClure and R. Collins (eds) *Bede: the Ecclesiastical History of the English People* (Oxford, 1994)

John of Worcester, *Chronicon* R. Darlington and P. McGurk (eds) *The Chronicle of John of Worcester. Vol. 2: The Annals from 450 to 1066* (Oxford, 1995)

MR   Mercian Register. Translations used in this book are mainly from Garmonsway 1954 and Swanton 1996.

Powel, *Historie*   David Powel, *Historie of Cambria, now called Wales*. Reprinted for John Harding (London, 1811)

William of Malmesbury, *Gesta Regum Anglorum*   R.A.B. Mynors, R.M. Thomson and M. Winterbottom (eds) *William of Malmesbury, Gesta Regum Anglorum*. Vol. 1. (Oxford, 1998)

Modern scholarship

Abels, R. (1988) *Lordship and Military Obligation in Anglo-Saxon England* (Berkeley)

Abels, R. (1998) *Alfred the Great: War, Kingship and Culture in Anglo-Saxon England* (London)

Abrams, L. (2001) 'Edward the Elder's Danelaw', pp. 128–43 in N.J. Higham and D.H. Hill (eds) *Edward the Elder, 899–924* (London)

Anderson, A.O. (ed.) *Early Sources of Scottish History, AD 500 to 1286*. Vol. 1 (Edinburgh, 1922)

Arman, J. (2017) *The Warrior Queen: the Life and Legend of Æthelflæd, Daughter of Alfred the Great* (Stroud)

Armitage, E. (1912) *The Early Norman Castles of the British Isles* (London)

Attenborough, F.L. (ed.) (1922) *The Laws of the Earliest English Kings* (Cambridge)

Baggs, A.P. et al. (1980) 'House of Augustinian Canons: the Abbey of Norton', pp. 165–71 in *A History of the County of Chester*. Vol. 3. (London, 1980) via British History Online http://www.british-history.ac.uk/vch/ches/vol3/pp165-171 [accessed 2 March 2018].

Bailey, M. (2001) 'Ælfwynn, Second Lady of the Mercians', pp. 112–27 in N.J. Higham and D.H. Hill (eds) *Edward the Elder, 899–924* (London)

Baker, J. and Brookes, S. (2013) *Beyond the Burghal Hidage: Anglo-Saxon Civil Defence in the Viking Age* (Leiden)

Baker N., Dalwood, H., Holt, R., Mundy, C. and Taylor, G. (1992) 'From Roman to Medieval Worcester: Development and Planning in the Anglo-Saxon City', *Antiquity* 66: 65–74

Baker, N. (2010) *Shrewsbury: an Archaeological Assessment of an English Border Town* (Oxford)

Bassett, S. (1991) 'Anglo-Saxon Shrewsbury and its Churches', *Midland History* 16: 1–23

Bassett, S. (1996) 'The Administrative Landscape of the Diocese of Worcester in the Tenth Century', pp. 147–73 in N. Brooks and C. Cubitt (eds) *St Oswald of Worcester: Life and Influence* (London)

Bassett, S. (2001) 'Anglo-Saxon Fortifications in Western Mercia', *Midland History* 36: 1–23

Bassett, S. (2007) 'Divide and Rule: the Military Infrastructure of Eighth- and Ninth-Century Mercia', *Early Medieval Europe* 15: 53–85

Bassett, S. (2009) 'Anglo-Saxon Warwick', *Midland History* 34: 123–55

Biddle, M. and Kjølbye-Biddle, B. (1988) 'The So-Called Roman Building at Much Wenlock', *Journal of the British Archaeological Association* 141: 178–83

Blair, J. (1986) 'Hook Norton, *Regia Villa*', *Oxonensia* 51: 63–7

Bollard, J.K. and Haycock, M. (2011) 'The Welsh Sources Pertaining to the Battle', pp. 245–68 in M. Livingston (ed.) *The Battle of Brunanburh: a Casebook* (Exeter)

Breeze, A.C. (1999) 'The Battle of Brunanburh and Welsh Tradition', *Neophilologus* 83: 479–82

Brink, S. (2008) 'Who Were the Vikings?', pp. 4–7 in S. Brink and N. Price (eds) *The Viking World* (London)

Brooks, N. (1989) 'The Formation of the Mercian Kingdom', pp. 159–70 in S. Bassett (ed.) *The Origins of Anglo-Saxon Kingdoms* (Leicester)

Campbell, E. and Lane, A. (1989) 'Llangorse: a 10th-Century Royal Crannog in Wales', *Antiquity* 63: 675–81

Campbell, J. (2001) 'What is Not Known About the Reign of Edward the Elder', pp. 12–24 in N.J. Higham and D.H. Hill (eds) *Edward the Elder, 899–924* (London)

Carver, M. (2010a) *The Birth of a Borough: an Archaeological Study of Anglo-Saxon Stafford* (Woodbridge)

Carver, M. (2010b) 'Four Windows on Early Britain', *Haskins Society Journal* 22: 1–24

Cavill, P. (2011) 'The Place-Name Debate', pp. 327–49 in M. Livingston (ed.) *The Battle of Brunanburh: a Casebook* (Exeter)

Chance, J. (1986) *Woman as Hero in Old English Literature* (Syracuse)

Charles-Edwards, T.M. (2001) 'Wales and Mercia, 613–918', pp. 89–105 in M.P. Brown and C. Farr (eds) *Mercia: an Anglo-Saxon Kingdom in Europe* (London)

Charles-Edwards, T.M. (2013) *Wales and the Britons, 350–1064* (Oxford)

Clark, G.T. (1889) 'Contribution Towards a Complete List of Moated Mounds or Burhs', *Archaeological Journal* 46: 197–217

Clarkson, T. (2014) *Strathclyde and the Anglo-Saxons in the Viking Age* (Edinburgh)

Coates, R. (1998) 'Æthelflæd's Fortification of Weardburh', *Notes and Queries* 45 (1): 9–12

Cowie, R. (2001) 'Mercian London', pp. 194–209 in M.P. Brown and C. Farr (eds) *Mercia: an Anglo-Saxon Kingdom in Europe* (London)

Cranage, D.H.S. (1922) 'The Monastery of St. Milburge at Much Wenlock, Shropshire', *Archaeologia* 72: 105–32

Darlington, R. and McGurk, P. (1982) 'The *Chronicon ex Chronicis* of Florence of Worcester and its Use of Sources for English History before 1066', *Anglo-Norman Studies* 5: 185–96

Davidson, M.R. (2001) 'The (Non-)Submission of the Northern Kings in 920', pp. 200–11 in N.J. Higham and D.H. Hill (eds) *Edward the Elder, 899–924* (London)

Davies, W. (1990) *Patterns of Power in Early Wales* (Oxford)

Dockray-Miller, M. (2000) *Motherhood and Mothering in Anglo-Saxon England* (New York)

Dodgson, J.M. (1970) *The Place-Names of Cheshire*. Vol 2 (Cambridge)

Downham, C. (2007) *Viking Kings of Britain and Ireland: the Dynasty of Ivarr to AD 1014* (Edinburgh)

Dumville, D.N. (2004) 'Old Dubliners and New Dubliners in Ireland and Britain: a Viking-Age Story', *Medieval Dublin* 6: 78–93

Dyson, T. (1990) 'King Alfred and the Restoration of London', *London Journal* 15: 99–110

Eagles, B. (1989) 'Lindsey', pp. 202–12 in S. Bassett (ed.) *The Origins of Anglo-Saxon Kingdoms* (Leicester)

Elmore Jones, F. and Blunt, C.E. (1958) 'The Tenth-Century Mint æt Weardbyrig', *British Numismatic Journal* 28: 494–8

Featherstone, P. (2001) 'The Tribal Hidage and the Ealdormen of Mercia', pp. 23–34 in M.P. Brown and C. Farr (eds) *Mercia: an Anglo-Saxon Kingdom in Europe* (London)

Fell, C. (1984) *Women in Anglo-Saxon England* (London)

Foot, S. (2011) *Athelstan: the First King of England* (London)

Ford, D.A. (1999) 'A Late Saxon Pottery Industry in Staffordshire: a Review', *Medieval Ceramics* 22–3: 47–65

Fraser, J.E. (2009) *From Caledonia to Pictland: Scotland to 795* (Edinburgh)

Frénée-Hutchins, S. (2014) *Boudica's Odyssey in Early Modern England* (Farnham)

Garmonsway, G.N. (1954) *The Anglo-Saxon Chronicle*. 2nd edn (London)

Garner, D. (2012) *Hillforts of the Cheshire Sandstone Ridge* (Chester)

Gelling, M. (1992) *The West Midlands in the Early Middle Ages* (Leicester)

Griffiths, D. (2001) 'The North-West Frontier', pp. 167–87 in N.J. Higham and D.H. Hill (eds) *Edward the Elder, 899–924* (London)

Hackwood, F.W. (1902) *Wednesbury Ancient and Modern* (Wednesbury)

Hadley, D.M. (2000) *The Northern Danelaw: Its Social Structure, c. 800–1100* (London)

Hall, R.A. (1989) 'The Five Boroughs of the Danelaw: a Review of Present Knowledge', *Anglo-Saxon England* 18: 149–206

Hanshall, J.H. (1823) *History of the County Palatine of Chester.* 2nd edn (Chester)

Harding, S. (2011) 'Wirral: Folklore and Locations', pp. 351–64 in M. Livingston (ed.) *The Battle of Brunanburh: a Casebook* (Exeter)

Hare, M. (1999) 'The Documentary Evidence for the History of St Oswald's, Gloucester, to 1086 AD', pp. 33–45 in C. Heighway and R. Bryant (eds) *The Golden Minster: the Anglo-Saxon Minster and Later Medieval Priory of St Oswald in Gloucester* (York)

Harmer, F. (ed.) (1914) *Select English Historical Documents of the Ninth and Tenth Centuries* (Cambridge)

Hart, C. (1992) *The Danelaw* (London)

Haslam, J. (2006) 'King Alfred and the Vikings: Strategy and Tactics, 876–886 AD', *Anglo-Saxon Studies in Archaeology and History* 13: 122–54

Heighway, C. (1984) 'Saxon Gloucester', pp. 359–83 in J. Haslam (ed.) *Anglo-Saxon Towns in Southern England* (Chichester)

Heighway, C. (2001) 'Gloucester and the New Minster of St Oswald', pp. 102–11 in N.J. Higham and D.H. Hill (eds) *Edward the Elder, 899–924* (London)

Herbert, K. (1997) *Peace-Weavers and Shield-Maidens: Women in Early English Society* (Little Downham)

Higham, N.J. (1988) 'The Cheshire Burhs and the Mercian Frontier to 924', *Transactions of the Lancashire and Cheshire Antiquarian Society* 85: 193–222

Higham, N.J. (1993) *The Origins of Cheshire* (Manchester)

Higham, N.J. (1995) *An English Empire: Bede and the Early Anglo-Saxon Kings* (Manchester)

Higham, N.J. (2001) 'Edward the Elder's Reputation: an Introduction', pp. 1–11 in N.J. Higham and D.H. Hill (eds) *Edward the Elder, 899–924* (London)

Higham, N.J. (2015) *Ecgfrith: King of the Northumbrians, High-King of Britain* (Donington)

Hill, D.H. (1996) 'The Calculation and the Purpose of the Burghal Hidage', pp. 92–7 in D.H. Hill and A.R. Rumble (eds) *The Defence of Wessex: the Burghal Hidage and Anglo-Saxon Fortifications* (Manchester)

Hill, D.H. (2001) 'The Shiring of Mercia – Again', pp. 144–59 in N.J. Higham and D.H. Hill (eds) *Edward the Elder, 899–924* (London)

Hill, D.H. and Rumble, A.R. (eds) (1996) *The Defence of Wessex: the Burghal Hidage and Anglo-Saxon Fortifications* (Manchester)

Hill, P. (2004) *The Age of Athelstan: Britain's Forgotten History* (Stroud)

Hill, P. (2008) *The Viking Wars of Alfred the Great* (Barnsley)

Hodder, M.A. (1992) 'Excavations in Wednesbury, 1988 and 1989: the Medieval and Post-Medieval Settlement and the Seventeenth-Century Pottery Industry', *Transactions of the Staffordshire Archaeological and Historical Society* 32: 96–115

Holland, T. (2016) *Athelstan: the Making of England* (London)

Hollis, S. (1992) *Anglo-Saxon Women and the Church* (Woodbridge)

Hollis, S. (2003) 'Æthelflæd of Mercia', pp. 5–7 in R. Pennington and R. Higham (eds) *Amazons to Fighter Pilots: a Biographical Dictionary of Military Women*. Vol. 1 (Westport)

Hooke, D. (1985) *The Anglo-Saxon Landscape: the Kingdom of the Hwicce* (Manchester)

Hooke, D. (1990) *Worcestershire Anglo-Saxon Charter Bounds* (Woodbridge)

Hookway, E.N. (2015) 'Archaeological Analysis of Anglo-Saxon Shropshire, AD 600–1066'. Unpublished MRes thesis, University of Birmingham.

Horovitz, D. (2017) *Æthelflæd, Lady of the Mercians; the Battle of Tettenhall; and Other West Mercian Studies* (Stafford)

Insley, C. (2016), 'Collapse, Reconfiguration or Renegotiation? The Strange End of the Mercian Kingdom, 850–924', *Reti Medievali Revista* 17: 231–49

Karkov, C.E. (1995) 'Æthelflæd's Exceptional Coinage?', *Old English Newsletter* 29.1: 41.

Keynes, S. (1998) 'King Alfred and the Mercians', pp. 1–45 in M.A.S. Blackburn and D.N. Dumville (eds) *Kings, Currency and Alliances: History and Coinage of Southern England in the Ninth Century* (Woodbridge)

Keynes, S. (2001a) 'Edward, King of the Anglo-Saxons', pp. 40–66 in N.J. Higham and D.H. Hill (eds) *Edward the Elder, 899–924* (London)

Keynes, S. (2001b) 'Mercia and Wessex in the Ninth Century', pp. 310–28 in M.P. Brown and C. Farr (eds) *Mercia: an Anglo-Saxon Kingdom in Europe* (London)

Keynes, S. and Lapidge, M. (eds and trans) (1983) *Alfred the Great: Asser's Life of King Alfred and Other Contemporary Sources* (Harmondsworth)

Lavelle, R. (2009) 'The Politics of Rebellion: the Ætheling Æthelwold and West Saxon Royal Succession, 899–902', pp. 51–80 in P. Skinner (ed.) *Challenging the Boundaries of Medieval History: the Legacy of Timothy Reuter* (Turnhout)

Lavelle, R. (2010) *Alfred's Wars: Sources and Interpretations of Anglo-Saxon Warfare in the Viking Age* (Woodbridge)

Loyn, H.R. (1984) *The Governance of Anglo-Saxon England, 500–1087* (London)

Lyon, S. (2001) 'The Coinage of Edward the Elder', pp. 67–79 in N.J. Higham and D.H. Hill (eds) *Edward the Elder, 899–924* (London)

Mac Airt, S. and Mac Niocaill, G. (eds and trans.) (1983) *The Annals of Ulster, to AD 1131* (Dublin)

Meijns, B. (2010) 'The Policy on Relic Translations of Baldwin II of Flanders (879–918), Edward of Wessex (899–924), and Æthelflæd of Mercia (d.924): a Key to Anglo-Flemish Relations?', pp. 473–93 in D. Rollason, C. Leyser and H. Williams (eds) *England and the Continent in the Tenth Century: Studies in Honour of Wilhelm Levison (1876-1947)* (Turnhout)

Molyneaux, G. (2015) *The Formation of the English Kingdom in the Tenth Century* (Oxford)

Naismith, R. (2014) 'Prelude to Reform: Tenth-Century English Coinage in Perspective', pp. 38–84 in R. Naismith, M. Allen and E. Screen (eds) *Early Medieval Monetary History: Studies in Memory of Mark Blackburn* (Farnham)

Nevell, M. (2002) *St Werburgh's Old Church, Warburton, Cheshire* (London)

Newark, T. (1989) *Women Warlords: an Illustrated Military History of Female Warriors* (London)

Nichols, P.W. (2005) 'Excavations at St Andrew's Church, Churchdown, Gloucestershire, 2000', *Transactions of the Bristol and Gloucestershire Archaeological Society* 123: 87–93

Nickson, C. (1887) *History of Runcorn* (London)

Parker, J. (2007) *'England's Darling': The Victorian Cult of Alfred the Great* (Manchester)

Parsons, D. (2001) 'The Mercian Church: Archaeology and Topography', pp. 51–68 in M.P. Brown and C. Farr (eds) *Mercia: an Anglo-Saxon Kingdom in Europe* (London)

Plummer, C. and Earle, J. (eds) (1899) *Two of the Saxon Chronicles Parallel*. Vol. 1 (Oxford)

Pollington, S. (2011) *Tamworth: the Ancient Capital of Mercia* (Tamworth)

Pretty, K. (1989) 'Defining the Magonsæte', pp. 171–83 in S. Bassett (ed.) *The Origins of Anglo-Saxon Kingdoms* (Leicester)

Quanrud, J. (2015) 'Taking Sides: North-West England Vikings at the Battle of Tettenhall, AD 910', pp. 71–93 in S. Harding, D. Griffiths and E. Royles (eds) *In Search of Vikings: Interdisciplinary Approaches to the Scandinavian Heritage of North-West England* (London)

Radner, J. (ed. and trans.) *The Fragmentary Annals of Ireland* (Dublin, 1978)

Rahtz, P. and Sheridan, K. (1971) 'Fifth Report of Excavations at Tamworth, Staffs., 1971 – a Saxon Water Mill in Bolebridge Street – an Interim Note', *Transactions of the Lichfield and South Staffordshire Archaeological and Historical Society* 13: 9–16

Sawyer, P. (ed.) *Anglo-Saxon Charters: an Annotated List and Bibliography* (London, 1968), accessible in electronic form via the online E-Sawyer database (http://esawyer.org.uk)

Sharp, T. (2013) 'Chronicles, Treaties and Burhs: the Burghal Hidage and the Mercian Register. Part 2: The Mercian Reconquest 910–919' http://www.academia.edu/5565935/Chronicles_Treaties_and_Burhs_the_Burghal_Hidage_and_the_Mercian_Register._Part_2_The_Mercian_Reconquest_910–919 [accessed 2 March 2018].

Sheridan K. (1973) 'Sixth Report of Excavations at Tamworth, Staffs., 1971 – a Section of the Saxon and Medieval Defences, Albert Road', *Transactions of the Lichfield and South Staffordshire Archaeological and Historical Society* 14: 32–7

Smallshire, J.L. (1978) *Wednesfield: the Field of Woden – Research into the History of Wednesfield* (Wolverhampton)

Smithe, F. (1889) 'Notes on the Church of St Bartholomew, Churchdown', *Transactions of the Bristol and Gloucestershire Archaeological Society* 13: 271–87

Stafford, P. (1981) 'The King's Wife in Wessex, 800–1066', *Past and Present* 91: 3–27

Stafford, P. (2001) 'Political Women in Mercia: Eighth to Early Tenth Centuries', pp.35–49 in M.P. Brown and C. Farr (eds) *Mercia: an Anglo-Saxon Kingdom in Europe* (London)

Stafford, P. (2008) 'The Annals of Æthelflæd: Annals, History and Politics in Early Tenth-Century England', pp. 101–16 in J. Barrow and A. Wareham (eds) *Myth, Rulership, Church and Charters: Essays in Honour of Nicholas Brooks* (Aldershot)

Stansbury, D. (1993) *The Lady Who Fought the Vikings* (South Brent)

Starkey, H.F. (1990) *Old Runcorn: Railway Extracts* (Runcorn)

Stenton, F.M. (1971) *Anglo-Saxon England*. 3rd edn (Oxford)

Stone, D.J.F. (2017) 'Mutually Assured Construction: Æthelflæd's Burhs, Landscapes of Defence and the Physical Legacy of the Unification of England, 899–1016'. Unpublished PhD thesis, University of Exeter

Swanton, M.J. (ed.) (1996) *The Anglo-Saxon Chronicle* (London)

Szarmach, P.E. (1998) 'Æthelflæd of Mercia: *Mise en Page*', pp. 105–26 in P.S. Baker and N. Howe (eds) *Words and Works: Studies in Medieval English Language and Literature in Honour of Fred C. Robinson* (Toronto)

Taylor, C.S. (1893) 'The Danes in Gloucestershire', *Transactions of the Bristol and Gloucestershire Archaeological Society* 17: 68–95

Thacker, A. (1982) 'Chester and Gloucester: Early Ecclesiastical Organisation in Two Mercian Burhs', *Northern History* 18: 199–211

Thacker, A. (1985) 'Kings, Saints and Monasteries in Pre-Viking Mercia', *Midland History* 10: 1–25

Thacker, A. (1995) '*Membra Disjecta*: the Division of the Body and the Diffusion of the Cult', pp. 97–127 in C. Stancliffe and E. Cambridge (eds) *Oswald: Northumbrian King to European Saint* (Stamford)

Thacker, A. (2001) 'Dynastic Monasteries and Family Cults: Edward the Elder's Sainted Kindred', pp. 248–63 in N.J. Higham and D.H. Hill (eds) *Edward the Elder, 899–924* (London)

Thompson, V. (2002) *Dying and Death in Later Anglo-Saxon England* (Woodbridge)

Varley, W.J. (1950) 'Excavations of the Castle Ditch, Eddisbury, 1935–8', *Transactions of the Historic Society of Lancashire and Cheshire* 102: 1–68

Vince, A. (1990) *Saxon London: an Archaeological Investigation* (London)

Waddington, S. (2015) 'The Shiring of Hereford', *Midland History* 40: 155–80

Wainwright, F.T. (1948) 'Ingimund's Invasion', *English Historical Review* 63: 145–69

Wainwright, F.T. (1959) 'Æthelflæd, Lady of the Mercians', pp. 53–69 in P. Clemoes (ed.) *The Anglo-Saxons: Studies in Some Aspects of their History* (London)

Wainwright, F.T. (1960) 'The Chirbury Excavation (1958)', *Shropshire Archaeological Society Newsletter* 10: 1–2

Walker, I. (2000) *Mercia and the Making of England* (Stroud)

Wallis, A. (2008) 'Archaeological Evaluation at St Mary's Road, Wednesbury', p. 7 in *Bournemouth University: Archaeological Investigations Project – West Midlands, Birmingham Area* (Bournemouth)

Ward, S. (2001) 'Edward the Elder and the Re-establishment of Chester', pp. 160–6 in N.J. Higham and D.H. Hill (eds) *Edward the Elder, 899–924* (London)

Welch, M. (2001) 'The Archaeology of Mercia', pp. 147–60 in M.P. Brown and C. Farr (eds) *Mercia: an Anglo-Saxon Kingdom in Europe* (London)

Williams, A. (1981) '*Princeps Merciorum Gentis*: the Family, Career and Connections of Ælfhere, Ealdorman of Mercia, 956–83', *Anglo-Saxon England* 10: 143–72

Winterbottom, M. and Thomson, R.M. (2002) *William of Malmesbury: Gesta Regum Anglorum. Vol. 2: General Introduction and Commentary* (Oxford)

Wolfe, J. (2012) *Æthelflæd: Royal Lady, War Lady*. 2nd edn (Chester)

Woolf, A. (2001) 'View from the West: an Irish Perspective on West Saxon Dynastic Practice', pp. 89–101 in N.J. Higham and D.H. Hill (eds) *Edward the Elder, 899–924* (London)

Woolf, A. (2007) *From Pictland to Alba, 789 to 1070* (Edinburgh)

Wormald, P. (1983) 'Bede, the *Bretwaldas* and the Origins of the *Gens Anglorum*', pp. 99–129 in P. Wormald, D. Bullough and R. Collins (eds) *Ideal and Reality in Frankish and Anglo-Saxon Society* (Oxford)

Yorke, B. (1989) *Kings and Kingdoms of Early Anglo-Saxon England* (London)

Yorke, B. (1995) *Wessex in the Early Middle Ages* (London)

INDEX